Women Entrepreneurs

Moving Beyond the Glass Ceiling

Dorothy P. Moore
E. Holly Buttner

 SAGE Publications
International Educational and Professional Publisher
Thousand Oaks London New Delhi

For information:

SAGE Publications, Inc.
2455 Teller Road
Thousand Oaks, California 91320
E-mail: order@sagepub.com

SAGE Publications Ltd.
6 Bonhill Street
London EC2A 4PU
United Kingdom

SAGE Publications India Pvt. Ltd.
M-32 Market
Greater Kailash I
New Delhi 110 048 India

Printed in the United States of America

Moore, Dorothy Perrin.
    Women entrepreneurs: Moving beyond the glass ceiling / by Dorothy Perrin Moore and E. Holly Buttner.
        p.   cm.
    Includes bibliographical references and index.
    ISBN 0-7619-0463-8 (acid-free paper). — ISBN 0-7619-0464-6 (pbk.: acid-free paper)
    1. Self-employed women. 2. Women in business. 3. Entrepreneurship. I. Buttner, E. Holly. II. Title.
    HD6072.5.M66 1997
    658.4′21′082—dc21   97-4854

This book is printed on acid-free paper.

97 98 99 00 01 02 03 10 9 8 7 6 5 4 3 2 1

Acquisition Editor:	Marquita Flemming
Editorial Assistant:	Frances Borghi
Production Editor:	Sanford Robinson
Production Assistant:	Denise Santoyo
Typesetter/Designer:	Christina M. Hill
Cover Designer:	Candice Harman
Print Buyer:	Anna Chin

Contents

Preface   xiii

Acknowledgments   xvii

1. Introduction   1
  Changing Times   1
    Female Entrepreneurship   1
    Women and Organizational Life   6
    The Global Environment   9
    Into Entrepreneurship   10
  The Research Field: What We Know and What We Don't   11
    Definitions and Fundamentals   11
    Data   13
    Typical Entrepreneurs?   14
    Organizational Interactions and Female Entrepreneurship   16
  This Study   18
    Observations   18
    Issues   18

2. Making the Leap   21
  The Decision Point   21
  Survey Data   22
    Rank Order of Departure Reasons   22

Scaled Ratings   23
Focus Group Data   24
  Content Analysis of Departure Influences   25
  Cluster 1: Self-Determination, Autonomy, and Job Freedom   25
    Autonomy and Freedom   26
    Self-Esteem   27
    Stifling Bureaucracy Effects   30
  Cluster 2: Challenge—The Attractiveness of Entrepreneurship   34
    Respect and Recognition   34
    Opportunity to Be in Charge   35
    Controlling One's Destiny   36
    Regaining Excitement   37
    Recognition of Accomplishments   37
  Cluster 3: Blocks to Corporate Advancement   37
    Not Fitting In   38
    Demonstrating Competence   39
    Career Barriers   39
    Lingering Discrimination   40
  Cluster 4: Organizational Dynamics—Power and Politics   42
    Compensation and Equitable Treatment   44
  Cluster 5: Balancing Career and Family   47
  Other Reasons for Leaving   48
The Decision Point   49
Summary   50

3. **The Organizational Incubator**   **51**
  The Organizational Incubator and Career Transition   51
  Part I: Incubator Transfer   53
  Part II: The Confidence, Credibility, and Creativity Transfer   58
  Part III: The Incubator Push Factor   60
  Part IV: Intentional Entrepreneurs, Corporate Climbers,
    and the Incubator Experience   66
  Incubator Perceptions   67
    Perception of Managerial Experience   68
    Perception of Marketing and Technical Experience   68
    Perceptions of Financial Expertise   69
    Perceptions of Similar Organizational Experience or
      Special Training Programs   69
    Intentionals, Corporate Climbers, and Corporate Flight   70
  Results   71
    Post Hoc Analysis   76
  Discussion and Conclusions   76

4. Career Transition Challenges   **81**

Transition Issues and Challenges   81

    Transition Challenges and Management Skills   82

        Research Questions   83

Transition Themes in Focus Group Discussions   86

    Perspectives   86

    Entrepreneurs as Innovators   88

    Roles   89

The Focus/Flexibility Paradox   89

    Delegation   90

    Finance   92

    Do Banks Discriminate Against Women Entrepreneurs?   94

    Establishing Credibility   94

    Support Versus Isolation   96

Conclusion   98

5. Interactive Leadership—The Hub Effect   **99**

Interactive Leadership   99

Leadership Styles   100

Findings   102

    Leadership Scale Relationships   102

    Exploratory Analysis   104

Focus Interviews   105

    Teamwork and Collaboration   105

    Caretaking and Support Versus Making the Hard Decisions   106

    Attitudes Toward Power   108

    Empowering Subordinates   109

    Empowering Clients   110

    Role Modeling and Creating a Vision   110

    Integration   111

    Multiple Roles   113

Conclusion   113

6. Networks as Vital Links   **115**

Entrepreneurial Networks   115

    Women's Networks   116

Questionnaire Data and Focus Group Analysis   118

    Questionnaire Responses   118

    Content Analysis of Focus Group Data   120

    Network Centrality   125

    Contacts, Teams, Teamwork, and Credibility   126

    Network Association and Perceptions of Performance   130

Value Added 131
Networking as a Cooperative-Integrative Strategy 132
Networks as Inclusion 134
Networks as Extension 135
Networks as Support Mechanisms 135
Questionnaire Data 135
Content Analysis 137
Sounding Boards 138
Sanity Check 139
Resource Access 139
Transition Strategies 140
The Corporate/Entrepreneurial Difference 141
Minuses, Limits, and Pluses 142
The Gender Difference? 145
Networks to Make a Difference 147
Summary 148

7. Success: Fulfilling the Dream 152
Fulfilling the Dream: Definitions of Success 152
The Women Entrepreneurs' Measures of Success 153
Survey and Focus Group Findings 153
Departure Factors and Success Measures 153
Making Money 154
Stability Rather Than Growth 156
Self-Fulfillment 157
The Internal Measure 159
Freedom and Autonomy 160
The Ethic of Care 160
Work and Family 162
Multiple Definitions of Success 163
The Interplay of Size and Success Measures 164
Conclusions 166

8. Summary and Advice 167
Summary 167
Corporate Exit 167
Transition 169
Incubators 170
Leadership 170
Networking Opportunities 171
Success 171
Implications 172
Starting a Business 172
Further Investigation 172
Organizational Dimensions 174

Advice   174
    Making a Difference   174
    Contacts and Influence   175
Making It Happen   175
    Having a Personal Plan   176
    Realism   178
    The Business Plan   180
    Spouse and Support   181
    Prudence in Developing and Using Support Systems   182
    Selling Oneself   182
    Being the Boss and Operating the Business   183
    Employees   184
    Getting Away From It All   184
Personal Networks   185
    Context   185
    Acquiring New Channels   186
Summing Up   187

Appendix 1: Methodology   **189**

Appendix 2: Questionnaires   **201**

Appendix 3: Acknowledgment and Appreciation   **218**

References   **229**

Name Index   **245**

Subject Index   **251**

About the Authors   **261**

List of Tables and Figures

Table 2.1   Ranking of the Most Important Reasons for Leaving a
            Prior Organization   23
Table 2.2   Factor Analysis Results of Entrepreneurs' Reasons for
            Leaving Their Prior Organizations   24
Table 3.1   Profiles of Intentionals and Corporate Climbers   72
Table 3.2   Multivariate Analysis of the Incubator Effect for the
            Corporate and Intentional Entrepreneur   73
Table 3.3   Multivariate Analysis of the Incubator Effect Among Venture
            Creators With Similar Organizational Backgrounds or Who
            Had Special Training Programs   74
Table 3.4   Multivariate Analysis of Reasons for Leaving the Organization
            by Intentionals and Corporate Climbers   75
Table 4.1   Overall Mean Ratings of Managerial Skills and Ratings by
            Level of Industry Turbulence   84
Table 4.2   Problems/Issues in Being an Entrepreneur: Mean Ratings and
            Ratings as a Function of Industry Turbulence   85
Table 4.3   Ranking of Entrepreneurial Issues by Time in Business   86
Table 4.4   Ratings of Managerial Skills and Business Issues as a Function
            of Expectations About Future Company Growth   87
Table 6.1   Descriptive Statistics of Networking Clusters   119
Table 6.2   Multivariate Analysis of Network Centrality   121
Table 6.3   Analysis of Supportive Role of Networks   122
Table 6.4   Multivariate Analysis of Transitional Functions of Networking   123
Table 6.5   Multivariate Analysis of Entrepreneurial Role of Networking   124

Table 7.1   Mean Ratings and Factor Scores of Women Entrepreneurs'
             Ratings of Success Criteria   154
Table 7.2   Correlations of Entrepreneurs' Reasons for Leaving Prior
             Organization With Measures of Success, Partialing Out the
             Effects of Demographic Characteristics   155
Figure 7.1   Women Entrepreneurs' Success Measures as a Function
             of Number of Employees   165
Table A1.1   Focus Format for Sessions   191
Table A1.2   Demographic Profile of the Female Entrepreneur Participants   193

Preface

In recent years, considerable attention has been paid to any number of highly touted business and economic revolutions. Reports range from the real and perceived impacts of new technologies to competition in the global market-place to the hammer blows of corporate change, usually cloaked in the slightly less threatening terms of relocation, reallocation, merger, divestiture, downsizing, rightsizing, de-recruiting, and the like. Numerous reporters have noted that small business has been the fastest growing segment in the American economy. The fact that women-owned business made up the fastest growing entrepreneurial segment was noticed less often. Between 1975 and 1990, women started businesses at more than twice the rate of men (Murphy, 1992). Women now own more than 7.7 million firms. They employ 35% more people in the United States than the Fortune 500 companies do worldwide (National Foundation for Women Business Owners [NFWBO], and Dun & Bradstreet Information Services, 1995, p. 4). By the year 2000, nearly half of all American businesses may be owned by women (Ando, 1990; U.S. Congress, House of Representatives, 1988).

We began this study of the ongoing revolution in the marketplace with the basic assumption that the modern entrepreneurial woman has passed many tests. The evidence is everywhere. Understanding that work is a path to success, quality of life, and self-fulfillment, women in business have changed the workplace substantially, creating opportunities for themselves and others in the process.

Many of the new female entrepreneurs had considerable exposure to corporate life before striking out on their own. We were intrigued with the numerous questions surrounding this phenomenon. Did women who entered organizations do so with intentions of eventually running their own businesses, in the manner of people we identify in this study as "intentional entrepreneurs"? Or did many female entrepreneurs begin in the mold of organizational women, thinking ahead to building careers in the company or industry, like the group we identify as "corporate climbers"? Are the women in these two groups similar? If not, how do they differ? What led them to leave the corporate environments? What did the female entrepreneur take from the organizational incubator? Does she now manage and lead differently from her former boss? How does she define and measure success? What observations, thoughts, and advice does she have to offer?

This study is based primarily on original information drawn from focus field interviews with 129 female entrepreneurs. The interviews were conducted in cities where the density of women-owned businesses is greatest. Data are drawn from the responses of the female entrepreneurs to an eight-page survey instrument, content analysis of the video-recorded field interviews, and responses to a follow-up survey questionnaire. The interview sites included 7 of the 10 major metropolitan areas with the greatest number of women-owned businesses as well as 6 other regional locations to counterbalance the research design: Atlanta, Boston, Charleston, Chicago, Cincinnati, Dallas, Lexington, New Orleans, New York, Orlando, Philadelphia, Winston-Salem, and San Francisco. Prospective participants were identified with the aid of the various chapters of the National Association of Women Business Owners, various governors' offices, the Small Business Administration, Chamber of Commerce groups, Women's Entrepreneurial Advocates groups, civic groups, and small business owners.

Who are these entrepreneurs? Many who participated in the study had achieved recognition such as an Entrepreneur of the Year award in their city or state. Some had been among the most accomplished female and minority managers in major corporations. Hardworking and motivated, many were on their way up the organizational ladders with aspirations for advancement until they hit a ceiling. Others had always intended to be entrepreneurs, but the time was not right when they started out. They went into organizations because the jobs represented their best personal or financial choices at the time. Once they acquired experience and contacts, they broke away.

The criteria for selection as a participant included such dimensions as organizational professional or managerial experience prior to launching a business, being established in business longer than a year, initiating a business, ownership of at least 50% of the business, and present service in a major managerial role. The typical female entrepreneur who participated in the study was 44 years old, white, college-educated, and married with at least one child at the time of the interviews. She operated an incorporated service business with sales in the $250,000-499,999 range. Her business was 7 years old on average. The entrepreneur defined her role as CEO, president, or owner. She worked an average of 52 hours a week. Her income primarily came from the business. She earned at least as much and usually more than she did in her former corporate position, where she had worked an average of 6 years. She was 37 years old at the time of business startup and had young children in elementary school. See Tables A1.2 and A1.3 in Appendix 1.

For this study, we contacted each entrepreneur by telephone and asked for her participation in a focus session consisting of a researcher and two to seven entrepreneurs. Prior to the focus group meetings, each entrepreneur was furnished with biographical data on the researchers, the purpose of the study, focal topics for discussion, and information on data analysis procedures, research outlets, and confidentiality of the information obtained. Each entrepreneur then completed a questionnaire prior to joining the focus group discussion. Nearly one year after the original focus interviews were completed, a follow-up survey was conducted. The survey questionnaire and focus group items were drawn from a careful review of the entrepreneurship and women in management literature, pilot tested on three groups of entrepreneurs, and then honed and clarified to measure the focal areas of interest in women's transitions from the corporate environment to establishing and operating successful businesses. (The complete questionnaires and focus interview format appear in Appendix 2.)

We begin by examining the corporate culture from which the entrepreneur launched her career. This is followed by a brief analysis of the driving forces that led her to leave the organizational environment, the effect of the incubator as a preparatory step in preparing for entrepreneurship, and how the organizational experience differed among intentional and corporate climbers. Later chapters look at initial difficulties encountered in starting the businesses, entrepreneurial networking, and successful strategies employed by these entrepreneurs after the corporate leap. In the conclusion, messages are provided for future entrepreneurs and for organizations that wish to halt the mass exit of talented women from their corporate environments.

Our thanks go to the Berkley Center for Entrepreneurial Studies, Leonard N. Stern School of Business, New York University, The Citadel Development Foundation, and the University of North Carolina at Greensboro, whose funding supported this lengthy research study.

Acknowledgments

This book grew out of a concern that successful women entrepreneurs were a relatively unstudied and unreported group. Small business research dealt primarily with male entrepreneurs. That many women entrepreneurs had previous corporate experience was well known, but there was little information on any impact this had on their own ventures. Speculations and assumptions were abundant, but we felt a need for a base of solid research from which other scholars could build.

We have many people to thank in getting our story into the hands of scholars, students, organizational and entrepreneurial women, and others. We express our sincere appreciation to the entrepreneurs who participated in this study. Their insights made this book possible. You will find that we have cited their remarks extensively. Although some preferred to remain anonymous, it is our privilege to acknowledge others by name or with a short bio-sketch in Appendix 3.

Many individuals and businesses identified potential participants and arranged facilities for our focus group interviews. The entrepreneurial centers and those who took key roles in facilitating the research also are acknowledged in Appendix 3.

This research was supported by funds from The Citadel Development Foundation, the Berkley Center for Entrepreneurial Studies, Leonard N. Stern

School of Business, New York University, and the University of North Carolina at Greensboro.

We especially appreciate feedback on an early proposal draft of our research by Professors Janet S. Adams, Michael J. Coles School of Business, Kennesaw State University; Robert F. Scherer, Small Business Development Center, Wright State University; and Howard D. Feldman, University of Portland.

Our heartfelt thanks go to Jamie W. Moore, who edited this book more than once and weaved many constructive changes into the chapters. His advice, encouragement, helpful suggestions, and spirit of equality and opportunity were supportive in the completion of this book. Thanks go to Marquita Flemming, our acquisitions editor at Sage, both for championing the project and for guiding the manuscript through the publishing process. Her flexibility in handling the special needs of acquiring permissions from each entrepreneur we have cited in the book made our working relationship ideal. We also appreciate the professional and constructive feedback we received from Sanford Robinson, Sage production editor, and the professional and meticulous work of A. J. Sobczak, the copy editor.

Sharon Kearns, a Ph.D. candidate, University of South Carolina, did a comprehensive ethnograph content analysis while a graduate assistant at The Citadel. Holmes Finch, of the University of South Carolina, offered statistical expertise and advice on the multivariate analysis designs in Chapters 3 and 6. Jamie L. Moore worked as proofreader and fact checker and contributed important revisions in several chapters.

Dorothy P. Moore especially acknowledges the encouragement and support of Belle and W. J. Moore, Judge Jeanette Harper of Mt. Pleasant, South Carolina, and George S. Vozikis, Bovaird Professor of Entrepreneurial Studies, the University of Tulsa.

E. Holly Buttner expresses deep appreciation to Lynn Baird; to Bud Miles, Department Head at the University of North Carolina at Greensboro, for his support; and to Mary Margaret Leverton and Beth Cox for their careful and thorough attention in the content analysis. Her parents, Sally and Doug Buttner, taught the value of education and instilled a love of learning. Jude Rathburn and Nur Gryskiewicz, friends and colleagues, rooted for her success. Her heartfelt thanks also to Christian Anderson for her support and encouragement during the data collection, analysis, writing, and revision of this book.

Introduction

Changing Times

Female Entrepreneurship

Between 1975 and 1990, 20 million women took jobs outside the home (Devine, 1994). Some sought opportunities and careers; others were driven by necessity. Whatever the reasons, by 1990, the 58% of all American women who were gainfully employed composed 45.6% of the total workforce. Women had become a major force. The trends continue. Over the next several decades, only 15% percent of the people entering the workplace will be male and white. By the year 2000, women will compose almost half of all people employed in the United States and in Canada (Dingwall, 1992; Hudson Institute, 1987). Female employment may account for more than two-thirds of the net alteration taking place in the size and composition of the labor market (Ries & Stone, 1992).

Women-owned businesses contribute powerfully to this transition. Between 1975 and 1990, the number of self-employed women more than doubled. The female self-employment rate increased 63% as women started businesses at more than twice the rate of men (Murphy, 1992). By 1990, 1 of every 10 women over the age of 35 was self-employed (Devine, 1994). The impact of these female entrepreneurs is considerable. "Women now own

1

7.7 million firms, employing 15.5 million workers and generating nearly $1.4 trillion in sales. These firms employ over one-third (35%) more people in the United States than the Fortune 500 companies worldwide" (National Foundation for Women Business Owners, and Dun & Bradstreet Information Services, 1995, p. 4). By 2000, 61% of all women of working age will have jobs (Johnston & Packer, 1987). Nearly half of all American businesses may be owned by women, according to a Congressional Report (Ando, 1990; U.S. Congress, House of Representatives, 1988).

Nothing like this has happened before. Historically confined to the private sphere of domesticity, prior to the 1980s, women had limited access to capital, business and technical education, and management experience. Self-employed women in managerial and professional specialty occupations fared somewhat better but still earned less than their male wage and salary counterparts (U.S. Department of Commerce, Bureau of the Census, 1986). Researchers (Demarest, 1977; Diffley, 1983; Schreier & Komives, 1973; Schwartz, 1976) thus suggested that when these women went into business, their motivations, psychology, and management styles reflected an approach that Gregg, in a 1985 study, defined as traditional: The typical female entrepreneur was most likely a person with a liberal arts background (Scott, 1986; Stevenson, 1986) and unlikely to be guided to start a business in male-dominated industries (Bowen & Hisrich, 1986; Buttner & Rosen, 1988b). She lacked experience with finance, marketing, and routine business operations, and consequently faced major problems in obtaining loans (Hisrich & O'Brien, 1981; Pellegrino & Reese, 1982). Her background, domestic orientation, and limited access to capital led her into sole proprietor service businesses that tended to have low income and low equity and to be small and slow growing (U.S. Department of Commerce, Bureau of the Census, 1986; Vesper, 1983).

The new group of female entrepreneurs that began appearing in the 1980s differed from the "Traditionals," so researchers began referring to them as a "Second Generation" (Gregg, 1985). These female entrepreneurs met Drucker's (1985) narrow definition of an entrepreneur as one who "drastically upgrades the yield from resources and creates a new market and a new customer" (pp. 21, 25, 33). Many were women who had left corporations to be their own bosses, to exercise their educational and technical skills, and, not incidentally, to make money (Fried, 1989; Rosener, 1989; Scott, 1986). Previous findings that had yielded a single profile of female entrepreneurs as being primarily sole proprietors with similar educational backgrounds and a basic interest in extending home skills into the marketplace no longer fit.

Now there were at least two distinct groups. Whereas the Traditionals focused on providing domestic types of services and skills, the new-generation "Moderns" entered a variety of occupations. Not only that, the second-generation female entrepreneurs in the traditionally nonfemale business areas of finance, insurance, manufacturing, and construction differed from women owners in the retail and wholesale trade areas by exhibiting traits more commonly associated with male entrepreneurs (Hisrich & O'Brien, 1981, 1982). Whereas traditional female entrepreneurs typically had needed assistance in acquiring capital, determining the availability and the use of credit, and managerial training, the Moderns more often valued advanced counseling in communication skills, training programs, and new business opportunities. Moderns heading corporations, more than sole proprietors, prized assistance in the more sophisticated business areas of short- and long-term planning, planning for cash flow, networking, and identifying and expanding into new markets (Moore, 1990). Demographically, the second-generation female entrepreneurs were likely to be white, older, married women with some postsecondary education, backgrounds in management or administration, and hardworking (Devine, 1994).

In this wave of second-generation entrepreneurs were women who were not only innovative and creative but also used to exercising authority and control. With professional expertise to match their ventures, they came to entrepreneurship with more exposure to the business world, were better prepared with technical and planning skills and network contacts, and were oriented to making money and creating new markets (Moore, 1987a, 1990). They averaged 10 to 12 years of experience before starting their businesses (Murphy, 1992). Many clearly had used their previous corporate and organizational environments as incubators (Cooper & Dunkelberg, 1987; Ireland & Van Auken, 1987) to provide them with training grounds and key contacts (Birley, 1989). Conservative and more concerned about the survival of their businesses than with high growth rates and profits (Chaganti, 1986; Hisrich & Brush, 1984), they strongly valued family security, personal accomplishment, freedom, and self-respect (Olson & Currie, 1992).

For some Moderns, entrepreneurship had not been their initial career choice. A number of female organizational aspirants in the 1970s belatedly discovered that, for women, the corporate ladder was never tall enough to reach the top (Rosener, 1989). So frequently did women leave firms because they found organizational life stultifying and confining that researchers linked their exit to career frustration (Winn & Stewart, 1992). Among those leaving were female business owners who had been pushed to entrepreneurship (Birley, 1989; Cooper, 1981). The most cited reasons for their leaving organizations were systemic attitudinal and organizational barriers to women's career advancement (Adler, 1993; Fischer, Reuber, & Dyke, 1993) and negative effects of the corporate culture (Hood & Koberg, 1994; Noble, 1993; Taylor, 1986). External observers suggested that business ownership was a means for women to obtain job satisfaction and bypass systemic discrimination against women in corporations (Belcourt, 1991). No studies, however, had been able to inquire deeply into the previous corporate experiences of these entrepreneurs or their effects, and the links between leaving organizations and female entrepreneurship were not altogether clear.

When she went into business for herself, the new modern entrepreneur was more likely to be a corporate owner than a sole proprietor. She thought of her business in terms of a career rather than a supplement to the family income (Moore, 1990). She sometimes had left her former organizational environment for opportunities not available in the massively bureaucratic and structured systems. Data from the Small Business Administration suggest that, during the period 1977 to 1982, the highest annual growth rates of female-operated businesses occurred in the segment populated by the new moderns. Overall, in the major industry divisions of agricultural services, forestry and fishing, mining, construction, and manufacturing, the growth rate of female-operated businesses exceeded that of the industry as a whole (U.S. Department of Commerce, Bureau of the Census, 1986). Despite the myth that women lack business savvy, these female-headed businesses had a success rate comparable to organizations headed by men (Birley, 1989; Hisrich & Brush, 1987; Kalleberg & Leicht, 1991).

Jill Martin Fugaro, Sudha Pennathur, Honi Stempler, and Linda Sahagian typify successful new modern entrepreneurs. All had extensive corporate experience prior to launching their ventures. Jill Martin Fugaro initially found corporate life exciting. Working for a large firm, she had opportunities to make crucial contacts, acquire and polish skills, and gain experience. She learned the basics of management: how to hire people, set employee goals, design personnel evaluation systems, and practice leadership techniques. Like all young managers, she made mistakes, and she learned from these, too. Doing various tasks, she learned how to identify markets, develop products, merge delivery and advertising strategies, and run a national sales campaign. Sudha Pennathur brought boundless energy to the wide variety of corporate management jobs she held over an 18-year span. An MBA holder from a respected university, she moved into senior executive management with a major clothing manufacturer. When she left the firm, she was the youngest general merchandise manager in the company's history.

Few companies had employees as devoted as Honi Stempler, who dedicated most of her time and energy to her company. To the detriment of her personal health and family life, for 9 years she worked an average of 60 to 80 hours a week, usually going to work at 7 a.m. and coming home at midnight. She was married and had that life, but her work always took precedence. After 6 years with the company, she took over the management of its newest subsidiary.

Few executives pursued careers as purposefully as Linda Sahagian. Raised to believe that she could succeed at whatever she wanted, after college she decided she wanted to become a broadcaster. She got her FCC license endorsed, which was required at the time, and then went job hunting. She went from station to station, only to be told, "You can't have that job because you are a girl." (Throughout the book, quotations from the entrepreneurs are taken from focus group interviews. Names are provided with permission; some respondents chose to remain anonymous.) "I had my credentials and everything," Linda says, "but this was before the outset of EEOC. People could make blatant statements at that time and say these things to you and you would have to suffer it." When she finally got a job in broadcasting in a major market, she had to change her name: "It was too ethnic and in New England, ethnic was not good." She was devastated until her parents wisely said, "Face it, the Lodges talk to the Cabots and the Cabots talk to God." So Linda changed her last name. She was in broadcasting and became a success, but she couldn't break into New York. Finally, someone told her, "Your real name is ethnic and you are using a name that isn't; don't you know that in New York ethnic is good?" So she went ethnic again. Coincidentally, 2 weeks later she landed a job with one of the major broadcasting networks. She loved it. She won the corporate battles she had to fight, like the time her superiors suddenly eliminated her job when they heard she was getting married. Linda told the powers that be, "You have a serious problem with this action. What you are doing is discriminating." Linda promised legal action. Suddenly, a new job materialized, and it was a dream job working on a major network news show.

In time, all four of these capable female executives left the corporate life to found their own businesses. Jill launched a West Coast designer label sportswear company. Her fast-growing organization produced five collections a year, manufactured and imported from three foreign countries along with production in the United States, serviced more than 1,400 accounts nationally, and grossed more than a million dollars in the first year of business. She sold her trademark to another apparel company, and today her trademark line is sold in better metropolitan markets and in catalogs nationwide. Sudha Pennathur is now the president of a firm that designs jewelry, accessories, gifts, and other objets d'art that range from reproductions of antiques to unique originals. Honi Stempler's first company was voted as one of Atlanta's top five in the prepress field. She still contributes these skills but devotes the majority of her time to Simple Solutions to Better Health with natural body balancing and immune system strengthening foods. Linda Sahagian, a Chicago entrepreneur, manufactures specialty snack foods and confections under a private brand name and label. She has developed a trademark packaging design known as A YARD OF and A FOOT OF.

Why did these accomplished corporate employees leave their positions? The four circumstances and stories differ, but the patterns show similarities. Jill puts it this way:

> I live in San Francisco, and I liken the disillusionment in a corporation to a creeping fog. In the night time, the fog slowly comes in from the ocean and goes under the Golden Gate Bridge. You are really not aware of it at first, and eventually you hear the fog horns in the distance, and those fog horns indicate a change in the environment, a slow creeping disillusionment. (Moore, Buttner, & Rosen, 1992, p. 86)

Women and Organizational Life

All four of these entrepreneurs experienced corporate environments that offered less opportunity for self-expression, individual creativity, or artistic skills than they desired. Could their organizations have avoided their problems and retained these capable female executives?

An organization culture is made up of shared values (Deal & Kennedy 1982; Sathe, 1985; Schein, 1983). These are the assumptions the organization has invented, discovered, or developed in coping with problems presented in the past. Because they bring success, traditional ways become well-grooved organizational routines. Over time, persistent organizational operating patterns can begin to veer greatly if the surrounding community or national culture begins to change. Firms anticipate the problem, of course, and management commonly addresses it, but changing organizational patterns often is difficult. When the organizational culture and people's private worlds differ greatly, an organization's management and working layers can be filled with individuals whose actions can reflect an internal determination to resist or slow the pace of change. Commitment to organizational social stability (Louis, 1980) and identification with the organization (Deal & Kennedy, 1982), neither of them intrinsically undesirable characteristics, can guide and shape people's behavior in ways that run counter to new organizational goals (Smirchich, 1983).

Organizations react to changing workforce and marketplace demographics. They decentralize decision making, combine job development and education, and seek more than one approach, often custom tailoring operations to local environments. Although flexibility is a real goal in some organizations, it is only a buzzword in others. Problems multiply when the organizational culture maintains a rigid and restricted outlook (Hill, 1990). Top-down management approaches and a reluctance to change can and do generate maladaptive behavior.

Demographic projections suggest that, in the coming decade, companies will not survive without recruiting and promoting women managers (Dingwall, 1992). Although strides have been made in achieving upward mobility for women into middle management, the corporate boards of Fortune 500 companies, predominantly male in the 1980s (Dipboye, 1987), have remained so. Findings in a 1996 census conducted by the New York nonprofit women's research group Catalyst showed that, for the first time, women held more than 10% of the directors' seats in the nation's 500 largest companies (626 of the 6,123 board seats), that the rate of increase in female directors had declined, that of the 1,216 inside directors at Fortune 500 companies only 11 were women (5 of whom were related to the chief executive or the controlling family), that the number of companies that had two female directors totaled 177 (up 11 from 1995), that the number of companies with three female directors totaled three, that the number of female executives in a large corporation correlates with having women on the board of directors, and that women constituted approximately 2% of corporate America's top earners (Dobrzynski, 1996). Depending on one's perspective, the news is either slightly uplifting or massively discouraging.

Female owners report a similar variety of corporate experiences that led them to initially consider entrepreneurship. Some get caught up in the system of organizational politics, in which the lack of trust drains energy from productive work and creates uncertainty about career advancement opportunities. Financial discrimination meant that males frequently made thousands of dollars a year more than females in comparable jobs. There also were the clear corporate messages. "I sure didn't fit in," remembers a Northeastern entrepreneur. "I got an award one time in this business and it's a baseball bat engraved with my name to indicate that I was a heavy hitter and also four volumes of novels about baseball." In some organizations, women had special requirements, like unofficial dress codes, while men did not.

In many firms, only a few women made it to upper management, and they had only limited access to power. Confined to advancement in staff jobs only, in highly centralized line organizations, female executives had little impact. Recalls Ann Grogan, now head of a retail firm, "The chain was absolutely vertical. During the entire 12 to 13 years I was never consulted nor did I have the authority to hire or fire a secretary who worked for me." In the sometimes highly politicized corporate environments, the team playing discussed in staff meetings was rarely practiced. Reports a San Francisco entrepreneur, "I had an overwhelming feeling of not fitting in. At first I had the feeling that this meant something was wrong with me instead of with the situation." Women managers found that turf guarding was often the norm, accomplished through such passive means as lack of contact, lack of communication, lack of action, and withholding critical information, the last an often unaddressed result of informal communication through male-bonded networks. "I knew I was going to leave," says Janet Bensu, Owner of BENSU, Inc., who is now involved in software and consulting services. "I reviewed my options, interviewed corporations and found that the same philosophy which had existed in the corporate environment in which I had operated was present in the new environments or possible environments. None of these would provide an improvement." Sudha Pennathur and others recall that colleagues lacked interest in taking risks, sharing information, or getting on with the work. Although the corporate path twisted endlessly, it never led to a feeling of accomplishment and success. Corporate loyalty and reward for those who stuck to jobs and did them correctly was lacking; indeed, rewards and corporate success often had nothing to do with each other. Rewards had more to do with who liked you and whether they wanted to keep you. Advancement meant you were "selected in" and not "selected out." No one ever said you were not selected. No one even said you had failed at something. You were just not on the inside track and ended up promoted to nonconsequential positions. Dedication did not always pay. Years of faithful and accomplished effort did not automatically mean that the companies intended to pay the promised bonuses or live up to other personal commitments (Moore et al., 1992, p. 87). After enduring the experiences, Sudha concluded, "I had gone as far as I could go. I was just tired of solving their problems."

These are not reports of isolated incidents. Although women have been entering the labor force in greater numbers than ever before and have made great strides in achieving upward mobility into middle management, only a limited number of top executives are female (Brenner, Tomkiewicz, & Schein, 1989). For years, women individually have learned this and collectively have left their corporate employers in large numbers. The frustration became so widespread and noticeable it was given a name: hitting the "glass ceiling" (Morrison, White, & Van Velsor, 1987). Women were becoming disillusioned with corporate politics and tired of being sidetracked in corporate downsizing after mergers and acquisitions, concluded researchers (Birley, 1989; Trost, 1990), and they came to desire the autonomy of entrepreneurship (Kaplan, 1988).

The Global Environment

The changes have been global. The percentage of employed women is increasing in most countries. The pattern holds across cultures, whether in economically developed or undeveloped countries. The number of women in management or holding executive positions, however, remains negligible almost everywhere (Adler, 1993; Brenner et al., 1989). Adler reports that evidence suggests that the underrepresentation, underutilization, and skewed distribution of female managers worldwide is neither coincidental nor random but rather a function of systemic cultural sanctions, educational barriers, legal restrictions, and corporate practices (Adler, 1993, pp. 291, 295). For women, doing all the "right stuff"—getting a similar education, maintaining similar levels of family power, working in similar industries, not moving in and out of the workforce, and not removing their names from consideration for a transfer—does not result in equal pay for equal work (Stroh, Brett, & Reilly, 1992). Gender-related factors, often in the form of office politics, along with work-related factors such as the lack of opportunity to progress, create dissatisfaction with working life for women (Rosin & Korabik, 1990). A review of proposed legislation for women's advancement in German enterprises found stiff barriers for women in the international setting. As noted by Protzman (1993), "From the board room down through the ranks of middle management, German women occupy just 5.9 percent of all jobs, although they account for 41.6 percent of the total work force" (p. 16). Although reforms have been made to guarantee equal rights in the workplace that specifically include provisions to protect women—from sexual harassment, for example—the corporate culture and the German social system, which promotes motherhood and not careerism, appears to resist change. Other European women face similar barriers. Antal (1992) cites a major European Community study that highlights the absence of managerial opportunities for women in the European Community:

> In 1987, women made up 4% of middle management in the Netherlands and Ireland, 7% in Belgium, 8% in Denmark, West Germany and Italy, and 9% in France. The proportion of women in top management was even lower—less than 3% everywhere except in France, where the figure was 7%. . . . Yet women across Europe account for between 36% and 48% of the labor force, and many of them are looking for managerial opportunities, but few are getting them. (p. 42)

Antal (1992) refers to the 1992 edition of *Crawfords Directory,* a United Kingdom company guidebook that "shows that of 7,103 top executives in the leading companies listed, 152 were women . . . and of the chief executives, just a handful were female" (p. 42). It is not surprising that women often value the concept of equality far more than do men (Fagenson, 1993).

As a former corporate representative overseas, a Southeastern entrepreneur had approached her job with an American work ethic. "I was an American," she says, "and American business people expect to have everything done yesterday." She had been trained to work very long hours, and she worked longer hours than anybody. To the local office, however, she was a pushy American female who "was never gonna be one of the boys," and her parent firm made it clear that she never would be accepted. For a while, she kept on implementing ideas that increased profits at American banking and manufacturing firms. She then elected to go into business for herself as a consultant to small businesses overseas. Looking back on the experiences, she muses, "I had this notion, this kind of American dream notion, that, if you really had some skills and were worth something, then you went out on your own and you became a millionaire and you kind of pulled yourself up by the bootstraps. What I did not realize was that I had to go down to my bootstraps in order to pull myself up to the bootstraps."

Into Entrepreneurship

Like men, many women entrepreneurs launched their businesses to achieve independence, personal development, and job freedom (Scheinberg

& MacMillan, 1988; Shane, Kolvereid, & Westhead, 1991). "I had an easy time deciding how to leave my old job," recalled Nancy Wonsavage.

> I was an account and marketing executive, burned out and pregnant: I said, "This is the time to leave" and so I did. My reason for leaving was primarily to get some balance in my own life and to regroup. I found that the transition at this key time from the corporate environment to owning my own business provided the opportunity to balance taking care of my children, spending time with my family, with working, and providing flexible hours.

In retrospect, we can see that changing attitudes over the last quarter century foreshadowed the appearance of the modern entrepreneurs. A 1984 replication of a 1974 study in occupational labeling revealed statistically significant differences within each of the perceptual categories of masculine, neutral, and feminine occupations and a statistically significant trend toward rating more occupations as being suitable for either sex (Moore & Rust, 1984). There is every reason to believe today that increasing numbers of young people will continue to see the world as a place where women and men have equally legitimate rights to seek whatever role they choose. This suggests that the numbers of modern female entrepreneurs will increase.

As we report in Chapter 3, many of these women use their previous organizational experiences as incubators for the businesses they create. As one entrepreneur says, "You don't start a money management firm without having a fairly long performance track record. Not if you want to succeed at it anyway." There is also a high probability that female entrepreneurs will use several corporate environments. "I've always had an entrepreneurial spirit, and, because of that, I would get bored with a job after a year and stay for two years and then leave," recalls Ethel Cook, owner of Corporate Improvement Group, Bedford, Massachusetts, "but I learned an awful lot."

The Research Field:
What We Know and What We Don't

Definitions and Fundamentals

Before we can begin to develop theories of entrepreneurship, it is essential to find some common definitions. This is not as easy as it looks. There are

many descriptions of an entrepreneur. Bart (1983) holds that an entrepreneurship is an "independently owned and operated business with less than 100
employees or less than $1,000,000 gross receipts per year." Quite often in
American business schools an entrepreneur is defined as one who owns and
starts a new and small business. Gartner (1985) calls "entrepreneurship the
creation of new organizations" (p. 697). Entrepreneurship, say Bowen and
Hisrich (1986), is "the process of creating something different with value by
devoting the necessary time and effort; assuming the accompanying financial, psychic, and social risks; and receiving the resulting rewards of mone-
tary and personal satisfaction" (p. 15). The U.S. Small Business Administration (1985) says that because 97% of all American businesses are small,
they can be considered entrepreneurial. A number of scholars of entrepreneurship have indicated that because so many definitions are employed
to define samples of business owners/entrepreneurs, a more important index
of ownership appears to be a clear definition of the sample.

In any new area of professional activity, researchers find it difficult to
agree on fundamentals or common constructs. This has been particularly true
in works on the entrepreneur (Wortman, 1987). If theory in the area of
entrepreneurship research is to develop, researchers will have to find com-
monalties so that comparisons can be made across studies (see Brockhaus,
1987). Empirical and descriptive scholarly studies of entrepreneurs and
small business owners cluster businesses into a homogeneous group despite
differences in their size, growth potential, sector of the economy, charter,
number of employees, revenue and mission, and type of ownership. Analysts
look at individual business units without employing a uniform definition of
entrepreneurship.

Over the last decade, researchers have projected new typologies that can
provide a foundation for model development. In the 1980s, state-of-the-art
research conferences and new publications appeared, among them the *Encyclopedia of Entrepreneurship* (Kent, Sexton, & Vesper, 1982), *The Art and
Science of Entrepreneurship* (Sexton & Smilor, 1986), *The Frontiers of
Entrepreneurship Research* (an annual publication of selected papers from
the Babson Conference), and the U.S. Department of Commerce (1986a)
report titled *The State of Small Business White House Conference on Small
Business—A Report to the President of the United States.* An Entrepreneurial
Division in the Academy of Management was formed in 1986, and a new
academic outlet, *The Journal of Business Venturing,* was launched.

Among the things revealed by the broader and more intense scrutiny was
that practically nothing was known about female entrepreneurs. Before 1978,

with the exception of a few isolated examples, entrepreneurial analyses considered only males (Stevenson, 1986). A decade later, there would be a major bibliography, *Women and Business Ownership* (LaSota, 1986). More recently, directories of female entrepreneurs have appeared. New theories would begin to explain who they were and where they came from. A number of well-established organizations began to contribute information about female entrepreneurs, among them the National Association of Women Business Owners (NAWBO)—at both the regional and national levels—and the centers of entrepreneurship that have sprung up around the country. An important development in the NAWBO was the establishment of the National Foundation for Women Business Owners (NFWBO) as a research and leadership development foundation. Other examples include the Women's Business Development Center in Chicago, Women Entrepreneurs, Inc., in Cincinnati, Ohio, and the Renaissance Entrepreneurship and Alumnae Resources Centers in San Francisco.

The number of well-structured, scholarly studies on the female entrepreneur still is not large. Only a few researchers attempt to define what made the business under study a female entrepreneurship. Lavoie (1984/1985) describes the female entrepreneur "as the female head of a business who has taken the initiative of launching a new venture, who is accepting the associated risks and the financial, administrative and social responsibilities, and who is effectively in charge of its day-to-day management" (p. 34). The U.S. Department of Commerce (1986b) suggests researchers commonly employ a broad definition for the concept of entrepreneurship; an entrepreneur is "one who takes an active role in the decision making and risk taking of a business in which s/he has majority ownership" (p. 10). In this study, we accept both definitions: A female entrepreneur is a woman who has initiated a business, is actively involved in managing it, owns at least 50% of the firm, and has been in operation 1 year or longer.

Data

Few data sources exist concerning female entrepreneurs. Most databases do not provide the gender, racial, or ethnic origin of the business owner. The United States government, for example, until 1996 has clumped all owners under the label "sole proprietor." Data are inconsistent across the four public sources of statistics on women-owned business (the Census of Women-Owned Business, the *Statistics of Income for Sole Proprietorships,* the statistics on self-employed individuals published by the Bureau of Labor

Statistics in *Employment and Earnings,* and the Current Population Reports). Each of these sources defines "woman-owned" differently. It means "51 percent owned, operated and controlled by a woman or women," according to the U.S. Small Business Administration's Office of Women's Business Ownership (U.S. Department of Commerce, 1986b, p. 17). Only recently has the Internal Revenue Service moved to the estimation of the broader spectrum of female business entrepreneurs. All immediate past estimates have been for sole proprietorships and have been calculated from the first names entered on Form 1040, Schedule C. The Bureau of Labor Statistics computes its total from the number of women reporting to be self-employed. More detailed reporting is needed on the number of businesses owned, shares of the business, and number of corporate ownerships (National Foundation for Women Business Owners, 1992; National Foundation for Women Business Owners, and Dun & Bradstreet Information Services, 1995).

Typical Entrepreneurs?

As Beggs, Doolittle, and Garsombke (1994) note, what are considered "typically entrepreneurial" values, experiences, and thought processes are based on conclusions drawn from studying men. The typology has become the norm against which women are compared. This is not always ill-advised. As noted by Birley (1989), when male and female entrepreneurs have been compared and contrasted, fewer differences than similarities have been found (Chaganti, 1986; Koberg, Feldman, & Sarason, 1992; Masters & Meier, 1988). Fagenson (1993) suggests that men and women who become entrepreneurs have similar values. Although the backgrounds, motivations, and previous experiences of male and female entrepreneurs are not generally thought to be uniform, only recently have investigations of female entrepreneurship moved beyond studies of entrepreneurship and self-employment that were all male (Denison & Alexander, 1986; Scheinberg & MacMillan, 1988), did not identify participants by gender (Birley & Westhead, 1993; Cooper & Dunkelberg, 1981; Shane et al., 1991), segmented entrepreneurs on the basis of occupational specialties (Shuman, Seeger, Kamm, & Teebagy, 1986), or included only small, select samples of professional women (Hisrich & O'Brien, 1981). The information deficiency was sufficiently great for one scholar commenting on the relative void of research on women entrepreneurs to call for more research in the little-studied field (Wortman, 1987). Since then, there have been some advances in theory. Moore (1987a, 1987b, 1988,

1990) has compiled studies of women entrepreneurs to attempt to develop a profile of modern female entrepreneurs as contrasted with former, more traditional entrepreneurs. Brush (1992) classified the existing empirical research studies on women business owners and their ventures and called for future research across a number of dimensions. Noting that diversity in the workforce is reflected in changes in the population of entrepreneurs, Beggs et al. (1994) called for new models and research approaches to address the changes, as did Baucus and Human (1994).

Drawing mainly on male-based research, Scheinberg and MacMillan (1988) suggest that entrepreneurs launch their own businesses for approval, independence, personal development, and welfare considerations, along with making money. Shane and colleagues (1991) conclude the one universal reason for business start-ups was a desire for job freedom. To these factors, Birley and Westhead (1993) recently have added tax reduction and other indirect benefits and a desire to follow role models.

There is, however, the strong suggestion that other reasons, unique to women, play a major role in the decision to become an entrepreneur (Brush, 1992; Fischer et al., 1993; Lee-Gosselin & Grise, 1990; Noble, 1986). One is perceived opportunities in the changing workforce. For example, Laurie Moore-Moore, Partner in Real Trends in Dallas, who today is a professional speaker and publisher, targeted the residential real estate industry because it uses numerous speakers, pays them well, and employs a large number of women who, she reasoned, would be interested in listening to a female expert. Devine (1994) notes that female self-employment versus wage-and-salary employment decisions appear intricately linked with a woman's decisions as an individual, as a household member, at any given moment, and over the course of her life. As an example, faced with choices between a lifetime devotion to a marketing career in the rapidly changing banking business, at potential cost to other areas of her life, Vickie Henry of Dallas channeled her expertise in surveying the elements of customer satisfaction into the operation of a business that today sells the service. She is now chair and CEO of Feedback Plus, Inc., known as "America's Mystery Shopper."

Brush (1992) suggests that "when a woman starts or acquires a business, the set of business relationships are integrated into her life" (p. 16). Strong evidence of the linkages between work and family requires that, for female entrepreneurs, measures of their performance must include such factors as social contributions, innovative management practices, customer satisfaction, quality of customer services, job security, social responsiveness, business goal achievement, and employee satisfaction, as well as the traditional measures of growth in sales and increase in employees and profits.

Organizational Interactions and Female Entrepreneurship

Historically, female entrepreneurs have tended to come from the ranks of women who grew up self-reliant. Some were encouraged by family mentors. One entrepreneur's physician stepfather advised her career development from occupational therapist to partnership in an 18-state corporation in the disability insurance area. Other female entrepreneurs simply developed self-reliance. Remembers one,

> Two things helped me have confidence. One was my education and that I focused on women as a student and a scholar. I wrote my undergraduate thesis in American History Literature on "Aspects of the Female Success: New England Women Living in the 1870's." And I graduated from college in 1961. And the reason I did that, I think, is because I was the child of a single parent. My father died when I was 11. I always wondered what would happen to me if I couldn't take care of myself.

Much of the expertise and motivation of female entrepreneurs (Birley, 1989; Brush & Hisrich, 1988) also appears to come from experiences in previous organizational environments (Moore, 1990; Moore et al., 1992). Susan Weiner, who now works in a company that gives her a great deal of freedom, previously started a business that developed customized training programs for Americans doing business with Japanese companies. The idea came from her experience in trying to help the members of her previous firm adjust to dealing with the Japanese.

Women entrepreneurs who have worked in corporate environments appear to benefit in the long run because the scope and variety of organizational experiences mean these environments function as learning laboratories (Murphy, 1992). By no means does this suggest that company principles became the lessons learned. One investment consultant recalled that she felt pressured by her former firm to increase the turnover in her clients' accounts so that the firm would earn more commissions. She knew that her clients' interests were not well served by this strategy. Her ensuing frustration eventually caused her to explore the possibility of opening her own firm.

We have noted already that the modern female entrepreneur, more likely to be a corporate owner than a sole proprietor, is here to stay. Like her male counterpart, her success often hinges on financial savvy, prior experience in the type of business venture, and a strong motivation for independence (Birley, 1989; Brush & Hisrich, 1988). Sometimes the female entrepreneur was driven into business by familiar economic necessities such as making a living after a divorce, the two-income requirement for a desirable standard of family living, or company downsizing. A management consultant depicts how many of the entrepreneurs responded to this last experience: "I was in a company that decided they were going to lay off and reorganize," she says. "I thought, Well, shoot. I'll just get out now because they're probably going to lay me off anyway." Brush (1992) and Devine (1994) have called for more research on female entrepreneurs, particularly studies that address the links between individual and organizational experiences and personal and corporate demands.

Bowers (1994) suggests that once people jump or are "pushed" out of the organization they are energized to become formidable competitors. Bored to tears in the rigidly discriminatory local office of a national financial services firm where the hierarchy expected little of her, for example, an Atlanta entrepreneur broke out to launch a successful competitive business. Many new companies are being developed or led by entrepreneurs who got their training at large companies. These smaller producers have been creating jobs at a steady clip. In the manufacturing industry, for example, the "13.4% jump in small-manufacturer employment exceeded the 11.3% job growth of the service sector, long viewed as the fastest-growing part of the U.S. economy" (Selz, 1993, p. A1).

Such competition is one reason why large American corporations are changing more rapidly than many major international firms. Large companies are hard pressed to keep up with their smaller, more flexible, and bureaucracy-free competitors. Keys to company success include more than product diversity, quality, service, holding down price, and focusing on what the customer wants; people and congenial working environments also are important. Many of the entrepreneurs interviewed in the course of this study were quick to point out that intelligent men had no problem working with creative and talented women. The higher in the organization these men were, the easier it appeared to be for them. Women reported numerous problems with male egos in middle management, by contrast.

Sometimes the reasons women leave organizations are gender neutral. "Following a merger, the new management was fearful of employee involvement and eliminated the Human Resources group I managed which ran the program," said one entrepreneur. As her department was phased out, she took the opportunity to start a meeting facilitation business. Other times, women leave because of gender-related problems. "I absolutely loved the company I worked for," says an entrepreneur who now owns a trucking company, "but I hated my boss. He was so arrogant and aggressive, and he would yell and swear and curse, and this created an unpleasant working environment."

This Study

Observations

We have observed already that female entrepreneurs are the fastest growing segment of the small business population, with numbers increasing dramatically since 1980. We see that women in large organizations are often disillusioned with corporate careers, slow advancement, and continued underrepresentation in top management levels (Dobrzynski, 1996). We have become familiar with the limited advancement opportunities women face, corporate downsizing, and the reality of glass ceilings (Morrison et al., 1987). Discrimination is also a factor. In one study, 46% of the female professionals surveyed reported that they experienced discrimination at work (Trost, 1990).

Worldwide, and particularly in the United States, successful and creative women are leaving organizations for opportunities not available in massively bureaucratic and structured systems (Taylor, 1986). Clearly, many women find what they seek in the new businesses they create, but we know relatively little about these female entrepreneurs.

Issues

This study addresses a number of research areas. Some questions involve organizational entry and exit. Why and how did women with exposure to corporate life decide first to enter the organization and then to leave it for entrepreneurship? Did some who entered organizations do so with intentions of eventually running their own businesses, the group we call "intentional entrepreneurs"? Did others begin in the mold of organizational women, thinking ahead to building a career in the company or industry, a group we term the "corporate climbers"? Or, at organizational entry, was planning short range at best—that is, did women take the organizational job as the best choice at the time?

Other questions relate to the organizational experience. Before entrepreneurship, what had been the female business owner's role in the organization: manager, executive, professional, or other? Did she feel successful at her work? Was she set to advance her career, or was she blocked? When she left to start her business, was she propelled by an internal drive for challenge and self-determination, or did she exit tired of dealing with unhappy organizational situations? In venture ownership, did she replicate a familiar organizational climate or create a new one? If she created a new organizational climate, what are its values?

Still other questions speak to broader topics. Was entrepreneurship a way for women to get control of their work and life? What role, if any, did concerns that time was running out for child-bearing and child-rearing play in decisions? What is the successful female entrepreneur's background? How does she network to get ahead? Will female entrepreneurs who always intended to be entrepreneurs differ from those who aspired to be corporate climbers?

We also wanted to pin down some of the characteristics of this modern female entrepreneur. Is her leadership style similar to or different from that of managers in organizations? Is she today more likely to be a corporate owner or sole proprietor? If she had prior business experience in more than one organization, did that play a role in her entrepreneurship decision? Does she think of her business as a career or as a supplement to a family income? If she benefited from her previous organizational environment as an incubator, did it provide her with a training ground and key contacts? Was she well prepared for private business, entering the market not only with knowledge, skills, ability, and ambition but also with experience and strategies for risk taking, campaigning, networking, and mentoring? Did she embellish her expertise before starting her business with firsthand experience gained through moonlighting or in some other fashion make a trial run before the financial commitment to the new venture? Does she consider herself successful? How does she measure success? What observations, thoughts, and advice does she have to offer to those who will come after her?

Finally, we examine an issue that has interested many researchers. We know that what society considers "typically entrepreneurial" values, experiences, and thought processes have been based on conclusions drawn from studying male entrepreneurs, not women (Birley, 1989; Chaganti, 1986; Fagenson, 1990; Koberg et al., 1992; Masters & Maier, 1988). Do the same measures apply to female business women? Are they, like men, mainly motivated by desires to make more money, achieve independence, and seize an opportunity (Cooper, Woo, & Dunkelberg, 1989; Sexton & Bowman-Upton, 1990)?

In the following chapters, we report what we have found.

2

Making the Leap

The Decision Point

This chapter presents themes in women's accounts of the factors leading to their organizational flight and creation of business ventures. Rich scenarios from the content analysis of the focus interviews along with data from the survey questionnaires provide considerable insight into patterns of organizational exit and the struggles of entrepreneurship, as exemplified by Ruth Ann Menutis, a recent White House Representative for Small Business. She summarizes a career spanning corporate America to the present ownership of The Grove, a $15 million retail and wholesale specialty fruit and nut business that operates in 18 of the nation's largest airports.

Certainly there are new roads for women to travel. We are paving roads so our daughters and granddaughters will be able to avoid the potholes. For 36 years I've traveled roads engineered for the "Good Ole Boy" network. Some roads were smooth, some unpaved, some rock filled and a lot had barricades. However, let's not forget that business men also travel those roads to success—but without the baggage.

For years the woman's role was defined as housekeeper and mom. This unrealistic perception has not disappeared. For those women who are blessed with great providers, I'm sure this can be a very fulfilling role, but still, there are some of us who had to break the mold of establishment thinking in order to survive the times. Now as the two-income family has become the must instead of the accepted, the misperception about roles can become more professionally damaging. It is our responsibility to change it. And as I travel the country, I feel it's clear that the women business owners of America will be the Fortune 500 companies of the 21st century and beyond.

Press reports blare that women have been making significant inroads into the management ranks of organizations, yet women are still vastly underrepresented at the top executive levels. Some suggest that women have been leaving corporations and starting their own businesses to bypass the "glass ceiling" (Morrison et al., 1987). Are there other factors, both personal and organizational, also at work? Because women who exit corporate environments are a unique and relatively unstudied set, we framed a set of questions.

1. What organizational and personal factors influenced the female entrepreneurs' decisions to leave their prior organizations to initiate their own ventures?
2. How important were the organizational and personal influences on these female entrepreneurs' departure decisions?
3. What role, if any, did discrimination play in women's decisions to leave their prior employers to start their businesses?
4. How important were family concerns in their departure decisions?
5. Did the female entrepreneurs who left organizations develop their own firms in ways to deliberately avoid cultural climates they had found onerous?

Survey Data

Rank Order of Departure Reasons

On the surveys, we asked the women to rank and rate a set of 32 possible reasons for their organizational departure and business start-up (see the main survey and follow-up survey in Appendix 2). The results are shown in Table 2.1. Thirty women entrepreneurs (23%) indicated that their most important reason in leaving the corporate environment was to advance themselves. Twenty-seven (21%) indicated their primary motivation was to create a work

TABLE 2.1. Ranking of the Most Important Reasons for Leaving a Prior
Organization

Most Important Reason for Leaving to Initiate Business	*N*
Launching out was the only way to advance myself	30
To create a work environment more consistent with my values	27
To be on the ground floor of a new and exciting business venture in which I am in charge	23
To regain the feeling of excitement about my work	14
To balance family and work	14
To become an entrepreneur	14
Total	122

climate more consistent with their values. Twenty-three (18%) wanted to be
in charge of a new and exciting venture. A smaller number of participants (*n*
= 14, 11%) reported a desire to regain excitement about work, or to balance
family and work (*n* = 14, 11%). Fourteen more (11%) reported that the desire
to become an entrepreneur was the most important motivation. The rankings
suggest that blocks to advancement and unsupportive work environments are
important influences on women's decisions.

Scaled Ratings

Respondents' ratings of organizational and personal influences on their
decisions to leave their organizations to initiate new ventures also suggest a
complex picture for entrepreneurial motivation. Five themes emerged from
a factor analysis of items on the questionnaire. Listed in order of importance
to our entrepreneurs, they are: Challenge, Self-Determination, Family Concerns, Blocks to Advancement, and Organizational Dynamics. (The results
of the statistical analysis appear in Table 2.2.)

Challenge, rated as the most important exit theme (*M* = 3.52), included
items related to the attraction of operating one's own business: respect, the
opportunity to be in charge, regaining feelings of excitement about work, and
recognition and reward for accomplishments. Self-Determination, the
second most important reason (*M* = 3.23), encompassed four reasons for
leaving: to try and make it on one's own, self-esteem, to become an entrepreneur, and freedom from bureaucracy. Family Concerns (*M* = 3.06), the
third theme in importance, had two items, balancing family and work and
gaining control of time. Blocks to Advancement, the fourth theme (*M* = 2.58),

TABLE 2.2. Factor Analysis Results of Entrepreneurs' Reasons for Leaving Their
              Prior Organizations

Reason for Leaving	Mean	Factor 1	Factor 2	Factor 3	Factor 4	Factor 5
Lack of shared information	4.28	**72**	30	18	11	−10
No urgency to finish	4.77	**80**	10	03	13	−00
Little motivation to produce	4.02	**84**	01	07	06	11
Low quality standards	4.28	**71**	16	13	−04	−05
Discrimination	3.99	21	**75**	06	−10	17
To overcome career barriers	2.48	05	**77**	25	08	−07
Didn't fit into corporate cultures	3.72	20	**71**	01	17	−13
Left for more respect	2.78	06	07	**79**	−09	21
Left to be in charge	2.22	20	11	**61**	22	16
Left to regain excitement	2.14	15	08	**80**	24	−07
Left to get recognition	2.83	05	11	**69**	23	−05
Left to make it on my own	2.59	−01	−11	18	**84**	−02
For self-esteem	2.60	03	12	35	**68**	−10
To become an entrepreneur	3.09	14	35	22	**52**	29
For freedom	2.73	16	09	−01	**72**	21
To balance family and work	3.61	−03	01	−05	−03	**86**
To control my time	2.28	−01	−06	26	23	**72**
Eigenvalues		4.51	2.24	1.46	1.40	1.29
Proportion of variance explained		.27	.13	.09	.08	.08

SOURCE: Buttner, E. H. & Moore, D. P. (1997). Women's organizational exodus to entrepreneurship:
Self-reported motivations and correlates with success. *Journal of Small Business Management, 35*(1), 34-46.
Used with permission.
NOTE: Decimal points are omitted from the factor scores of each item.

included the items discrimination, career barriers, and a feeling of not fitting into the corporate culture. The final theme, Organizational Dynamics
($M = 1.66$), was composed of organizational obstacles to getting work
accomplished: others failed to share critical information, lack of urgency in
completing tasks, demotivating aspects of the organizational climate, and
low quality standards.

Focus Group Data

The mean ratings of the five themes that emerged from the analysis of the
questionnaire data suggest that, when reflecting on their entrepreneurial
motivation, entrepreneurs were influenced by the attraction of entrepreneurship more than by negative organizational factors. Discussions in the focus

groups, however, were free from the questionnaire structure, and conversation flowed. As the numerous focus group comments revealed, many entrepreneurs had left their former employers because they felt exploited ("I was experiencing stress-related physical health problems and sexual harassment. It really was necessary for me to leave my last position," said one) and because opportunities were lacking:

> My view of the corporate world was that you continually go up. It was when I got to the most senior levels of the corporation, I was one of the 10 highest ranking women in a 15,000 person corporation. That's when I found the glass ceiling.

Content analysis of the focus group discussions highlighted a number of negative organizational experiences. This may suggest that perhaps the entrepreneurs were concerned about the social acceptability of their survey responses when they filled out the questionnaires, a phenomenon previously observed by Rosener (1995).

Content Analysis of Departure Influences

The content analysis of focus interview data reveals deeper and more comprehensive reasons for the organizational exits. The first item to cluster in the content analysis was Self-Determination. This cluster was largely composed of the factor dimensions Autonomy and Job Freedom ($n = 42$, 33%). The item Challenges and Attractions of Entrepreneurship clustered second. It included all the items identified in the factor analysis of the questionnaire data: Desire for Recognition and Respect ($n = 35$, 27%), Being in Charge ($n = 30$, 23%), and Regaining Excitement About Work ($n = 13$, 10%). The third cluster, Blocks to Corporate Advancement, was largely influenced by the items Lack of Career Advancement ($n = 28$, 22%), Discrimination ($n = 24$, 19%), and a Feeling of Not Fitting in the Corporate Culture.

Cluster 1: Self-Determination, Autonomy, and Job Freedom

As noted above, the Self-Determination cluster composed of the autonomy, job freedom, and self-esteem dimensions clustered first in the content analysis. This was not entirely unexpected. Research has suggested critical differences in the values of entrepreneurs and managers. Fagenson (1993) found that entrepreneurs gave significantly more weight than did their managerial counterparts to the values of self-respect, freedom, a sense of accomplishment, and an exciting life and such methods of achieving these values as ambition, capability, and independence. Fagenson (1993) concluded that entrepreneurs want something different out of life than do managers. Such differences in values may make it more difficult for aspiring entrepreneurs to succeed in large organizations and may contribute to the impetus for departure for business initiation.

Autonomy and Freedom

The search for autonomy and freedom and the desire to make it on one's own was referenced in the interviews by 42 of our women entrepreneurs (33%). This item ranked first in our content analysis cluster for the dimension of Self-Determination and was the second ranking explanatory component in our questionnaire data. These findings are consistent with previous research findings that entrepreneurs value freedom and autonomy, have a preference for personal responsibility, and exhibit a high need for achievement (Cromie & Hayes, 1988; Fagenson, 1993; Hornaday & Aboud, 1971; McClelland, 1985; Neider, 1987).

Elizabeth Morris, president and founder of Insight Research Corporation in Dallas, described her quest. "I never wanted to take the risk of having somebody else make the decisions. I always thought, 'If I make the decision wrong, we'll have to turn the lemon into lemonade. It's my decision and I'm going to live with it.'" Other women entrepreneurs described similar desires for autonomy. "I knew that I was going to be a working person for my life. And I wanted something that wasn't just a job. It would have to be more fulfilling than working as a job in somebody else's business," recalls Andrea Coates, owner of ChiroCare Plus in Brookline, Massachusetts. "And for me, it was very important to be able to go into a field where I would never have to compromise my ethics."

Gender has been found to influence the career resources and power that command and enhance one's managerial advancement (Tharenou, Latimer, & Conroy, 1994). Perhaps this is one reason only 14 of our entrepreneurs (11%) felt their former organization helped them develop a feeling of autonomy. Janee (Gee) Tucker, president and chief operating officer, Tucker & Associates (TAI), and vice president of Integrated Logistical Support, Inc. (ILSI), New Orleans, reflects on this organizational barrier to independence:

You know, "You do the work, you're our little woman." I'm not that type. I like to work on my own and I like to get there and get things done. I think I was doing a little too much and getting too much publicity for the training department and training programs and test stores. They didn't like the idea, so they decided when promotion opportunities came up it was time for me to stay where I was and that my training programs could be duplicated through the hiring of key personnel to do the same work in the operations department making that department responsible.

Brodsky (1993) and Rosin and Korabik (1991) have observed that women tend to leave male-dominated organizations that have limited leadership opportunities and responsibility, where schedules are inflexible, and where the lack of autonomy and presence of office politics predominate. The experiences of most of the entrepreneurs in this study appear to support this conclusion and also the research findings of Fagenson (1993) that women who wanted to command their work viewed the corporate environment as confining and without much opportunity to feel personal empowerment. Elizabeth Morris, a Dallas entrepreneur, remembers:

I think I have consistently felt that every organization that I've worked in, from a large private to a public agency, that I had only one wheel on the ground. I was only allowed to do what they needed me to do in the niche. Of course, that's the way an organization works. You have to fit into the team slot where you're needed. I felt that I wasn't . . . able to live up to my capacity. The only way I could do that was to steer out on my own, where all four wheels hit the ground. What I got as an entrepreneur was head and shoulders above where I had been as any-body's employee.

Self-Esteem

Part of the challenge for the woman manager in organizations, particularly large ones, is to maintain her identity and her sense of what is important in environments shaped and largely determined by men. Lindsay and Pasquali (1993, p. 35) described the dilemma as "the internal struggle of each woman to define herself, and especially her femininity, in a world and workplace dominated by images of successful men and masculinity." Gilson and Kane (1987) and Ely (1995) report that women experience a struggle to retain their sense of identity at work. In their holistic approach to women's careers,

Powell and Mainiero (1992) emphasize life's totality. It is reasonable, they say, to assume that there are many shifts in focus within a single career, and, at times, for women to place a greater emphasis on their personal lives and make sacrifices in their personal career development.

Sixteen of the entrepreneurs (12% of the sample) reported that beginning their new venture was the result of a personal search, an internal focus, rather than a direct response to some external event or series of events, such as discrimination. A theme of these women's comments was that they were seeking to acknowledge parts of themselves that had been suppressed or had not yet been developed. In all, 24 (19%) entrepreneurs mentioned the difficulty of maintaining self-confidence in their previous incubator organizations. Said Susan Brown, an owner of The Avalon Consulting Group in Pennsylvania, who left a corporation in the financial services industry,

> What I felt I was good at and what my skills were and what I liked about myself, they were the things I wasn't using anymore because I became almost afraid. I mean, my confidence in my own ability was lost in trying to adapt to this corporate identity. And when I didn't have meaningful work, I didn't feel like I had a meaningful life.

Reevaluating her career, Rebecca Carney, owner of BECCA et al, a Philadelphia-based company in the industry's Multi-Million Dollar Roundtable, said:

> I remember feeling so trapped. I remember thinking that they just owned me. I had grown up in this company. I mean I felt like my whole identity was wrapped up in who I was there and how I was perceived there and I mean, I began to feel just boxed in. Let me out. Let me be whoever I am, whatever that is. But, I didn't even know who I was then.

A California entrepreneur described how her former job as a state's attorney was inconsistent with what she wanted. "I developed some ideas of what I would like to do with the rest of my life. The question came when I asked myself, 'What is it that you create in your job?' The best I did was to reduce someone's misery. I wanted to create happiness."

In some cases, it was a lack of organizational commitment or the changing of the guard within the incubator organization in an unexpected way that forced an entrepreneur out. At every stage of her career, Susie Marshall, owner of CompuTactics, Inc., a Dallas firm, had focused on developing and honing her skills to keep up with the newest advances in technology. She

became an expert in computer systems, city government, and banking. She
was also a certified public accountant, specializing in public accounting and
money transfer. She rose to become a vice president in her firm, then joined
a special management team for a major manufacturing subsidiary. What led
her to leave the corporate incubator?

> We grew that company from 6 to 250 people. I left because we had a
> 5-year contract. We ran it very much as an entrepreneurial company. We
> made all the decisions, but we didn't have an ownership interest, only
> a contract and some strong commitments from the company. While we
> knew that the major corporation planned to come down and take over
> the company in 5 years, we did not expect them to take over in $3\frac{1}{2}$. They
> sent their team down to reorganize everything. I was chief financial
> officer, but instead of reporting directly to the president, I was reporting
> to another vice president. I had about twice as many people reporting
> to me as before—they had just doubled all my responsibilities—and I
> had no decision-making authority. I thought, this is not really what I
> want to do.

In addition to the search for autonomy, findings from this group of
entrepreneurs support Gabor (1994), who concluded that many entrepreneurs
come from the ranks of women who had been successful in corporate life,
who sought a range of professional experiences, cultivated industry contacts,
and changed jobs whenever they felt they reached a dead end. Said Marilyn
Sifford, an owner in Philadelphia, tracing her varied career:

> In my career, since graduating from college, I have worked in about six
> or seven different industries and organizations. I was a truant officer,
> then I worked for the state employment security commission. This was
> followed by a personnel job at a newspaper and then I got involved in
> training. After that, I worked for an insurance company and from there
> went into organizational development in an oil company. The oil com-
> pany had a major restructuring and eliminated my department. My next
> job was at a university hospital. The man who hired me died of cancer.
> The man who succeeded him called me in his office one day and said,
> "I want my own team." My next job was starting an internal consulting
> function inside a financial corporation. I'd been there about 2 years
> when I was recruited for a job with a major corporation in another state,
> a position that basically put together everything I had done up to that

point. I passed the six-figure mark with that job. But I ended up with a boss who, while I had more responsibility and was being paid more than I ever had before in my life, refused to let me make decisions on my own.

Phelps and Mason (1991) suggest that older women, after careful consideration of alternatives, may opt out of the corporate track altogether because they are more excited about entrepreneurial and consulting prospects. Fifteen of our entrepreneurs gave this reason for leaving the corporate culture. Another organizational trail to entrepreneurship is the well-trod path made by successful women who once were on the threshold of senior management (Aldrich, 1989; Brush, 1992; Dingwall, 1992; Powell & Mainiero, 1992). Carol Scarano, a New York entrepreneur who established Helping Hands Network, Inc., defines how the previous organizational environment had affected her:

I worked my way up to senior vice president of operations in a $4 million company. My responsibilities included finance, the day-to-day operations, personnel review, hiring and firing and so on for the whole company. During the last 3 years I was there I was getting very unhappy because there wasn't anywhere for me to go according to my boss, who was the owner. All of a sudden I needed special degrees in the things I had been doing for the last 12 years.

Stifling Bureaucracy Effects

Long-standing research suggests that bureaucracies are premised on hierarchical principles that conflict with the entrepreneurial values of independence and freedom (Weber, 1947). Specific references were made by 29 of our entrepreneurs (22%) in the focus interviews to a desire to be free of the bureaucratic environment. Elizabeth Morris recounted the divergence between what she sought in her corporate position and what she found:

I think I just wanted a chance to work and to be the best I could be. What I found in the corporate environment was that they didn't encourage you to be the best you could be. They encouraged you to fit into a niche or slot. They encouraged you to fit into their expectations. If you outperformed your peers, then your staff had to work harder. Some resentments built up. Under some circumstances you were a threat to the organization when you overproduced.

Research has shown that entrepreneurs often find the structure and procedures of large organizations cumbersome and frustrating, prefer innovation rather than routine, and in their attempts to implement their ideas may seem abrasive to their organizational colleagues (Buttner & Gryskiewicz, 1993). Part of the frustration reported by the women entrepreneurs may be a function of the inherent incompatibility of their values and *modus operandi* with organizational rules, modes of conduct, and reward systems. Recalls Evelyn Eskin, president of Health Power Associates, Inc., in Philadelphia:

> I worked for a man who resigned a month after I got there and the department became very chaotic. The job became very undoable very quickly and I didn't want to work in that kind of environment. It was also a very, very bureaucratic process-oriented environment. It allowed me to see that, contrary to what they told me in MBA school, I am not a bureaucrat or process-oriented person. What I wanted in the workplace was very different from what people expected in that environment.

Speaking about elements in the environment where conflict occurred, Evelyn also referred to the deadly effects of the homogenization of the work product, the absence of standards of accountability, and her desire "to build up people's skills rather than trying constantly to force square pegs into round holes." Saralyn Levine, owner and founder of Delectable Dining in Chamblee, Georgia, once a manager at a major communications company, spoke about the loss of individuality:

> The reports that I would send up to the home office in another state might have had my name on them, they might not have. I don't think anyone really cared where they came from, and I just didn't care that much about what I was doing, because I knew everyone else in the different areas of the country was doing the exact same thing.

Time-consuming politics often led to a feeling that an organizational dead end had been reached (22%, $n = 28$). Says Susan Brown:

> I left the corporate environment essentially because the work that I was doing wasn't consistent with my value system. It wasn't at all energizing

in a learning sense. I felt that I was getting to be a couple of tricks pony. What I was best at doing, bringing an organized and thoughtful sense of inquiry into a corporate situation, was not very highly prized the higher I got in the management ranks.

Changing business climates had led Vickie Henry to a dead end.

My primary reason for leaving a job in banking I had for 15 years was because you could see what was happening to the financial industry. As vice president of marketing, I began to watch all the de-clustering that was going on. Being in charge of nine banks and doing the marketing, I could see no future when the mergers began.

Suppressive environments caused some women to begin finding a way out of the organization. "I much prefer to be my own boss than to report to somebody else," said Ann Angel, president of Technologies Training of the Triad, Inc., Winston-Salem, North Carolina:

I decided I would go to another corporate environment. But the feelers didn't result in anything I could put my hands on or that I felt comfortable with. When the opportunity to explore a small business came along, I took a major step on blind faith alone and went for it. But because I was the procurer of the services that I am now delivering, I knew what was unavailable in the market place. I knew what companies needed and what they didn't need. I had learned that in my corporate experiences.

Another bureaucratic characteristic with which these female entrepreneurs had difficulty was the reliance on rigid rules and regulations that hampered one's productivity and thereby closed off opportunity. Says one entrepreneur:

[T]he three people who owned the company were all ex-service people and they ran the place like boot camp. It did not really matter what kind of job you did if you were not plugged in to that network. There were no women in management. It really didn't make a difference if you saved the company a million dollars, and I did, purchasing all of 13 million dollars a year in raw materials.

Another entrepreneur who is currently a management consultant and previously held various positions in state and federal government recounted both her satisfaction and her frustration in a high-level position:

> I made a number of contributions, but when it reached a certain point, I found the system to be unyielding. For example, I was in charge of research contracts for $50 million and seven financial departments. There was always a blockage of some sort. I could fix everything under my control but there were other things I coulan't fix.

Wendy Norden Ginn, CEO of Convert!, Inc., a San Francisco high-tech company, observed of her former corporate environment:

> A lack of vision—the mundane approach to operations. This brought about the beginning of my desire to leave. No one took accountability for their work. Responsibility was passed onto someone else. Enthusiasm was missing. Endless meetings occurred which appeared to only slow down the decision-making process.

Bureaucratic frustrations took a toll, as an East Coast entrepreneur related in describing an earlier event in her career.

> When I came to the city, I became a police officer and worked for the chief for a while. I was able to make some changes in efficiency and proficiency but only to a certain level. Somehow, someone from somewhere else made decisions and then everything I did was lost. One incident: The city was going to invest in a whole bunch of word processors and I had just come off working on a case where a little girl was snatched and murdered. I had set up a computer that could track all the kick sheets that came in because we didn't have a computer that could do that. When they decided to set up a word-processing system, I said, "Why don't you buy a computer system that will do the tracking as well as the word processing?" I gathered the data. I came in with a system that would allow us to track serial killers around the country with a competitive price that was also much lower than what they were going to pay just for the word processing. When the time came, they purchased the word processors, not the computers. Two or three years

later they dumped all the word processors, but that sort of thing I found personally frustrating.

Many entrepreneurs clearly felt that adjustments to the corporate culture came at too high a price. "I could have stayed if I had swallowed my self-respect and swallowed my self-esteem, but I wasn't willing to do that," says one entrepreneur, who then turned her discouragement into building a clientele and preparing for the day she would launch her own business. Twenty-nine of the entrepreneurs in this study (22%) referred to organizational conditions that had left them with no space to work or no opportunities for advancement.

Cluster 2: Challenge—The Attractiveness of Entrepreneurship

The item Challenges and Attractions of Entrepreneurship was the second to cluster in the factor analysis of the focus group discussion.

Respect and Recognition

Thirty-five women (27%) cited the desire for increased responsibility and recognition as a part of their departure deliberations. In their own businesses, the women asserted, they had been able to develop companies with values more consistent with their own, where their input made a critical impact on the success of the business. Honi Stempler explains, "I never had the American dream of opening my own company." After taking over the management of a subsidiary of the company where she had been for 6 years, however, "I began to have the sense of what I could do, who I was, that I was capable of doing more than I had ever thought, not just churning out the work, but the hiring and firing, and the billing and the increasing the sales, and all that . . ., and I began to wonder whether I was happy where I had been." After working hard and successfully running the subsidiary, her bosses were aggravated, not pleased.

Because the first year they were supposed to have a loss. They had opened up this subsidiary as a tax shelter to the corporation, and being as naive as I was in these matters, I never thought they would put me down there with that in mind. I showed a $200 profit that year, and it drove them crazy. I was just so naive, so trusting, so absolutely fooled.

So I configured a vision for my own company; I wanted a place where people could be appreciated, people would do the work they were supposed to; where I could rely upon them, where everyone could be adult about it, where one would not have to worry about all this political garbage.

Opportunity to Be in Charge

Gilson and Kane (1987) reported that 86% of the women in their study sample felt that they lacked sufficient authority to accomplish their work. Ibarra (1993) says that inadequate authority to accomplish assignments means that women must rely to a greater extent on the informal networks in the organization and use personal influence because they lack organizational resources afforded to male managers. This is particularly a problem when women are excluded from the informal organizational networks. Men, like women, have a preference for associating with others similar to themselves. Although the exclusion may not be intentional, it has the effect of denying women access to information about the unwritten rules of conduct, support from others at their organizational level, and useful contacts. Thirty women in this study (23%) talked about the desire to be in charge as a primary reason for their organizational exit.

In addition to the professional toll resulting from the exclusion, there is also a psychic cost for women, an issue raised by the entrepreneurs in discussing their reasons for leaving. Laurie Moore-Moore, a former manager, remembers that having her authority usurped was "demoralizing, a horrible thing to go through, because when you're used to being able to make decisions and have authority, then have that taken away from you, it is extremely stifling." A Midwestern entrepreneur recounts how preconceived notions about what women could and could not do prevented her from being able to complete the assignments for which she was specifically hired:

I got a call from the VP of human resources for a Fortune 500. I went in and talked to him and he said, "I know what you can do. I have heard time and time again what you have done, how you have done it, I am so impressed, I have always wanted to meet you and I want you to work for me. I have interviewed other people and nobody quite fits the position that I want to fill and I think you are the one." So I was hired. A year and maybe 2 or 3 months later I was out of the organization. And the reason I was out of the organization was because I was the first female manager of human resources in the entire system. I found that the industry was so male-dominated in its attitudes towards women, especially in management positions, it was an absolute nightmare. It was so bad with one senior vice-president in particular that my male boss confided: "I never will admit this in court, but quite frankly 'X' is a male chauvinist pig. He sees you as a threat to him and his power." I was forced to be accompanied by two men whenever I visited the field force—for my "protection," they said. I was dealing with such a pile of baggage on the part of senior management that I knew I couldn't cut through it. I didn't feel that I could or should be the savior of the company or the savior of women in the company. It just wasn't worth it.

Findings here are consistent with research that has found that women managers with low perceived support and lack of authority experienced high job anxiety as well as depression (Greenglass, 1985, 1987). Obstacles to job success such as insufficient authority or the absence of a supporting environment push people to overcome a painful situation by leaving the organization (McCauley, Ruderman, Ohlott, & Morrow, 1994).

Controlling One's Destiny

Motivation to leave corporate environments also came from a desire for control over one's life. Julie Thomas is a co-owner of Thomas & Thomas Architects, Ltd., of Evanston, Illinois. She is a licensed architect and interior designer whose work has been featured in *Art by Architects*. She explained, "I always wanted to be in charge. I wanted to strike out on my own at a very early age." Other entrepreneurs believed, after observing bosses in their old organizations, that they could do a better job. Impatient about waiting for a promotion to have that opportunity, they took the alternate route of branching out on their own. High productivity records were a driving force, as illustrated by Jeanne Tighe, an owner of Blue Grass Advertising Specialties in Lexington, Kentucky.

I became the second highest salesperson out of a force of 12. All the other salespeople were men. I beat them all in sales except one. I was the only woman. The man that owned the company sold it. The man that bought it did not know anything about the business. I decided that I knew more about it than he did, so I would start my own company.

Regaining Excitement

Thirteen of our entrepreneurs stated that they started a business of their own to regain excitement about themselves and their work. Joan Holliday, one of four partners of Women in Process Consulting, in Chadds Ford, Pennsylvania, wanted to test her business competence but could not in her prior organization: "You had a sense that you had something of value to offer and there was a limit to that. The culture did not encourage initiative." L. Elaine Green, president of Video Features, Inc., in Cincinnati, summed the feelings of many women, saying,

> What I have come to think over the years is that we are always wanting equality and consideration in male-owned and dominated companies. We are creating our own opportunities now. We are creating companies and some of these companies are going to be major corporations in the future. We are creating our own opportunities, we are not having to ask permission for them.

Recognition of Accomplishments

Entrepreneurs spoke about the lack of appreciation they perceived for their input into their former organizations. Says Mary B. Hopple, "I wrote a memo stating, 'Why don't you have a purchase order system and get the merchandise out the moment it hits the door. Let's sell this before we have to pay for it.' I was 25 and they didn't listen." Recalls Renee Peyton, a computer consultant from Atlanta, "In every company I ever worked, you were expected to play politics and, excuse the term, 'suck up' to your superiors or you got nowhere. I mean the fact that you were creative and had ideas that could help the company advance had absolutely no bearing on what was actually happening."

Cluster 3: Blocks to Corporate Advancement

Blocks to Corporate Advancement, the third item to cluster in the content analysis of the focus group discussions, incorporated the dimensions of not fitting into the corporate culture, barriers, and discrimination.

Not Fitting In

As women begin to move into the upper levels of their organizations, they often found themselves alone, female pioneers in male-created and -dominated environments. Kanter (1977) coined the work "tokens" to describe this pioneering status. Token status often encourages social segregation while simultaneously making members of the dominant group more aware of their commonalities. This "contrast effect" makes it likely that men in the dominant male group will be uncomfortable and uncertain in working with a token. Consequently, Snavely (1993) argues, although the effectiveness of women's abilities and behaviors in organizations has been documented, women still are not accorded the respect and recognition deserved by their performance. The token thus will have to go to greater lengths to prove her loyalty to the group and her worth than would a new member from the dominant group. McKeen and Burke (1990) found that female tokens were less satisfied with their jobs and were more likely to quit to find more hospitable organizational climates than were their male colleagues.

Their status as outsiders ran through the comments of a number of the female entrepreneurs in this study. On observing the interactions of the top executives in her company, Marilyn Sifford, a former manager, reported that she changed her mind about the attraction of a top management position for herself in the company. "I had the opportunity to facilitate some meetings with the top group and there were maybe a couple of women and 25 or 30 men in that group. Being in there and feeling like what it felt like to be there and seeing how they operated didn't make me want to be there."

It was the "good old boy" system that drove one in every five of the entrepreneurs in this study out (20%, $n = 26$). A former vice president of marketing and education for a major corporation recruited to another organization describes the 13 months she worked in the second firm as the most miserable time of her life. After this experience, the Texas entrepreneur resolved to never work directly for another man again. Another entrepreneur echoed, "I bought the business because the determining factor was that I would never work for a man again. That was for me a very conscious decision." Another resolved to break the pattern. "I had been in an environment that was very hierarchical, very male oriented, not much personal feedback, not much opportunity for females to advance. I was determined that was not going to happen in any business I created," says Dale Whitmer, executive director of The Colin A. Ross Institute for Psychological Trauma in Dallas.

Demonstrating Competence

The sex role stereotype of the American woman is that she is passive and compliant (Broverman, Vogel, Broverman, Clarkson, & Rosenkrantz, 1972; Moore, 1986). This expectation creates a dilemma for women seeking to demonstrate their ability to handle complex business problems and their competence to move up in organizations. Marilyn Sifford talked about how this dilemma played out for her:

> I don't think I am bragging when I say I knew I had very good managerial skills. I had a track record for being able to build a team and have a group of people work together to really accomplish exciting things. Well, this manager—whenever I made a decision, which I thought was a little decision, if I didn't consult him first, he saw it as me going around him, leaving him out. What he wanted from me was compliance. He wanted me to do whatever he said to do and to accept whatever he said. And when I didn't do that, you can't imagine the anger that evoked.

Powell (1993) concludes that although there are some stylistic differences, there are no differences in the effectiveness of male and female managers. Kelly (1991) also reports that men and women are similar in personality traits including dominance, self-control, achievement via independence, intellectual efficiency, capacity for status, and responsibility.

Career Barriers

Rosener (1989) reported that of 124 women attending a business conference, 70% had worked in a corporation prior to becoming an entrepreneur. Of the women entrepreneur expatriates, 80% reported that, in their prior positions, they had to work harder than males to advance. Similar findings were reported by Lawler (1994). Of the 250 women executives in Gilson and Kane's (1987) study, 97% agreed with the statement that " 'women have to work harder to reap the same rewards'—the same salary, authority, status, perks, and bonuses" (p. 142).

In the focus group discussions, the entrepreneurs discussed the barriers they had encountered. Factors that had affected them included Reorganization ($n = 15$, 12%) or Downsizing ($n = 14$, 11%); a Lack of Managerial Ethics ($n = 25$, 19%) that surfaced in unkept commitments, often in terms of pay

(n = 17, 14%); being involved in dead-end jobs with no possibilities for promotion, growth, or advancement (n = 28, 22%); running headlong into the good old boy system (n = 26, 20%); or simply facing burnout or unexpected blows (n = 17, 14%). Each of these items either directly or indirectly tied back to performance and the distribution of organizational reward systems.

Their own focus on superior performance often brought the women in the present study in conflict with organizational standards. Several entrepreneurs said that their former bosses and organizations did not know what to do with competent, capable women seeking more responsibility and autonomy. One entrepreneur, who had worked with several presidents of universities, had been in the office of her boss when he was called for a reference. She recounted:

> When I asked to leave, he said "No, you sit right here." He put on the speaker phone and talked to this guy and said all these wonderful, flowery, flattering things about me. And the other guy said what anybody would say, "If she is so good, why aren't you keeping her there?" My boss said, "Because the organization doesn't know what to do with her." When I think about it, that's why the organization couldn't keep me. It was such a profound statement.

Said one entrepreneur of the political frustrations of her former job, where she had risen as far as she could within the firm, "I was let go from a major corporation. It really left a bad taste in my mouth. I was determined that I wasn't going to put myself in this position again."

Many of the organizations clearly were not used to having women in high management positions. "When we looked at the organizational structure," said Susie Marshall,

> the women were indeed in the lower supervisory and mid-manager positions. When you got to the home office and corporate environment, there were no women. When they took a very bright woman and demoted her from a regional position, they couldn't justify it to me. That told me that my career path was going to be blocked at some point.

Lingering Discrimination

Evidence of discrimination has been demonstrated in decisions concerning selection, promotion, performance evaluation, access to training opportunities (Rosen & Jerdee, 1973, 1974), and salary assignment (Dipboye, Arvey, & Terpstra, 1977). In a study of 466 employed women by Konek and Kitch (1994), two-thirds reported that they had experienced one or more episodes of discrimination. Salary discrimination was the most frequently reported form, followed by bias in promotion and assignment of job responsibilities, selection, and hiring. In spite of government and corporate efforts to ensure equal opportunity, women still report a significant amount of bias. Discrimination was referenced by 24 (19%) of our entrepreneurs in the focus interviews. Some women had experienced sexual harassment. Says one who did, "I was fired because I wouldn't sleep with my boss. I was just kicked out, kicked upstairs actually. I just couldn't do that. I scrambled to use my skills and started marketing myself around the business."

Compared with other themes from the survey data, however, for these entrepreneurs discrimination appears to be a less important influence in departure decisions than other organizational and personal factors. For example, many of the 17 entrepreneurs who cited pay as a primary factor in their decision to leave the corporate environment to start a business of their own tied the inequity not to discrimination but to factors such as the lack of organizational ethics, reorganization, politics, and the good old boy system. Their observations are consistent with current research findings. Women recognize that discrimination exists but often decide to "play by the rules" and not to protest, with the result that only a small proportion of women leave organizations solely or primarily as a result of discrimination (Loudermilk, 1987; Williams, 1988). Freeman (1990) found that female mid-level managers would rather change jobs than attempt to change coworkers' attitudes.

Discrimination occurred frequently enough to affect many entrepreneurs in this study, however. Remembers one:

I was in a unique position in that I was the highest ranking female in the company. I was the pioneering female, the only one for many years. As I got higher up, I really started experiencing more discrimination. Which was really such a shock and I had a hard time figuring it out. But the higher I went up, the more I experienced the resistance of "Well you've gone too far and you're too big for your britches."

Discrimination appeared in a variety of forms. "What depressed me," says one entrepreneur,

was that I felt like a female every single day of my life there. There were colleagues who would never give me an assignment because I was a female. If I had a shot at doing some work and proving myself, that is one thing, but when they won't even allow you to work, that was a problem. So it was an oppressive atmosphere.

A Southern entrepreneur remembered the frustration she felt at being discounted, "sitting on a management team of predominantly men and not being taken too seriously. Encountering traditional males, I just got this pain, 'Ooh, this stuff does exist, this chauvinism, this discrimination.' Finally I decided that to really have control over a situation I would have to do it on my own." Evelyn Eskin remembers discrimination in the form of management "[i]gnoring what you said or having what you say ignored or dismissed until it's later said by a man, in which case it was then determined to be a brilliant idea. After you see that happen a number of times, it is very disturbing."

Cluster 4: Organizational Dynamics—Power and Politics

Kanter (1977) suggested that power is controlled by a small number of people in large organizations. Those who wish to get things accomplished are therefore dependent on these powerful few. Because many corporations are large, managers must work with and through others over whom they lack formal authority. These bureaucratic characteristics lead to the predominance of politics. Although fourteen (11%) of the entrepreneurs in this study reported that they had a sense of autonomy in their prior organization, and 7 (5%) of these felt empowered, many of the other entrepreneurs had exactly the opposite experience. Ann Angel, now operating a highly successful computer training company, said of her former organization:

The political environment there was very, very oppressive, even before the takeovers. I found that my need for self-expression, my need for creativity, my need for just value in who and what I was, to be unacceptable in that environment. It was politics pure and simple. People who did not do a good job were rewarded in spite of that.

Long before Wendy Ginn left, she knew her ideas did not mesh with those around her. "Because of my experience in the corporate environment I know the political things to do to survive, but I will not run my business that way," she now says. "I realize that people in the trenches get it done." Ethel Cook notes, "I was working for CEOs. It's a position that, if the CEO goes, you go. One position I got in, I started work on Monday, working for the president of the company, and Friday he was fired. I stayed with that company 6 months, but ultimately, they were trying to replace me behind my back and I found out about it." Joanne Pratt, president of Joanne H. Pratt Associates, holds advanced degrees from Oberlin and Harvard University. She operates a consulting firm specializing in the virtual office and provides a perspective on how the rituals in the organizational culture worked to thwart empowerment opportunities.

We moved into a new building. The men in every office had a big desk. The assistants—some male, some female—had a smaller desk. My mentor took one look at our new office and he shoved the small desk out and down the hall. He then went down the hall and got me a big desk. And all hell broke loose. Men at my mentor's level in the organization just couldn't stand the symbolism of my having a desk the same size as his. With clients, he would make sure that I went with him to out-of-town business meetings. I had a professional position rather than a subservient role. That's one of the things that helped me when I later became an entrepreneur. I had been given self-confidence. It was a wonderful example of mentorship. But I also saw the kind of organizational symbolism that is intended to keep women in their place.

Power shifts, organizational redesigns, and the absence of mentors left many of the entrepreneurs disillusioned with corporate life. As the only designer on staff, one entrepreneur had flexibility, opportunities to take charge, and responsibility, but no one from whom to learn. Later, after advancing rapidly, she worked for a very good manager who focused on developing people. During this 4-year period, he convincingly painted a bright, long-range picture of opportunities that would open up. An overnight power shift in the company, however, collapsed this designer's future opportunities. She reported that her new manager was egotistical and inexperienced and had limited people skills. "He felt threatened with the fact that I was 15 years his junior and making twice the money he was. Rather than understanding that my success was his success, because in a sales management structure it is like a pyramid with goals based on the people below you, I was a vehicle to help him reach his goals and to help him earn income. He considered me too much competition."

Twenty-three (18%) of the women cited organizational politics as a decisive exit factor. Said Sherie Conrad, a New Orleans human-resource and small-business management expert, in pointing to the restraints placed on her duties, "I worked to get a job with an employment agency as an apprentice. I held it for 6 months and was very successful. The person that I worked for had a real problem because I did more than the five people he had in the job prior to me. Instead of exciting him, it scared him. My decision to leave there was based on the fact I did not have control over my work." "I left there because I wanted to be the boss," says another entrepreneur with a similar experience. "I felt repressed by not being able to have creative freedom." At worst, deeply embedded politics determined how all organizational tasks were carried out. "I had an identity with a mentor," says Janet Bensu, a California entrepreneur.

When he fell, I fell. There were six senior managers and all of us left. There was no honor, no ethics. Everything I now did was discounted. There was no one to turn to. There were some women in the organization. I turned to a woman lawyer and I was able to create a nice situation monetarily. I had not prepared other options. Now in business for myself, I prepare myself for risks. At one point in my own business I lost everything and I had no money. It never entered my mind to go back into the corporate world. I developed a whole new concept of the decision-making process. Small business is not as bureaucratic. Nor does it have as many hurdles as the corporate world.

Compensation and Equitable Treatment

Expectations among women in management and the professions are changing. Hardesty and Jacobs (1986) found that many successful women professionals want fair treatment, improved compensation, and a more balanced life. When these were not available in the corporate environment, career shifts—among them self-employment—were not uncommon, as noted in the following transition for Dale Whitmer.

I had been creating businesses for other people for about 12 years by starting laboratories from ground up. For the past 5 years I started a physicians management group and grew that business. What I didn't realize at the time was that while what I was doing was exciting, I would move from one project to the next challenge and always ended up hitting a ceiling. I was dissatisfied financially and with the fact that my knowledge went unrewarded. I was ready for the challenge and the freedom. Now no one else is calling the shots and no one else is taking the paycheck.

Another entrepreneur puts it this way: "I had been figuring out that they had a lot of men in the company and all of the promises that had been made about promotions and partnership never came across. To preserve a number of solid business relationships, I decided I wanted to just go ahead and start my own company."

Our study also found direct references to overt discrimination and inequitable pay among our focus group members. "I was 'Girl Friday' at the newspaper, the editor, the publisher, wrote the news and ran a small office supply inside the newspaper and I didn't get paid for my work. A guy they hired after me didn't do nearly as much as I did. Now I was to train him and he was making a higher salary." The experience of Patty Breeze, who has an insurance practice, Mass Mutual, The Kentucky-West Virginia Agency, in Lexington, Kentucky, represents the recurring theme of the lack of opportunities in the organization for women. "There was no supervisory position that I would have enjoyed doing that was available. Appropriate compensation for the time and effort I was putting into the job would have made a difference."

Not just inequity in pay, but nonrecognition also led to an acute sense of dissatisfaction with an organization. An entrepreneur illustrates how this became a driving force to leave the organization:

A partner and I co-edited the features section of the newspaper. We worked our little hearts out on that section of the paper. We had total responsibility for it. When we won the University of Missouri School of Journalism award for the best section of that type in the Southeast, our male boss was the one who went to accept the award and the two of us never received a word of recognition for all our creativity and work. Within 3 months we were gone.

Experiences with female stereotypes abounded. One entrepreneur was told that because she was married, she should consider her pay "pin money." Twenty entrepreneurs (16%) had been told they should be satisfied with less pay because they were women. One entrepreneur had gone into a field that was nontraditional for women. With no role models, in a predominantly male-based occupation, she opted out of her previous organization because of perceived inequity in pay and treatment. Another entrepreneur, a design and marketing specialist, reported that she had advanced in the corporate structure and earned a salary several times as high as her immediate supervisors. They saw her as a threat. Women in the study had found it difficult to make headway after butting heads, for whatever reasons, with autocratic and bureaucratic managers. Some women had experienced retaliation that was unending and unmerciful after they had complained. Terri Parker-Halpin is a principal in International ISO Group, Cincinnati, Ohio, and the author of more than 100 technical books and numerous technical articles. She has spoken nationally on technical writing and documentation management:

> An ex-Marine colonel was hired as the director of my computer center. It was obvious that he did not like women. Two talented and qualified women were passed over for promotion in two rounds. I later applied for the position. He not only ignored my application, he then placed two males in succession in the job who had no prior experience or the interest that I had. I sued. He let me know in no uncertain terms that he would not retire from his position until the case was settled, and made it very miserable for me.

Anita Porco, the president and founder of Nurses Today, Inc., in Dallas, remembers the experience of being the victim of unethical practices:

> I started a business not because I wanted to become an entrepreneur but because I was working for an organization in a similar business. The owner decided to close the company. I was the one signing the payroll checks. [Chuckles from the focus group.] The checks bounced all over the city with my name on them. It was one of those deals where I could have crawled into a hole because I couldn't believe this would happen to me and that I really would be responsible for all this money out there. And we were getting summonses from the district attorney's office and all kinds of things. My life had really turned into a mess. My attorney said that he felt the thing for me to do was start my own business and let people know that I hadn't known the company was closing, that I did not know the company didn't have money in the bank, that the owner hadn't paid his payroll taxes or anything else. It seemed like a pretty risky thing to do. But it also seemed like a really good challenge to me. At the same time, I was getting calls from clients asking "Why don't you do this on your own?"

Cluster 5: Balancing Career and Family

For most American women today, employment is a financial necessity. The Families and Work Institute (1995) reports that 24% of working women who are married expect their own jobs to provide more financial security for their families than their partners' jobs. There has been much press coverage in recent years about the conflict women experience over managing the simultaneous and sometimes competing demands of family and career. Research shows that, in spite of the fact that most women between 21 and 65 years of age in the United States work, they still assume the primary responsibility for home and child care activities (Googins & Burden, 1987; Jick & Mitz, 1985).

Such evidence has led to suggestions that women with families might be opting to start businesses of their own to achieve greater control over their time and energy and to better manage their dual roles. Data from both the women entrepreneurs' questionnaire surveys and the content analysis of the focus group interviews fail to support this assumption. Although ratings by the entrepreneurs on the survey instrument indicated that career and family had greater explanatory variance of entrepreneurial behavior than did discrimination, we did not find this to be the case in the focus group content analysis. We conclude that, although important, family factors held a lesser priority than other reasons for women to begin a business. Our finding is consistent with the prior work of Rosin and Korabik (1990). Like them, we find that women who left their organizations were not basing their decisions on family concerns. Rather, the decisions were a function of work-related issues, including politics and lack of opportunity.

This is not to say that career and family concerns have not been important. Among our entrepreneurs, 20 (16%) referenced dual career or home responsibilities as being major determinants in their career development. One entrepreneur had left a good organization after finding it difficult to explain to her company why she could not take an international assignment. She had risen to the vice presidential level and was involved in creative and strategic planning. She was fascinated with the position, liked her colleagues, and had every intention of staying in the company for the long haul. The problem of a family trade-off involving her husband's career, however, was not understood by senior management. The experience of dealing with similar conflicts between family and corporate advancement opportunities was common among our entrepreneurs. Commented Mary Tanner, a Cincinnati entrepreneur:

The last year I was there I got the top rating and I was ranked as the top manager out of my group. They were talking to me in terms of "We would like you to take the next level, we would like for you to be on our management intensive program." Well, I had one small child and I was thinking in terms of having another child. I really didn't want to sit there and tell my manager, I just want to get a paycheck. I want to put my career on hold for a little bit and not work 70 hours a week. I don't want to hop on a plane at the drop of a hat. I simply cannot do that. I was starting to feel so anxious about the position. The final straw was that I got put into a job that was like half a level higher than the position I was in but it was doing something that I simply did not want to do. It had no flexibility and it started interfering with my family schedule. And that was really the final push that I had to leave there.

Susan Brown reflected, "Organizations force you to make an either/or choice: family or work life."

Other Reasons for Leaving

Entrepreneurs in this study left their organizational environments for other varying reasons. Thirty-two (25%) of them picked up the expertise to run their own businesses by "moonlighting" in the same type of business prior to deciding to leave the corporate environment. Another 25 (19%) indicated that they had also moonlighted prior to opening their own businesses. Shirley Schwaller, owner of Horizon Communications Group in Dallas, had been writing about successful entrepreneurs for about 10 years as part of various positions in journalism. "I wasn't terribly unhappy at the paper," she said, "although I knew it was going to go under eventually. Everybody in town knew that."

Twenty others (16%) left because of the client demand for their areas of expertise. Unexpected blows from dead-end jobs also caused many to never place their trust in an organization again. Suzan B. Kotler, a certified financial planner who is associated with Money Concepts, remembers the devastation of being laid off: "I was working in a firm that was relocated down here and got laid off and I was in a strange city with no friends, and no job. I decided that I would not allow anyone else to control my destiny the way this event had. And as long as you work for someone else, somebody else always pulls the strings."

The Decision Point

In the focus group interviews, entrepreneurs spoke of the growing realization that they intended to leave a corporate position. Many had remained in their jobs for a while, uncertain when to depart. Dianne Semingson, owner of DLS International, Inc., and its affiliate New Source Management, in Philadelphia, listened to women in her focus group describe their decisions to leave. She had held a series of positions, including a high-profile job in the mayor's office of Philadelphia and one as chamber of commerce regional director for the Mid-Atlantic states. She commented, "Whatever I did was just not enough. I think I should have read the writing on the wall."

The first exit was not always to entrepreneurship, but women with one negative organizational experience were particularly alert to similar environments. Remembers Lisa Adkinson, a partner in the Strategic Eight Consulting Group of Greater Cincinnati and owner of Inner Applications:

> I went out in search of other positions and interviewed pretty much every company of interest in the industry. My final count was 12 job offers that I turned down for one reason or another. I began to realize the reason I was uncomfortable with the offers was because of too many similarities in the relationship I had in the previous job or there was no growth potential. The positions were either at a comparable level or a setback and going nowhere. So why do it?

Often it was a critical but unplanned event that served as a turning point or prompted the decision to leave. An entrepreneur who left the office of a state district attorney general recounted the coincidental events that propelled her out of the legal profession: "The push to leave the organization was twofold. First, the earthquake pushed me because of the relocation of the offices. Second, I developed some ideas of what I would like to do with the rest of my life." Another entrepreneur was faced with the dilemma of advancement. "The reason I left was they offered me a promotion, but it was to Manhattan. And it was a choice between my career and my marriage. My husband was from Maine and he would have lasted about a week in Manhattan. But there were other issues too. Ethical issues. And my boss was a real jerk. I didn't want to stay where I was and I didn't want to go to Manhattan." Marilyn Sifford had 18 years' experience in human resources and organization development at the time she was commuting from Philadelphia to her job in Minneapolis. She was very unhappy working for an autocratic boss.

Her husband had a heart attack on a plane trip to visit her. She came home to care for him in Philadelphia. Five years earlier, she had considered going into business for herself but had rejected the idea, feeling she just was not ready. Now back in Philadelphia, with an ailing spouse, she knew the time was right. She also knew she had the experience, the confidence to go out and sell herself, and the strong network she needed to succeed.

Summary

Our findings suggest that women's decisions to leave their prior organizations are a complex function of organizational influences and personal aspirations. The entrepreneurs here indicated that they were seeking to escape a stifling corporate atmosphere in search of a new challenge and the opportunity to prove to themselves that they could succeed on their own. Many of the reasons the women cited have also been identified in studies of male entrepreneurs. Other reasons appear special to women. Although there is probably considerable overlap in motivations and aspirations, the relative importance of the departure influences appear to differ somewhat for women and men. Gender, only occasionally in the form of discrimination, makes a difference.

3

The Organizational Incubator

The Organizational Incubator and Career Transition

Over the past decade, small businesses have grown more rapidly than any other sector in the American economy (U.S. Bureau of the Census, 1991; U.S. Small Business Administration, 1995). Small businesses now make up 99.7% of all employers and account for more than half of private sector output and employment. By the year 2005, small businesses will engage 70% of the workforce (U.S. Department of Labor, Bureau of Labor Statistics, 1995; U.S. Small Business Administration Office of Advocacy Report, 1995).

The changes in the business landscape can be attributed to a number of factors. More than 43 million jobs were eliminated in corporate America between 1979 and 1995. White-collar workers confronted downsizing and outsourcing (Uchitelle & Kleinfield, 1996, p. Y16), higher pay in many small companies for skills less rewarded in corporate environments, the absence of stability and tenure for survivors of the waves of job cuts, and a growing disillusionment about the prospects for long-term careers in big corporations. Middle managers and up increasingly focused on using the experiences they accumulated in the corporate environment to launch small businesses.

Information about how people have used organizations as incubators is limited (Barrett & Christie, 1994; Brush & Hisrich, 1991; Cooper et al., 1989; Moore, 1990; Moore et al., 1992). There is also a paucity of research in the areas of self-employment career theory (Dyer, 1994; Katz, 1994; Ornstein & Isabella, 1990), career separation (Ornstein & Isabella, 1993), and the role of intentions in establishing entrepreneurial ventures (Learned, 1992). Two things are known: (a) that the traditional career models (Hall, 1987), mostly developed prior to recent corporate restructuring and downsizing (Powell & Mainiero, 1992), do little to explain the entrepreneurial or professional development of women (Dyer, 1994), and (b) that a new generation of entrepreneurs clearly has benefited from organizational incubator experiences (Baucus & Human, 1994, p. 45; Cooper, 1986; Feeser & Willard, 1989; Moore, 1990; Perkins, Nieva, & Lawler, 1978; Van de Ven, Hudson, & Schroeder, 1984). Research suggests that the more successful of these entrepreneurs launched firms in the sector or industry where they had gained experience, training, and skills (Brush, 1992; Fischer et al., 1993) or firms that dealt in products and services similar to those of their prior organizations (Cooper et al., 1989).

How information is transferred from the organizational environment to an entrepreneur's business is a key question. Some women clearly joined the corporate world with the idea of using the environment as an incubator—a training ground—for the business they always intended to create. Planning from the beginning to start a business of their own (Schein, 1990), they worked for others because this was a best initial personal or financial choice. Others who later became entrepreneurs entered organizations with clear career aspirations to advance within them. These corporate climbers hoped to find environments that met their expectations (Holland, 1973) and intended to remain in the fields or firms they had entered (Hall, 1987, p. 307). When things did not work out, the attraction of being one's own boss (Knight, 1987; Scott, 1986; Shaver, Gatewood, & Gartner, 1991) outweighed the advantages of staying put (Brockhaus & Horwitz, 1986), and many left to start a business. Changes ranged from corporate downsizing (Uchitelle & Kleinfield, 1996) to some combination of organizational push and entrepreneurial pull factors (Birley & Westhead, 1993; Cooper & Dunkelberg, 1981; Denison & Alexander, 1986; Dubini, 1988; Scheinberg & MacMillan, 1988; Shane et al., 1991).

Once in business, female entrepreneurs with former organizational experience draw from their previous organizational environments, using them as training grounds (Birley, 1989; Brush & Hisrich, 1988; Moore, 1990; Moore et al., 1992; Murphy, 1992), incubators (Cooper & Dunkelberg, 1987; Ireland & Van Auken, 1987), and sources of contacts (Birley, 1989). This chapter examines how this process worked for our 129 entrepreneurs. In addition to analyses of questionnaire data and focus interviews, we examine some hypotheses that evolve out of the literature. Among other things, we find that the unique properties of the organizational incubator make it a decisive tool in developing an entrepreneurial career strategy.

The analysis is at four levels. First, we compare the types of businesses women worked in prior to becoming an entrepreneur (the incubator experiences) with the type of business they elected to start. Within this frame of reference, we then analyze how entrepreneurs use or transfer the skills acquired in the previous environment to run their own business and the degree these acquired skills are general, task-specific, or absent. Of special interest here are the effects of direct and indirect transfer of contacts, business and professional experiences, training programs, and any skills acquired while working in the management, marketing, finance, sales, legal, and other areas of organizations. Second, we look at the perceived developmental potential of the incubator organization in establishing self-confidence and interpersonal skills. Our third unit of analysis looks at the culture within the organizational incubator to see what led the women entrepreneurs to decide the time had come to leave and start their own businesses. Our final analysis section focuses on hypothesized differences, developed on a careful review of the literature, between those entrepreneurs with long-range intentions to become entrepreneurs—whom we have labeled the "intentionals"—and those whose entrepreneurial intentions emerged later, the "corporate climbers."

Part I:
Incubator Transfer

We begin by addressing the period of organizational gestation, the "incubator effect," as it contributes to how well prepared entrepreneurs think they are as they leave the organization to construct their own businesses. Brush and Hisrich (1991), Cooper and Bruno (1977), and Cooper and colleagues (1989) all say that a strong relationship exists between corporate field experience and new venture creation. Of the 129 entrepreneurs participating in this study, 112 (87%) said there had been a direct transfer of information from the prior organizational setting to the business they now own. The type of business in which 92 (71%) of the entrepreneurs previously worked was very similar to the new business they started. Where the new business was dissimilar, many of the entrepreneurs said they employed skills similar to those they used in the previous organizational environment. In some cases, the new business came about directly or indirectly from outsourcing by the incubator firm. Says Dianne Semingson:

> My business came about because a competitor to a former employer asked if I would help with their business development. Layoffs in construction and downsizings left people in the company overworked. No one was marketing the firm and building up a project pipeline. My company developed to fill this niche.

Relates Elizabeth Morris, a Dallas entrepreneur who runs a research firm that has contributed to location decisions affecting the workplace of more than 1.3 million workers:

> I think the business kind of came and got me. It developed out of the previous work I had done. I spent 7 years in city management. We were responsible to everyone. Everything we said, everything we did was screened through different filters to be sure it conveyed accurate information. I had moved from that position into real estate brokerage where I saw a totally different business pace but very little research to accompany it. So on one side we had extraordinary levels of research and on the other side we had none. I moved to a corporation that developed office buildings, warehouses, and apartment complexes. I was in on the ground floor. Inside 3 years I had an opportunity to build an office building, a shopping center, and a 120-unit condominium complex virtually unsupervised because the company was growing so fast. I got a real quick education as a developer. I became convinced that the industry was going to hell in a hand basket because the research was not being done to support all the development. Because I did an extraordinary amount of research on my projects, people kept asking me if I would help with theirs. The firm I was with didn't pay me commensurate with what I was producing—nothing close to the salaries of less experienced men. So I said, "OK, I've got two kids, a mortgage and a car payment and I'm going to make a success of this. I want to see if I'm as good as I think I am." I got a white knuckle grip on the table and

submitted my resignation. My research company is now in the top tier of international competition.

The organizational incubator can also provide security while an entrepreneur is preparing for the new venture launch. "I began by developing a clientele and working insane hours for about 3 years prior to striking out on my own," said Julie Thomas, in a focus group, "so when I left, I had a client base." For another entrepreneur, the new business allowed incubator skills to be used in a setting free from organizational headaches. "In a nutshell," she said, "we design licensed apparel. Requests from licensers allowed us the opportunity to spin ourselves off from the company. It also got us out of the loop of the manufacturing and its frustrations and so forth." Still another entrepreneur started her business while fully employed. "I received telephone calls from attorneys in the state who I had worked with. They said, 'You know, could you help us out?' This led me to starting a business."

What did the new entrepreneurs value most after starting their businesses? In the follow-up study completed 1 year after the initial focus and questionnaire data had been collected, the group as a whole rated the experiences they had gained in an organizational incubator in facing major setbacks and achieving success as the most influential. The experiences gained from supervising managers and workers ranked next. The industry identity of these entrepreneurs was highly associated with the incubator firms. Most of the entrepreneurs were in the same or similar businesses or dealt with similar products or services, customers, suppliers, competitors, and technology.

The three incubator transfer factors provide some support for the work of Cooper et al. (1989), who found that, among other things, entrepreneurs who started businesses closely related to their former jobs were more likely to succeed. Deborah Hueppeler, an independent financial consultant in Dallas, related how she planned the incubator experience to launch out on her own:

I have always been directed in business. Really focused on business, never interested in anything else. And particularly the financial aspects. So I started my career in the financial services in New York on Wall Street with the ultimate goal of landing in the Sunbelt. Here I started with financial services to gain the financial background and familiarity with a lot of different companies and industries. This would provide an important building block for the company I later created.

There were also other important transfer elements. Forty-four (34%) of the entrepreneurs in this study brought from the organizational environment the key contacts that they later used in their own firms. Sixty-three (49%) said they directly transferred business expertise. The strongest direct transfers took place in managerial skills (51%, 66 members of the focus group), technical proficiency (55%, $n = 71$), and professional credentials (43%, $n = 56$). The transfer of managerial and technical expertise was matched by the value the entrepreneurs placed on developing the proper educational background (43%, $n = 56$) and followed closely by access to training programs (39%, $n = 50$). Mary Tanner, a Cincinnati entrepreneur, emphasized the positive image her incubator organization placed on training: "I rose fairly quickly within the organization. I had tons and tons of very expensive training, within the organization and training outside. They pumped a lot of money into me as a manager. They paid for my master's degree. So I think they would have liked for me to stay because they had a lot of investment in me in training and experience." Other entrepreneurs who had been exposed to training programs found the experience equally invaluable. Says Ann Angel, a Winston-Salem entrepreneur, "I was invited to write on a new slate, create the firm's first computer training department. I got a blank check to go research it, put it together. Nobody was doing anything like it in the early eighties. It provided an incredible learning opportunity for me."

Women who did get the training in the corporate environment later saw the benefits. "I was in the training department," said a New Orleans entrepreneur, "that allowed me exposure to financial planning and projections and provided an understanding of how businesses operate from the ground up, personnel matters and so forth." Many entrepreneurs, however—even some who had benefited from their organizational experiences in other ways—felt they had been excluded. More than half of our entrepreneurs said they had not benefited from formal or informal organizational training programs. The work of Ragins and Sundstrom (1989), who found that organizations regulated access to training as part of a pattern of tracking and grooming men—but not women—for powerful positions, may suggest an explanation.

Some entrepreneurs said that the skills acquired in previous organizations prepared them in a general way rather than in the specifics of running the businesses they would create ($n = 43$, 33%). In retrospect, others felt that they had lacked important skills when they launched their firms ($n = 26$, 20%). Specific areas mentioned included management and human resource management. Fewer than one-third of the entrepreneurs felt that their former educational and corporate experience had prepared them in the areas of finance ($n = 42$), marketing ($n = 37$), sales ($n = 35$), and legal expertise ($n = 12$). Janet McCann, an interior designer in the Chicago area, says:

> When I think back about all the pain, I remember that I learned every-thing as I went along. If I had planned on having my own business, I would have watched the financial, the marketing, but I didn't. I just liked what I was doing. I was learning my particular skill and I had no thoughts about all the rest of it. I remember thinking after beginning my business, well, I must be nuts, I know nothing about finance, nothing about marketing, I know nothing about any of this stuff. What am I doing here?

Eighteen entrepreneurs felt the skills they had transferred were too special-ized. Fifteen more felt there was no direct transfer between the incubator environment and the business they created, making it necessary for them to learn everything from the "hard knocks school" or a "hands-on approach." One said, "I realized upon reflection that I've worked for many fine large corporations. And I'm really grateful for that experience. But that experience did not give me any help in preparing to run my own business. Each company gave me just a sliver of information."

One group of entrepreneurs placed great importance on advanced educa-tion. The idea that without higher education something was lacking was particularly felt by those who had not had the opportunity to attend college. How had they learned? Gee Tucker, an entrepreneur who has been regionally and nationally recognized for her outstanding accomplishments, climbed over the hurdles.

> So I started going to the business seminars and conventions. I didn't get what I needed through the school system. I always felt like I was inadequate because I didn't. I always felt I had to do it better. I had to work harder. I had to work longer hours. I had to make my mark because I didn't get the necessary formal educational tools to prepare me to be where I am now. I learned the hard way, on the job, things I could never have learned in school. But I think the formal training in school would have made it easier.

Another self-taught entrepreneur, Michele Babineaux, proprietor of Michaul's Cajun Restaurant on St. Charles, has been named Entrepreneur of

the Year in both the city of New Orleans and the state of Louisiana. She
reflects:

> It is amazing to me. I have gained all my information from the hard
> knocks school. I thought it would be wonderful to go to college. When
> I did go, I was older. I sat there in the classroom and all I could think
> about was how I needed to be out working and making money. I asked
> the professor if I could get what she was saying on my own. She said,
> yes, you have worked all your life. You can take the book and learn what
> I am teaching in this class. It was such a relief. It would have been a
> luxury to sit in the class and learn, but I decided that I would take the
> book and learn on my own. So I brought the book back to the restaurant.
> Every day I got my employees together and we had a lesson from the
> book. We all learned the material together. All of my new employees
> have college degrees, especially in sales and management. I want to use
> this extra edge.
>
> But some of these people have no appreciation of what that college
> degree means. Education is the most important thing. I cannot believe
> the lack of respect for the degree and the opportunity that these people
> have. The best wisdom available is to get the most out of your schooling.
> And realize that you are going to have to work extremely hard if you
> want to succeed. Know food costs, know beverage costs, I had to learn
> all of these things. Luck is nothing more than labor under controlled
> knowledge.

Part II:
The Confidence, Credibility, and Creativity Transfer

Findings in our analysis support a generalization that one role of the incubator is its importance in acquiring survival skills, coping with setbacks, and
learning to deal with special challenges. One entrepreneur learned: "I had
the experience and the confidence to be able to go out and really market
myself. I had a lot to sell and I had a very strong network." Still another
entrepreneur says, "The biggest thing I gained was credibility. I can go into
an important client and say I have done this for an industry leader. Then they
listen." Twenty-four entrepreneurs in the focus groups specifically referred
to similar organizational triumphs. Says Gee Tucker, "My husband can sell
an Eskimo a refrigerator. But I have put the system in place that enabled this

growth based on what I learned working in my former organization." A Cincinnati entrepreneur acquired the self-confidence needed from her environment: "I felt that the company had been a wonderful training ground; I started seeing that I wasn't helpless."

Gender does not have to get in the way. Burke and McKeen (1994) have found that when they are available, women value the support and development opportunities the same way men do. Some of our entrepreneurs experienced such benefits. Cynthia Toivenon, formerly in health care management, recalls, "I got a lot of support from a lot of great guys. I am sure half of them probably hated it anyway. But they didn't let me know it. It really was very rewarding." Debra Rust, president of Alpha Communications Technologies, Inc., in Warrenville, Illinois, remembers:

> The company wanted me to stay because they are a big corporation and they wanted female managers. My boss kept saying that in 5 years I will probably be working for you because they are really putting a push on to increase the female roles in the corporation. They offered me just about anything I wanted, international assignments, anywhere I wanted to go. I liked the work, which is why I decided to start my own business. When I left I didn't make any enemies.

Sometimes a positive mentor relationship developed out of what looked like a bad start. "When I first went to work, the first thing my boss said to me was, 'You can be replaced.' I was horrified, I was young, and innocent. Then he turned out to be a wonderful mentor, a wonderful teacher. I follow his advice to this day."

The seven entrepreneurs in this study who mentioned a sense of empowerment, benefit from a mentor, or other experience of support in the incubator firm looked back with gratitude. "I really do feel fortunate to have had that earlier experience with a good company where I felt valued and had the opportunity to make decisions, where I was encouraged by several managers, all men, about thinking of this business. Those things have helped me enormously since I've been out on my own," Rebecca Carney recalls. Such feelings may be directly attributable to organizational bonding. "There is something about struggle that bonds people," she remembers, "There were about 50 of us who were charged with keeping this one product from bleeding us dry. Once the company sold that product, we were integrated into all the other products, which were very successful. Then it was almost routine.

There was never that original kind of work effort again. At least 35 of us are still bonded in a very special way."

Part III:
The Incubator Push Factor

Women's careers can be affected by a variety of barriers. As Newman (1993) puts it, the obstacles women encounter as they attempt to advance in their careers are not related to gender differences but rather to the differences that gender makes. The suggestion is that women have a span of career objectives as they balance personal and corporate or professional career life. Encountering barriers anywhere across the span can make leaving an organization more appealing than staying on the organizational career track.

Considerable evidence suggests that barriers to female advancement are real. In the corporate suites of the biggest companies, women play marginal roles at best (van Oldenborgh, 1992). Women are only slightly represented in top public sector jobs. Although women represent 51.4% of the U.S. population, they hold only a small portion of top government decision-making posts (Guy, 1994). The absence of women in high positions in business and government is attributed to such architectural organizational characteristics as formal and social structures, position classification systems, designs of work, the effects of the informal organization on operating style, and the processes for selection, socialization, and development of personnel (Blum, Fields, & Goodman, 1994). Although advances have been made in reducing organizational barriers for women, the process is slow. The rate of progress suggests that the outlook for women is not likely to change soon (Hill, 1993). Anne Sadovsky, CEO of Anne Sadovsky & Company, a Dallas-based marketing consulting and seminar provider, summarizes it this way: "The only way through the glass ceiling is to go out on your own. There are relatively few women who have become CEOs, CFOs, or CLOs in major corporations, compared with the number of us who have not been able to overcome the obstacles. The guys still run the major corporations in America today."

Organizational features that discouraged women and caused them to consider leaving were discussed in the previous chapter. Prominent among the negative elements was the "good old boy" system. Several of the entrepreneurs had expected to meet it and contrived ways either to deal with the system in pursuit of larger goals or to turn it to their advantage. They went deliberately into male-dominated environments operating with male rules because there was much to learn. One established three criteria for evaluating her next job move: "First, I wanted to deal with decision makers. Second, I wanted to develop expertise in repeat sales. Finally, I wanted a creative selling environment with input into the sale." She acquired a job in a major company that met all the criteria,

> I knew going in this was the most influential organization. They had made me a job offer which I accepted. Then they told me that I was going to have to pay my own fee. So I knew, going into the company, that I didn't like them. But I wanted the training. It was a very male-oriented industry. I worked there for 2 years, took my act out on the road, worked on straight commission. They started playing games and actually forced me into starting my own company. There was no place else to go.

Coping with organizational politics required honing survival skills. While they were in the incubator organizations, entrepreneurs learned how to stay on top of the political game. One, who had developed training films, constructed a unique corporate climate. "People were thrilled by my role-playing exercises in management techniques and interviewing, problem-solving customer service techniques, so my modules were a hit and brought a lot of attention to my work." Then, as she notes:

> The VP who brought me in was kicked out because there was a battle for second place next to the source of power in the organization. Once the person who brought me in was killed off, I found myself in a memo battle with the second man. He was trying to find a way to eliminate me from the operation. But while he was trying to find a way to push me out, I continued to steadily make my mark in the training department by getting national exposure for my personnel service training modules. The company philosophy was based on building the operation through training. When our leader went around the country he found himself being asked how I was and what was I doing and he heard "boy, she's fantastic."

Lessons were learned from the bad corporate environments as well as from the good ones. "I grew to dislike the corporate environment because of so much bureaucratic and political hoopla," says Catherine Marrs, owner of Liaison, Inc., in Dallas, "and three years after learning the system I realized I could do the work better with a greater level of integrity and a higher quality service to the customer than the company did." Kris Schaeffer, founder of Kris Schaeffer & Associates, a San Francisco-based company, built entire training departments from scratch and has developed a long list of "first-evers," including sales training, product knowledge training, and plant supervisor training and team building. She recalled the limits of bureaucratic routines.

Corporations reduce everything down to 6 or 10 steps. Everyone wants an "add water and stir" solution. It ends up not being performance driven. There is a great fear of not having the information that is going to influence others. In the corporate environment, this approach is supposed to make things happen. In your own business, things happen because you make them happen. You create the 9,000 options. You figure all the contingencies. In the corporation human interactions with differing perspectives create bottlenecks and get in the way of completing successful projects.

Entrepreneurs noted that sometimes the corporate politics produced results that ran counter to the professed purposes of the organization. Remembers one:

Over a 3-year period the employee involvement/quality improvement function I managed became much more important. But the senior people who had supported it, including the president, were eliminated from the company due to a merger. The new leader eventually cut all the programs and killed all the things he had not created.

Stereotyping women into perceived female roles in the organization had been among the reasons a number of the entrepreneurs had left their former employers. Fagenson (1993) suggests that women who give up managerial roles because of stereotyping will be very careful to create different environments in their own businesses. The story of Wendy Ginn bears this out.

In my first big job assignment with a multinational corporation I became associated as a secretary because I saw we needed to type a manual on operations in the company. The fact that we were in the computer business with some of the most high-powered equipment available and our operators did not know how to operate it blew my mind. It appeared to me that, in order to sell the equipment, at a minimum, we had to know the equipment inside out, how to operate it, to demonstrate it. This was not happening. The company attitude, not being able to see the important relationships among training, operation, and selling, was "We should make you a secretary." This was the beginning of my desire to leave. The company could have recognized the relationship between selling the product and understanding the array of uses which the product had. They could have placed more emphasis and backing on the training programs. But the training programs were charged to the department you worked for. Because the departments wanted favorable balance sheets indicating high profit and productivity, training was de-emphasized. It was obvious to me that fear of the new technology existed in the market. If we were to be successful with our product, we had to not only train our own people but we had to find ways to alleviate that fear among our clients. My attitude in the company could best be described as "They can't sell it if they don't understand it."

I knew how to play the corporate game. I used the mentor system but I always felt I had a better understanding of what was going on in the company than did my mentors. In time, I came to understand the hopeless mismatch between my ideas and those of the company. No one seemed interested in whether or not one was competent to sell this product. No one seemed to understand the importance of customer trust. The snap answers and the inhumane way customers who had problems with our product were treated did not create trust. Because my ideas did not mesh with those around me, I felt responsible. I took a career changes class to find out what was wrong with me.

At the same time, I could see clearly the relationships necessary to make the computer business work. I more than anyone realized how dehumanizing machines and data can be. Through much anguish, I had learned each new process and realized that advancement would come when one could personalize the work for computers. I started my own company as a test. My objective was to provide a personal service built on trust. My business plan was successful because it should have been;

it took more than 400 hours to complete. The real power lies in understanding other people's jobs.

For entrepreneurs who were in nontraditional fields, discrimination did
not end even after they started their firms. Patt Gallagher, owner of Evergreen
Supply Company in Chicago, whose customers knew her in a suit and a hard
hat, remembers:

> I searched out my customers and my market. I picked five large corpo-
> rations and found out what their needs were. Then I searched out the
> competition. I needed to know more. So I stopped my research and went
> to electrical school to learn what I needed to know. Then I went back
> and asked the manufacturers if I could handle their parts. The answer
> was "No, because you are a woman and it's a man's field." I worked
> very hard to get where I am. I started in the basement of my home,
> moved into a warehouse, and now I have three trucks on the street,
> moving from one warehouse to another. It was marketing and seeing
> those people and finding out their needs from the beginning. Now men
> will come and want to know what was my key to get where I am now.

For others, the problem was the culture in a male-dominated industry.
Deborah Hueppeler points out how this affected her in an auto-related
business:

> When I made the acquisition there was a lack of recognition that I was
> the boss now. So I had to earn their respect. And their attitude was "Who
> are you and what do you know?" So the first 2 years was winning their
> trust, winning their support and really to underline it all, meshing our
> cultures. Because here I was, a female, a white-collar professional with
> degrees and Yankee. And tall, I was taller than all of them. And then
> coming into an operation that was blue-collar, male-dominated and
> operationally driven rather than financially driven. So the first 2 years
> were absolutely hell.

Many of our entrepreneurs were the sole supporters of households with
children. They went into business to solve financial problems. Relates one:

> I had two children to support and I was a single parent. I had financial
> obligations. When it became apparent I was not going to be promoted

or appreciated in the organization, I ruthlessly used them to put a $30,000 cushion under myself before I stepped out into this no man's land of entrepreneurship.

Another entrepreneur felt so intensely the need to earn a living to support herself and her daughter that out of desperation alone she struck out on her own, breaking the pattern that had kept her down throughout her earlier married life.

I worked during the day making $4 an hour for a man who owned two printing companies and worked at an insurance company at night. I was the sole support of my daughter. I would take her to work with me at night where I was making $5 an hour. I was so disgusted because I was doing the art work for both printing companies and was bringing in more work than the owner had when I started there. Yet I could not get the raise I was promised. I did the selling, cleaned the place up, raised his prices, I dealt directly with customers, did the billing; I did everything. One weekend I had just had enough; my daughter, disgusted, had gone back to live with her dad. I confronted my boss about my raise, and he gave me an increase of 25 cents an hour. Out of desperation, I went and bought used equipment, named my company, did the logo, all in one weekend. I started small, I rented a small storage area in an office building. For a short time I continued to work for the printing company during the day and at night for myself.

Gail Withers, another entrepreneur, with a $13,000 salary and close to being eligible for Medicaid and food stamps, determined to fight her way out of poverty.

Because I'd seen the poverty cycle and how it engulfs generation after generation, I decided that I wasn't going to fall into it. So I decided after 11 years to leave social services and start a business that I really didn't know anything about. I had the gut feeling that I was strong enough to do it. I had survived the divorce. I had kept my family together, my children, held on to my house and other things. And I said, if I'm strong enough to survive this, I'm strong enough to take on a business. So I left with about $11,000 in retirement. Knowing that retirement would carry me for about 11 months. And started my business with $1,000.

Part IV:
Intentional Entrepreneurs, Corporate Climbers,
and the Incubator Experience

Entrepreneurial studies have sought to identify the relationship between intention and entrepreneurial start-ups. We examine these concepts here by using our classifications of "intentionals" and "corporate climbers." The distinction is based on an entrepreneur's long-range or latent intentions to start a business.

Intention, "a conscious state of mind toward the goal of founding a business" (Bird, 1992; Bird & Jelinek, 1988; Hansen & Wortman, 1989, Katz & Gartner, 1988), may be a critical factor in beginning a business (Learned, 1992, p. 42). There is limited information, however, on the specific role that intentions play in one's becoming an entrepreneur (Krueger & Brazeal, 1994). On one hand, Shapero (1982) has proposed that long-range entrepreneurial intentions, which can span a lengthy period, are critically important to understanding small business start-ups. On the other hand, Katz and Gartner (1988) and Katz (1994) see intention as a label describing people who seek out information they can use to create a business. In this definition, not only may entrepreneurial intentions be short-range, but initially an entrepreneur also may be unaware that the intention exists. The profile fits Fran (Raglin) Johnson, owner and founder of Elite Travel Services in Cincinnati.

As I look back on my life though, at the age of 53, probably I was always an entrepreneur and totally unaware of it. As far back as I can remember, since I was 5 years old, I was helping my aunt make lamp shades. I was paid by the shade. And if you look at it, that was an entrepreneurial experience. Because I calculated how much money I wanted to make for certain activities/products and I made that number of shades. As a very young teenager I purchased items from wholesale houses and marketed in apartment buildings going from one apartment to another selling merchandise. I cringe when I think about that now. How dangerous it was. As far back as I can remember I found ways to make money. I cooked chicken dinners and went to barber shops and beauty shops to solicit orders for dinners. And even though I was working a full-time job, if I needed money, I would do those kinds of things. I relied upon my sales skills to fund furniture purchases and to start my business. I sold things at college sales and to flea markets. So probably I was always an entrepreneur and never thought about it.

For L. Elaine Green, a corporate climber who had risen successfully in her corporate environment over a 15-year period, the move to consider entrepreneurship had been forced by radical changes in her life. There was a corporate restructuring. Because she had outstanding performance reviews and prestigious national awards, in spite of the organizational shake-ups she was told she could stay on in her job for a reasonable time. Then a client made a request. She had done a video feature on Arabian horses and later had been asked to do a very large horse show in Arizona. "The Arabian horse owner said, 'Why don't you put yourself on an airplane and come out here and be our guest for a week?' That airplane ride was probably the most important ride in my life. I thought, this is what I want to do—to be in video arts."

Incubator Perceptions

Studies have suggested that the managerial experience acquired in the incubator period provides an important training ground and contacts key to business venture creation (Birley, 1989; Cooper & Dunkelberg, 1986; Feeser & Willard, 1989). Research also suggests that entrepreneurial and professional management skills may be mutually exclusive (Daily & Dalton, 1992; Schein, 1985; Whisler, 1988). Stuart and Abetti (1990), for example, say that it was previous entrepreneurial experience, not managerial expertise, that was the significant factor in the relative early performance of 52 new technical ventures. Bridging the gap are findings that suggest that skills developed in an incubator contribute to performance in both arenas (Bird, 1988, 1992; Bird & Jelinek, 1988; Cooper, 1981; Feeser & Willard, 1989). There is also research suggesting that the move to entrepreneurship may be less a complete break than a series of sequential decisions to change one's career direction (Naffziger, Hornsby, & Kuratko, 1994, p. 34). All of this leads to intriguing questions about how the organizational experience is perceived by our two groups. One group, the intentionals, had lifelong ambitions of ownership, whereas the intentions of the corporate climbers surfaced later.

Perception of Managerial Experience

Entrepreneurial success has been heavily correlated with extensive managerial and start-up experience and the ability to react quickly to environmental change (Daily & Dalton, 1992; Duchesneau & Gartner, 1990). Drucker (1985) notes that people can have both entrepreneurial and professional management skills. It also seems true that professional managers generally come with administrative experience from larger corporations (Hambrick & Crozier, 1985). Research shows that managers in large organizations have different experiences and values than do entrepreneurs (Fagenson, 1993). Managers may value management experience more highly because it is key to upward mobility in their organizations. Intentional entrepreneurs may value it less because they do not see managerial experience as instrumental in their entrepreneurial venture. The competing findings suggest that intentionals and corporate climbers will perceive the value of previous managerial experience quite differently. Our first hypothesis examined these differences.

Hypothesis 1: Because they initially had planned to advance in the corporate ranks, corporate climbers will consider their organizational managerial experience significantly more important than will intentional entrepreneurs.

Perception of Marketing and Technical Experience

The development of marketing and technical expertise, either on one's own or by putting together a team, often occurs within an organization prior to the launching of a business. Market information advantages come from acquiring a clear identification of marketing niches (Morgan & Hunt, 1994). Technical information such as product timing, quantity, and quality, as well as customer preferences, also is critical (Baye, 1995). Members of founding teams of entrepreneurial ventures often meet in the incubator organization (Cooper, 1985) and later combine their skills to form a business (Brush, 1992; Cooper, 1993). It appears plausible that intentional entrepreneurs more than corporate climbers will be driven to acquire insider information about the market they intend to enter and will perceive marketing strategies and technical skills to be more important to later entrepreneurial success (Cooper & Dunkelberg, 1986). Our second hypothesis addressed this possible difference.

Hypothesis 2: Intentional entrepreneurs, those who always intended to start a business of their own, will perceive a greater value of the incubator experience in acquiring technical expertise and marketing knowledge than will corporate climbers.

Perceptions of Financial Expertise

Developing financial expertise is important to managers in any organization (Cooper, 1985; Hisrich, 1990; Mainiero, 1994; Ostgaard & Birley, 1994). Because a strong understanding of the financial aspects of doing business is critical to success (Brush & Hisrich, 1991), we did not expect that intentional and corporate climbers would differ in their perception of the incubator value to acquiring this information.

Hypothesis 3: Because financial expertise is necessary for advancement within an organization or to creating a business of one's own, significant differences are not expected in the ratings of the two groups for the incubator value in acquiring this information.

Perceptions of Similar Organizational Experience or Special Training Programs

Research has clearly established that the road to advancement in organizations owned by others is through the recognition and selection for special training programs. Cianni and Romberger (1995) suggest that such developmental opportunities convey the message that the selectees are "promotable" and have "potential" (p. 446). Similarly, among successful new ventures, owners tend to have more management experience and managerial goals (Cooper et al., 1989). The experiences most valuable, say Reuber and Fischer (1993), are those most directly linked with performance: start-up experience, management experience, and industry experience. Chandler and Hanks (1991) found that the combined effect of pre-ownership training and experience in a similar business is positively related to venture performance and that managerial flexibility is important in high-growth companies. Building on the research findings of Fischer and colleagues (1993) and Vesper (1990) that the best way entrepreneurs can prepare themselves to do business in a particular sector or industry is to acquire experience in that setting, and then taking into account the mixed findings on direct correlations between management/industry experience and entrepreneurial success (Dyke, Fischer, & Reuber, 1992), specifically on findings that entrepreneurs who remain closely related to their original organizations do better because they can draw on the technical and market knowledge (Cooper et al., 1989, p. 319), we proposed that, although the intentional and corporate climbers would have experience and goals that are managerial in nature (Cooper et al., 1989), the corporate climbers would value the special training opportunities significantly more than would intentional entrepreneurs.

Hypothesis 4: Corporate climbers who now operate in similar fields or industries or who had special training programs prior to starting their own businesses will value their managerial training more than intentional entrepreneurs with similar backgrounds.

Intentionals, Corporate Climbers, and Corporate Flight

As discussed in the previous chapter, a number of studies have found that the driving forces for starting a business are the desires for job freedom (Katz, 1994; Schein, 1990; Shane et al., 1991), for autonomy and control over one's life (Belcourt, 1991; Cromie & Hayes, 1991; Scott, 1986), for challenge (Scott, 1986), and to create something new (Katz, 1994; Schein, 1990, pp. 29, 30). Other research suggests differences between entrepreneurial and managerial types of people (Fagenson, 1993). Brodsky (1993) found that managers were more trusting and required lower levels of control than entrepreneurs. Managerial types may view the corporate environment as safe and supportive; entrepreneurs may consider the same environment confining. If intentional entrepreneurs and corporate climbers leave organizations for different reasons, understanding basic differences may lead to a better understanding of apparent differences in the performance of new firms depending on whether they are managed by founders or professional managers (Daily & Dalton, 1992; Dyer, 1986; Schein, 1985; Whisler, 1988; Willard, Krueger, & Feeser, 1992). Other, more subtle changes may occur in the perception of the entrepreneurial and managerial experience. As indicated by Elaine Green:

In the beginning, I felt like an entrepreneur. As I got more staff, I became more like a manager and spent less time thinking creatively than I wanted to. My goal now is to find someone to do day-to-day management so I can spend time being an entrepreneur. Management per se takes up so much time that you're not doing what you wanted to do when you first started the business. Management does not create money, the entrepreneur does.

No studies have examined differences in how the perceptions of intentional entrepreneurs and corporate climbers may differ in these attributes.

Hypothesis 5: Although intentional entrepreneurs and corporate climbers will differ in their ratings of reasons why they leave organizations, intentional entrepreneurs will place a significantly higher value on self-determination (the entrepreneurial spirit) than will corporate climbers.

Results

The results of the tests of these five hypotheses are presented in Tables 3.1-3.4. Table 3.1 shows the profiles of the corporate climbers and the intentional entrepreneurs. Table 3.2 provides the results of the MANOVA analysis with the discriminant functions for the first three hypotheses. Table 3.3 provides the data for the analysis of Hypothesis 4. Table 3.4 shows the MANOVA used to analyze the value placed on self-determination as predicted in Hypothesis 5.

Findings from our analysis support Hypothesis 1, that corporate climbers consider managerial experience significantly more important than do intentional entrepreneurs. We also found support for our second hypothesis, that intentionals would perceive a greater value in the incubator experience from acquiring marketing and technical expertise than would corporate climbers. In both cases, the mean values are higher for intentional entrepreneurs.

In our analysis of Hypothesis 3, regarding further distinctions between corporate climbers and intentional entrepreneurs, we found that corporate climbers, with businesses from a similar organizational environment or who had special training programs prior to starting their own businesses, consider managerial training significantly more important than do intentional entrepreneurs.

TABLE 3.1. Profiles of Intentionals and Corporate Climbers

	Intentionals		Corporate Climbers	
Characteristic	Mean	SD	Mean	SD
Age	44	5.65	44	8.20
Business profile				
Full-time employees	16.54		15.82	
Years of ownership	7.0		7.6	
Percentage earnings from business[a]	85.9		94.0	
Years of work experience	6.7	6.29	6.3	4.75
	n	Percentage	n	Percentage
Demographic profile				
White	40		77	
Nonwhite	1		6	
Married		61.0		67.0
One or more children		66.0		58.0
Operational role/owner		93.0		91.0
Type of business				
Service		76.0		74.0
Construction or manufacturing		8.0		12.0
Finance, insurance, real estate		12.0		5.0
Transportation/communication		4.0		5.0
Wholesale trade		2.0		

NOTE: $N = 124$; 5 additional entrepreneurs participated in the study but did not identify themselves as a corporate climber or an intentional entrepreneur and are not included in this table. In total, there were 9 nonwhite entrepreneurial participants in the study. Median sales revenue = $250,000-500,000 range.
a. For the majority of the entrepreneurs, all income came from the business.

Hypothesis 4 predicted that intentional entrepreneurs more than corporate climbers will perceive value in being in an industry with products, customers, suppliers, competitors, technologies, and size similar to a previous firm or in experience gained from starting a business before. Results concerning this hypothesis are mixed. We found support at the univariate level but not at the multivariate. Neither did we find differences between the two groups in the value placed on financial information.

We found support for Hypothesis 5 (Table 3.4), that although intentional entrepreneurs and corporate climbers are expected to differ in their ratings of reasons why they leave organizations, intentionals will place a significantly higher value on self-determination (the entrepreneurial spirit) than will corporate climbers. For the scale as a whole, and also as demonstrated

TABLE 3.2. Multivariate Analysis of the Incubator Effect for the Corporate and Intentional Entrepreneur

Variable	Intentional Mean	Corporate Mean	Canonical r^a	Correlations With SD on Diagonal					Univariate F	Significance of F
				1	2	3	4	5		
Technical	2.23	2.79	-.45	1.49					3.82	.05
Marketing	2.20	2.79	-.50	.03	1.38				4.81	.03
Financial	3.30	3.16	.11	-.09	.36	1.54			.21	.65
Networking	2.23	2.50	-.24	.07	-.001	.04	1.36		1.10	.30
Management	2.93	2.30	.52	-.01	.23	.09	.07	1.41	5.26	.02

Multivariate tests of significance

Pillais: .14, $F = 3.70$, 5/114 df, $p < .01$

Hotelling's: .16, $F = 3.70$, 5/114 df, $p < .01$

Wilks': .86, $F = 3.70$, 5/114 df, $p < .011$

Eigenvalue = .16 (100% variances), canonical correlation = .37.

NOTE: N for intentional entrepreneurs = 40; N for corporate climbers = 80. Responses are scored on a 6-point scale where 1 = *most* to 6 = *least*.
a. Correlations between dependent and canonical variables. Canonical variable 1, Parameter 2 = .43.

TABLE 3.3. Multivariate Analysis of the Incubator Effect Among Venture Creators With Similar Organizational Backgrounds or Who Had Special Training Programs

Variables	Intentional Mean	Corporate Mean	Canonical r[a]	Correlations With SD on Diagonal			Univariate F	Significance of F
				1	2	3		
Management	2.81	2.09	.76	1.34			4.62	.04
Technical	2.23	2.75	-.53	-.007	1.40		2.26	.14
Marketing	2.23	2.43	-.22	.22	.003	1.28	.40	.53

Multivariate tests of significance

Pillais: .11, $F = 2.62$, 3/66 df, $p < .06$

Hotelling's: .12, $F = 2.62$, 3/66 df, $p < .06$

Wilks': .89, $F = 2.62$, 3/66 df, $p < .06$

Eigenvalue = .11889, canonical correlation = .32597

NOTE: N for intentional entrepreneurs = 26; N for corporate climbers = 44. Responses are scored on a 6-point scale where 1 = *most* to 6 = *least*.
a. Correlations between dependent and canonical variables. Estimates of effects for canonical variables. Canonical variable 1, Parameter 2 = .35.

TABLE 3.4. Multivariate Analysis of Reasons for Leaving the Organization by Intentionals and Corporate Climbers

Variable	Mean Intentionals	Mean Corporates	Canonical r^a	1	2	3	4	5	6	7	8	9	10	11	12	13	14	15	16	17
Organizational dynamics																				
Lack of shared information	4.00	4.47	.21	1.66																
Lack of urgency in completing projects	4.88	4.78	-.05	.65	1.45															
Absence of motivation to be productive	4.32	3.90	-.16	.50	.54	1.68														
Low maintenance of quality sStandards	4.29	4.30	.00	.40	.37	.56	1.66													
Organizational blocks																				
Experienced discrimination	3.56	4.25	.27	.31	.17	.27	.28	1.90											
Method of overcoming barriers	2.35	2.59	.10	.28	.17	.14	.18	.44	1.77										
Lack of cultural fit	3.32	3.82	.19	.39	.26	.12	.21	.34	.42	1.95									
Challenge																				
Respect for talents and skills	3.00	2.58	-.20	.14	.06	.13	.18	.20	.23	.01	1.52								
Be in charge	1.97	2.26	.15	.23	.14	.23	.18	.12	.22	.11	.36	1.42							
Regain excitement	1.97	2.18	.10	.35	.19	.12	.13	.05	.22	.18	.50	.53	1.54						
Recognition	2.97	2.48	-.25	.22	.10	.05	.09	.14	.25	.13	.46	.28	.50	1.46					
Self-determination																				
Independence	2.32	2.49	-.08	.03	.04	.03	-.06	-.08	.01	-.02	.06	.22	.30	.20	1.63				
Self-esteem	2.32	2.52	.09	.17	.11	.08	.06	.02	.23	.18	.22	.20	.36	.37	.52	1.56			
Entrepreneurial spirit	2.27	3.38	.50	.14	.25	.16	.18	.19	.30	.19	.24	.44	.33	.22	.33	.26	1.63		
Freedom in work environment	2.24	2.82	.25	.12	.14	.22	.08	.03	.12	.08	.15	.10	.08	.19	.42	.30	.36	1.69	
Family concerns																				
Balance family and work	3.74	3.52	-.08	-.05	.00	.03	-.10	.12	-.04	-.07	.12	.08	-.03	-.03	.00	-.03	.20	.08	1.98	
Control time	2.23	2.30	.13	-.03	.01	.05	-.08	.02	-.03	-.03	.28	.17	.13	.13	.13	.14	.15	.19	.47	1.54

Correlations With Standard Deviations on Diagonal

Multivariate tests of significance
Pillais: .29, F = 2.15, 17/89 df, $p < .02$
Hotelling's: .41, F = 2.15, 17/89 df, $p < .02$
Wilks': .71, F = 2.15, 17/89 df, $p < .02$
Eigenvalue = .41046 (100% variances), canonical correlations = .54

NOTE: N for intentional entrepreneurs = 34; N for corporate climbers = 73.
a. Correlations between dependent and canonical variables. Canonical Variable 1, Parameter 1, Parameter 2 = -.68.

(Table 3.4), intentional entrepreneurs have higher mean scores than corporate climbers, indicating a greater value placed on self-determination.

Post Hoc Analysis

After we had completed the initial part of our study, Barrett and Christie (1994) developed scales designed especially to measure the incubator effect. We adapted their scales in the follow-up survey, for which we received 77 responses. A MANOVA analysis of this data supports significant differences between corporate climbers and intentional entrepreneurs at the univariate level for the way the groups perceive value from participating in an industry with products, customers, suppliers, competitors, technologies, and size similar to the previous organization or experience acquired from starting a previous firm.

Discussion and Conclusions

In this chapter, we have examined the responses from questionnaire data, the content analysis of focus discussions, and follow-up data to analyze the perceptions of how the 129 female entrepreneurs used their previous organizational environments as incubators. We examined differences in how corporate climbers (those who became entrepreneurs after first aspiring to corporate careers) and intentional entrepreneurs (those with lifelong aspiration to be entrepreneurs) used the incubator organizations. Findings here support suggestions that entrepreneurial career orientations emerge from using the organization as an incubator. In addition, primary differences appear between those who always intended to be entrepreneurs and those who were initially corporate climbers in perceptions of the skill development and value of the incubator experience in marketing, management, technology acquisition, and training.

Our findings support the attribution of greater importance to managerial experience among corporate climbers than among intentional entrepreneurs. This distinction also occurred when the entrepreneur opened a venture similar to previous organizational experience or previously participated in corporate training programs. Intentional entrepreneurs without previous special corporate training programs or who went into dissimilar organizational environments valued marketing and technical training more than did corporate climbers. The above suggests that those who had aspired to advance in the organizational hierarchy place higher value on the development of managerial skills, which are directly correlated with corporate advancement, than do intentional entrepreneurs. Although previous research has not addressed how the two groups of entrepreneurs would use the organizational environment in their own ventures, there is support for a suggestion by Baucus and Human (1994) that corporate acculturation in management and technical skills is considered an important entrepreneurial career anchor, especially for those who previously intended to be professional managers. The results suggest a tendency among the latent entrepreneurs to underestimate the importance of technical expertise such as marketing and for intentional entrepreneurs to underestimate the importance of managerial experience, important dimensions for entrepreneurial success. Enhancing awareness of the importance of these differing areas of expertise may encourage aspiring entrepreneurs to balance their management team and seek advice in the less developed areas.

Our sample distribution did not permit the opportunity to subdivide the corporate climbers and intentional entrepreneurs by firm size to examine managerially oriented goals, to relate firm type—as reported for entrepreneurs in the studies of Cooper et al. (1989) and Dyke et al. (1992)—or to examine level of professional and administrative experience, as done by Hambrick and Crozier (1985). These are all worth further investigation in future studies of how entrepreneurs use the incubator experience. At the univariate level, there appear to be differences between the groups on the importance of the incubator industry similarity, with the intentionals valuing this more than do corporate climbers. This avenue of research, too, is worth further investigation.

In the post hoc analysis of data collected in a follow-up study, no significant differences were found at the multivariate level in the perceptions of specific areas of managerial experience that contributed most to running a business. Across both groups of entrepreneurs, support was found for the findings of Cooper et al. (1989), Duchesneau and Gartner (1990), Stuart and Abetti (1990), and Vesper (1990), who suggest that organizational and management experiences relevant to the new business are especially important. Factors found here include acquiring experience dealing with the challenges involved in facing major setbacks and successes, supervisory experience, and the similarity of the organizational and industry type, product, service, customer, competitors, technology, and size to the entrepreneurial venture. Although our findings support those of Fischer and colleagues (1993) that acquiring expertise in a particular sector or industry and start-up exposure are perceived as important components in successful venture operation, it is important to note that the entrepreneurs in this study saw their experiences in facing challenges and setbacks and in supervision as more important. This area is worth further investigation, as there is much to be learned from the transfer of managerial experience from the corporate environment to private ownership.

As predicted, intentional entrepreneurs placed a higher value on expertise acquired in marketing and technical areas than did corporate climbers. This supports the research findings of Morgan and Hunt (1994) in the importance of the perception of the market niche advantages acquired while still in the incubator organization among those who intended to start businesses. Also supported here are the research findings of Cooper (1985, 1986) on the importance of marketing and supplier expertise for those who have long-range intentions of creating their own businesses. One of the key advantages of entrepreneurial firms competing with much larger rivals is the ability to identify and serve a specific market niche in a superior fashion. The results of this study indicate that intentional entrepreneurs appreciate the importance of this strategic advantage. Latent entrepreneurs, however, may be less aware of the importance of this critical competitive competence and, therefore, less sensitive and responsive to shifts in the marketplace. This could have implications for firm survival and deserves further analysis of how intentionals use the previous environment to specifically acquire insider information.

Our hypothesis that significant differences would be apparent in the perceptions of reasons for flight of corporate climbers and intentional entrepreneurs is supported here. Primary differences between corporate climbers and intentional entrepreneurs appear to be centered in the self-determination of intentional entrepreneurs and their desire to start their own businesses. This driving force to start a business by intentional entrepreneurs may be comparable to the two career anchors previously identified by Schein (1990) as Autonomy/Independence and The Creation of Something New. Included are the motivations to overcome obstacles, run risks, and develop personal prominence in whatever is accomplished. In our study, these attributes had higher average ratings (means) among the intentional entrepreneurs than among those who perceived themselves as corporate climbers. This supports the thesis of Katz and Gartner (1988) and Cromie and Hayes (1991) that intentional entrepreneurs have the goal of starting their own business and a higher propensity and drive to do so than do corporate climbers.

Although we expected to find differences between corporate climbers and intentional entrepreneurs in reasons for leaving the organization and expected these reasons to be similar to the profile used to describe distinctions between entrepreneurs and managers by Fagenson (1993), we did not find this to be the case. We found that, irrespective of whether an entrepreneur was an intentional or a corporate climber, the areas of autonomy, freedom, and control were important dimensions of the reasons for leaving the organization. Autonomy, operationalized here as the desire to make it on one's own, freedom, and self-esteem (Capowski, 1992; Cromie & Hayes, 1991; Scott, 1986; Shane et al., 1991) accounted for most of the variance. This finding supports the hypothesis of Schein (1990) that autonomy/independence is an important stable career anchor that emerges from work experience.

Organizational climate was most associated with the desire to create an environment to fit a personal value system and a reaction to the bureaucratic environment. Control was more associated with time and the potential to regain excitement and be in charge. This supports the concept of the stable anchor of entrepreneurial creativity, as proposed by Schein (1990) and Katz (1994). Our research also supports Brodsky (1993), who found that entrepreneurs seek to define their own work environments and parameters. There were no significant differences between these ratings for those who had always intended to be entrepreneurs and those who had more latent intentions to become an entrepreneur.

Although we did not find reasons in line with the characteristics (Fagenson, 1993) discovered for people taking flight from the organization, at our point of analysis both the intentional entrepreneurs and the corporate climbers had made the decision to operate a business. Fagenson (1993) postulated that once the female manager leaves the organization, she perhaps adapts entrepreneurial characteristics quickly and gives up the managerial characteristics that earlier differentiated the two groups. The conclusions of both studies may bear on research presently being conducted regarding threshold management decisions in entrepreneurial organizations; that is, situations in which an entrepreneur must decide to let go of some power and turn management over to someone else. The combination of these sets of findings would make for an intriguing study of entrepreneurial decisions and characteristics important to career development of entrepreneurs and managers.

To aspiring entrepreneurs, what all of this may suggest is that, because the future can be guaranteed to be uncertain, a solid strategy is to join an organization in one's target field that has a strong training program, has a favorable nurturing environment, and offers opportunities to acquire marketing, financial, new technology, and management experience. The education and experience to be gained are portable commodities, useful to either corporate advancement or a transition to entrepreneurship.

4

Career Transition Challenges

Transition Issues and Challenges

Moving from a large organization to venture initiation—to a business that requires the near total commitment of one's time and energy for a significant period—is a big step. For the entrepreneurs in this study, the transition sometimes involved giving up many of the tangible and intangible benefits offered by a corporate career in hopes of gaining benefits such as independence and autonomy, and sometimes making more money. Among the rewards at the outset were the excitement and exuberant enthusiasm that comes from making a dream into reality. The risks, however, can be very real, and in the beginning unknown. Karen Kline, president of Accent Chicago, Inc., which she launched in 1979, has seen her business grow to five stores. It now includes an advertising specialty distributorship, Accent Promotions, and a wholesale distributorship, Sunburst Souvenirs. As she looks back:

> This is the third career that my husband and I have shared. The first two were in the nonprofit sector. We were successful and had security but there wasn't much financial potential. Going into this business reversed

81

that. The business gave us the opportunity for growth, but at an enormous risk. We put ourselves in a "go for broke" situation. We didn't
start small, we started big, because we were a little bit older. That puts
you in a place where you really have to work hard. We put in 14-, 16-
to 18-hour days, because the alternative, to go back to an apartment and
start all over again, was grim. That provides enormous motivation. Now
looking back, it was tumultuous. We managed to pass through it. I wish
there had been some preparation to help us or that it could have been
different. I don't think before we did it I was as keenly aware of just
how gutsy it was, and I am not sure that I would have done it if I had
truly appreciated the situation.

The commitment required to succeed in one's own business also involves
changes in one's life. Often these changes are not appreciated at the outset.
An entrepreneur who has operated her business more than 5 years in a large
city reflects, "I think it is a love affair with the business in the beginning.
There is a point when you ask, am I going to really run with this love affair?
Or, wait a second—do I have other things that are important that are going
to be with me forever, that I don't want to mess up?" The leap to business
ownership also involves giving things up, as this entrepreneur explains, with
a touch of nostalgia:

The flip side I think is that it makes you appreciate what you have a lot
more. I always made big bucks doing what I was doing before and now
it is the complete opposite of that. I look back and think how I handled
my money then, how I looked at what I was doing and I realize how
fortunate I was, comparatively. I didn't think about it that way then. I
always complained about it, then. The amount of work then and what I
got paid and the amount of work I do now for what I get paid is
dramatically different, like night and day. So you learn to appreciate
those things a lot more. I think you learn an appreciation of everything
in a different fashion when it is coming out of your pocket.

Transition Challenges and Management Skills

Previous studies have identified problems common in the start-up and
early phases of women-owned ventures. These include obtaining start-up
capital (in part because of a lack of collateral), marketing the product or
service, and shortcomings in business training such as financial and em-

ployee management skills (Alpander, Carter, & Forsgren, 1990; Hisrich & Brush, 1984; Humphreys & McClung, 1981; Kuratko & Hodgetts, 1989; Terpstra & Olson, 1993).

Research Questions

We asked our study participants to rate various management skills to determine whether their present entrepreneurial environments require talents different from those on which they relied in the past. We posed the question of whether or not they had been challenged by the entrepreneurial start-up problems identified in previous research, and we asked these successful women business owners to rank various start-up problems. Because there is some evidence that over time a venture moves from being entrepreneurially driven to a more administratively driven organization, we compared the participants' ratings of management skills and business problems based on their time in the business. We also compared the ratings as a function of industry turbulence and growth expectations. The analyses and related research are described below.

Ratings. The entrepreneurs' mean ratings of management skills are presented in Table 4.1. The participants rated decision making as their most important skill, followed by marketing and human resource skills and activities. Financial skills were rated as less important. These findings were consistent with previous research by Alpander et al. (1990), Hisrich and Brush (1984), Humphreys and McClung (1981), and Kuratko and Hodgetts (1989). It appears that start-up challenges are consistent over time, even for highly successful former corporate women managers and professionals.

The mean ratings for problems and issues are provided in Table 4.2. The most important issue confronting the entrepreneurs was their responsibility for their employees' welfare, followed by time management and the stress they experienced in making decisions in running their businesses. The concern for employee welfare is consistent with the strong interpersonal orientation of many of the entrepreneurs, which is described in greater detail in the next chapter.

Time in Business. Hisrich and Brush (1984) reported that among their 468 women entrepreneurs, different problems appeared depending on how long the business had been operating. We examined the questionnaire ratings of management skills and problems to determine whether they differed as a

TABLE 4.1. Overall Mean Ratings of Managerial Skills and Ratings by Level of Industry Turbulence[a]

		Amount of Turbulence		
Managerial Skill	Mean Rating	High or Moderate	Little or None	t
Decision making	1.32	1.38	1.24	
Focus on consumer needs	1.48	1.36	1.52	
Managing employees effectively	1.55	1.53	1.62	
Determining market niche	1.60	1.45	1.71	
Delegating	1.73	1.75	1.95	
Use presentation skills	1.95	1.83	2.29	1.70*
Direct the business	1.98	1.88	2.20	
Use negotiation skills	1.98	1.72	2.57	3.63***
Plan for the future	1.99	1.96	2.29	
Employ marketing and sales strategies	2.06	1.85	2.67	3.75***
Use financial savvy	2.13	1.89	2.90	4.03***
Supplement technical with nontechnical skills	2.38	2.36	2.14	
Network with other entrepreneurs	2.77	2.57	2.81	
Obtain managerial experience	2.93	2.87	3.05	
Acquire outside capitalization	3.02	2.68	3.29	
Entrepreneurial self-efficacy		393.67	309.19	2.30**

a. The question about industry turbulence was posed in the follow-up survey, so t tests are only on respondents to the second questionnaire, a subset of the whole sample.
*$p < .10$; **$p < .05$; ***$p < .001$.

function of the entrepreneurs' time in business. As shown in Table 4.3, entrepreneurs in business fewer than 2 years ranked responsibility for employee welfare, isolation, unmet expectations, and a lack of freedom as their most pressing problems. Those in business longer than 2 years identified responsibility for employees as an important problem and also ranked highly the issues of worry about making the right decisions, lack of freedom, and ethical issues. The rankings are consistent with the entrepreneurs' comments in the focus groups, in which many discussed their concerns about employees. The rankings also showed that these entrepreneurs, once established, developed networks of clients, vendors, and colleagues that helped them overcome the isolation experienced in the early years. The networking effects are discussed in greater detail in Chapter 6.

There were significant differences in the entrepreneurs' ratings of management skills depending on their time in business. Experienced entrepreneurs (in business more than 2 years) rated their ability to direct the business

TABLE 4.2. Problems/Issues in Being an Entrepreneur: Mean Ratings and Ratings as a Function of Industry Turbulence[a]

Problem/Issue	Mean Rating	Amount of Turbulence		*t*
		High or Moderate	Little or None	
Lifestyle changes	2.79	2.83	3.19	
Time management	1.80	1.91	1.90	
Not having enough family time	2.39	2.43	2.95	
Managing the stress of decision making	2.31	2.26	2.76	
Responsibility for employees' welfare	1.56	1.53	1.43	
A feeling of isolation	2.79	2.53	3.38	2.35**
Unmet expectations	2.79	2.52	3.38	2.29**
Worry about making the right decisions	2.70	2.57	2.95	
Conflicting new roles	3.02	2.85	3.57	1.86*
Lack of personal freedom	2.61	2.58	3.19	1.86*
Ethical issues	2.77	2.77	2.67	

a. The question about industry turbulence was posed in the follow-up survey, so *t* tests are only on respondents to the second questionnaire, a subset of the whole sample.
*$p < .10$; **$p < .05$.

as more important ($M = 1.9$) than did the newer entrepreneurs ($M = 2.5$, $t = 2.02$, $p < .05$) and reported significantly more stress along three dimensions: making decisions ($M = 2.21$ versus 2.94, $t = 2.14$, $p < .03$), more role conflict ($M = 2.93$ versus 3.61, $t = 2.38$, $p < .02$), and increased ethical concerns ($M = 2.67$ versus 3.41, $t = 2.14$, $p < .04$).

Turbulence. The entrepreneurs also indicated the degree to which they perceived their industry as turbulent. As Table 4.1 indicates, entrepreneurs in turbulent industries rated marketing, financial, and negotiation skills as significantly more important and presentation skills as marginally more important than did entrepreneurs who saw little or no turbulence in their fields. As the difference in the perceived self-efficacy scores indicates, perhaps because they had survived and succeeded, entrepreneurs in the more turbulent environments had more confidence in their managerial skills than did their colleagues in less turbulent fields. As Table 4.2 shows, the entrepreneurs in more turbulent environments also reported a sense of isolation and unmet expectations to be significantly greater problems and role conflict and lack of freedom as marginally greater problems than did their counterparts in more stable business environments.

TABLE 4.3. Ranking of Entrepreneurial Issues by Time in Business

	Time in Business (years)	
Issue	*1–2*	*3 or more*
Felt responsible for employees' welfare	1	1
Isolation	2	6
Unmet expectations	3	5
Lack of freedom	4	3
Worry about making the right decisions	5	2
Ethical issues	6	4
Role conflict	7	7

Expectations. We compared the entrepreneurs' mean ratings of the importance of management skills and problems as a function of growth expectations. Results are presented in Table 4.4. Entrepreneurs who expected their firms to grow rated delegation and presentation skills as significantly more important and marketing and financial skills, along with management experience, as marginally more important than did entrepreneurs who expected no change or a decrease in the number of employees. The growth-oriented entrepreneurs also felt less responsibility to employees and anticipated role conflict and lifestyle changes to a marginally greater degree.

Transition Themes in Focus Group Discussions

In the focus groups, we asked the entrepreneurs how they defined their business roles, about the challenges and problems they faced in making the transition to entrepreneurship, and about their business challenges. Themes that emerged included the change in perspective as entrepreneurs moved from a bureaucratic environment to an independent venture, the challenges of delegating authority, the difficulties of managing the financial dimensions of entrepreneurship, struggles to establish credibility, and their new isolation, especially in the early phase of their entrepreneurial careers.

Perspectives

Not unexpectedly, the entrepreneurs in the focus groups reported great changes in their lives after going into business. One consistent theme was

TABLE 4.4. Ratings of Managerial Skills and Business Issues as a Function of Expectations About Future Company Growth[a]

	Projected Change in Number of Employees		
	No Change/Decrease	Increase	t
Skill			
Delegate	2.29	1.63	2.35**
Determine market niche	1.86	1.47	1.69*
Use financial savvy	2.57	2.05	1.80*
Get management experience	3.57	2.70	2.53*
Use presentation skills	2.79	1.84	3.34**
Issue			
Lifestyle changes	3.57	2.75	1.98*
Felt responsible for employees	.86	1.72	2.36**
Role conflict	3.79	2.88	2.00*

a. Growth was measured by projected change in number of employees. The question about projected change in the number of employees was posed in the follow-up survey, so t tests are only on respondents of second questionnaire, a subset of the whole sample.
*$p < .10$; **$p < .05$.

the need to feel the drive to create one's business despite any obstacles. As Janet McCann said:

> I think that tremendous drive is probably the universal characteristic among business founders. It wasn't being the entrepreneur. It wasn't running the business. It was the drive for doing what you wanted to do under your own terms. And that burning desire puts you in a situation where you can't fail. I had years which I could not describe as successful, but I never, ever gave up. I remember thinking that I could work anywhere for better hours and better pay. But I knew that eventually it was going to be good and I wouldn't accept less than that. And that's what it takes.

For some entrepreneurs, the challenge was learning how to project themselves to operate their businesses effectively. Linda Horn, owner of L. R. Horn Capital Concepts, Inc., in Harrison, Ohio, put it this way:

> I am five feet tall and female and people do not take me seriously right off the bat. You need to be bigger and more masculine to intimidate people; then they pay attention to you. It's like an elephant. An elephant

gets more attention than a mouse. But if the mouse is the president of the company and it needs to be run effectively, then the mouse needs to learn how to manage the elephant. And that is what we do. We manage at least one elephant every single day.

Nearly all the women business owners found they were making adjustments in their personal lives. Suzan Kotler related her business sense to being a woman:

We have had to experience these difficulties in terms of trying to juggle your schedule around, so we are a lot more receptive to someone in the same situation. And we just learn to be more flexible. That expression: the reed that bends with the wind is the one that doesn't break. We learn that early on and have to make compromises and be flexible in ways that I think men don't.

Entrepreneurs as Innovators

In research on entrepreneurs, Buttner and Gryskiewicz (1993) found that entrepreneurs are more innovative than their managerial colleagues in larger organizations, prefer unstructured situations, and enjoy incorporating new and untried strategies in problem solving. Comments from several entrepreneurs illustrated these dimensions. Said Lisa Adkinson, a Cincinnati entrepreneur:

I consciously go from the entrepreneur role with the ideas that are creative and having a vision and make a conscious switch to being the doer and the implementer. I can put on my administrative hat when I need to and put on my financial hat when I need to. I can put on my systematize and organizational structure hat but that is not where I want to stay. I can stay there for a short period of time but I have to move back to the big picture.

Ethel Cook, in defining her role as business initiator, noted that "I love the semi-structured chaos in my life. It's got to be a part of the mix for me." Said Mary Louise Stott, co-owner of Bioplans, Inc., in Winston-Salem, North Carolina, "I enjoy starting new things. To me that's the excitement. I don't ever want to just be bound to the office."

As businesses moved beyond the start-up phase, some entrepreneurs felt a conflict between their preference for new challenges and the needs of their firms for administrative oversight. One Cincinnati entrepreneur explained, "In the beginning I felt like an entrepreneur. As I got more staff, I became more like a manager and had less time to think creatively. My goal now is to find someone to do day-to-day management so I can spend time being an entrepreneur."

Roles

Some entrepreneurs defined their role as related directly to their definition of the business. Marilyn Sifford, a Philadelphia entrepreneur, named her business after her vision, explaining, "The name of my company is STAR Consulting. STAR is the acronym for Systems Tapping All Resources. I felt creating that was really exciting for me, because I wanted to have a business that really stood for my values and the things that I wanted to do in my work." Joan Holliday had a similar perception about the intertwined nature of her business and self: "I'll describe my business as a mission," she said. "It comes from that base. I need to be the product of the work I am doing. I need to be the example of what I am teaching, and I think a lot of the work comes from the idea that if I am living it then I will sell it. So, I am the product."

The Focus/Flexibility Paradox

From a strategic perspective, the competitive advantage of small companies is their flexibility, the ability to adapt quickly to changes in consumer demand in the marketplace and to customize products and services to individual clients. It is critical for an entrepreneur to develop a distinctive competence, a unique capability or service or product that differentiates one's business from the competition. Chaganti and Schneer (1994) found the most profitable strategy for entrepreneurs was to appeal to customers by offering a customized, high-quality, competitively priced product. The paradox is that entrepreneurs must also hone in on and capitalize on what they do better than their rivals; that is, they must maintain their distinctive competence or focus. Entrepreneurs thus must remain flexible and adaptable, at the same time specializing in a narrow niche, one too small to be viable for their larger competitors.

Issues of distinctiveness and adaptability were discussed by 10% of the entrepreneurs in the focus groups. Lorena Blonsky, president and owner of LMB, an executive and professional search firm based in Chicago, talked about her struggle to create a unique identity for her company in a very competitive marketplace. "I have no overhead, and while that is an advantage, it's very easy for competitors to enter. That's why, in my business, there is lots of competition. Part of the problem starting up has been learning how to differentiate myself." Saralyn Levine, an Atlanta entrepreneur, found how to adapt from her customers' needs.

> I started out not as a catering business, but as a gourmet dinner delivery service for 2 to 12 people. Talk about a narrow range. Then people started asking, "Well, do you do hors d'oeuvres?" "Yes, I can do hors d'oeuvres," and I made a list up of hors d'oeuvres, and then people said, "Well, you need more desserts." I made a whole page up of desserts. That's how my menu has evolved, when people ask me for different things, and that's why I have a real menu now instead of just a photocopy of a few items.

Conversely, Karen Kline, a recipient of the Chicago Woman Business Owner of the Year Award in 1992, found that

> [w]hat has led to success is my tenacity about our focus. We have an extremely narrow focus. We have a store with a 3,000 square foot area that sells nothing but city memorabilia. Since we are in a high traffic area there are all kinds of temptations to add this or that. When business slows down there is a tremendous temptation. But that focus and sticking to the focus is what has made us successful.

Delegation

Studies have found that ability to manage employees is also important to the success of a business (Alpander et al., 1990; Cuba, DeCenzo, & Anish, 1983; Humphreys & McClung, 1981). Hisrich and Brush (1984) report that one of the problems for women entrepreneurs was hiring competent staff. Neider's (1987) in-depth study of 52 women entrepreneurs cites the inability to delegate authority as a major problem. Analysis of the focus group discussions, in which 18% of the comments involved delegation of authority, provided some information on why it is a thorny issue for entrepreneurs.

The delegation question appears to have two components. The first consists of the difficulty the entrepreneurs have in hiring competent, high-performing employees. Because the businesses are small, each employee plays a critical role, and there is little margin for an employee who fails to perform. Recalled one entrepreneur about an employee who seemed to lack initiative:

> I had a person who left because she said she had no one to call on. I said, "We have this list of thousands of clients. Sixty-six new people called in three months." She never even thought to follow up. I would have said, "Give me the list." She never made the connection that a follow-up was needed. You can't light the match for the fire in the belly. You've got to have it in you.

Relating similar frustrations, entrepreneurs pinpointed the difference between their perspectives and an employee's. "I can't get my people to not depend on me," said one. "Even when I had a partner, a full 50/50 partner, she would not follow through with things. You have to have someone there to be sure that the least little things are followed up, and if you don't you're going to begin losing customers. If I go away everything is right there, waiting there for me when I return." Employees do not necessarily feel the same responsibility for the business, says another business owner. "In my situation, I am overseeing every operation in the business. I did hand over the buying responsibility to someone else and she almost put us in the ground because she didn't have that financial tie that makes you smart in the business."

The second component of the delegation dilemma is the difficulty entrepreneurs have in giving up control over various aspects of the business. On one hand, the entrepreneur has a major risk and investment. "It's a tough transition," says one, "especially growing from a certain size business to a larger business. Delegation's so hard because as an entrepreneur, you can't afford mistakes." On the other hand, once the business grows beyond a one-person operation, the entrepreneur can no longer do it all. "I think as you grow, and we averaged over 45% growth for 9 straight years," said another entrepreneur, "you can't oversee everything. If you're not willing to give it up, you can't expand." As one New Orleans entrepreneur acknowledged, however, giving up control is not easy. "It's very difficult to delegate. I want to know everything that is going on. I want that control." Adds a Kentucky entrepreneur, "We work so hard to get our power that it is hard to turn it over."

Delegating authority was a learning experience for many of the entrepreneurs. Part of the challenge lies in identifying what is important to each employee and designing rewards to fit that individual. Said one entrepreneur, "Some of our managers are not motivated no matter how much we pay them. You have to find out what makes them tick. Once you start to do that it gets easier, but it's difficult at first." Another entrepreneur explained, "I have a lot of problems with dependability. The commitment needs to be there. I have three people. I know what motivates them. I feed them that. It's not always money."

A second element in successful delegating was creating an atmosphere in which employees could grow. As one entrepreneur acknowledged:

> I suddenly realized I was in charge of everything and I started releasing some of the responsibility to those employees I could trust. I had to learn how to let this work out to employees without looking over their shoulders and taking the work back from them that they didn't do exactly as I wanted it done. I think that is very important and it is also a great sense of taking risks. I had never taken those sorts of risks before.

Other entrepreneurs reported:

> I give my employees more opportunities to make decisions. They know these decisions will be backed up. It is important to link clients to staff members because this creates customer loyalty and satisfaction and frees up the valuable time all entrepreneurs need. No one can do it all, and it is not desirable to have customers think you are the only one in the organization who can handle their problems.

Finance

Hisrich and Brush's (1984) survey found that female entrepreneurs frequently reported that they lacked financial training, particularly in the areas of financial planning and obtaining credit. In Humphreys and McClung's (1981) study of female entrepreneurs, 34% of the participants reported difficulty in raising capital. Financial management, including obtaining outside funding, was the second most frequently cited problem among the INC. 500 fast-growing companies in 1993 (Terpstra & Olson, 1993). Financial issues have been identified as significant start-up and small business problems by other researchers (Alpander et al., 1990; Kuratko & Hodgetts, 1989; Scott, 1986). Numerous studies have reported that it is harder for female entrepreneurs to obtain funding than for their male counterparts (Hisrich & O'Brien, 1982; NFWBO, 1996; Pellegrino & Reese, 1982). This is particularly important because bank financing historically has been second only to personal savings and family loans as a source of start-up capital for female entrepreneurs (Hisrich & O'Brien, 1982).

Fully 25% of the focus group participants in this study said that financing their business had been a transition and start-up problem. Several entrepreneurs had started their businesses using personal savings. One explained the impact on her first several years of operation:

> I was in a situation where I had no income. I had zip, I had to go from ground zero. So that the transitional problems for someone like myself was to rearrange all my finances. I had to downsize all my expenses because I recognized if I were going to be in business and had no idea what my income would be for the first couple of years, I would have to give myself a fighting chance. I moved out from a big, lovely apartment to a smaller, half-as-lovely apartment. I kept my business expenses minimal. The problems I see with start-up companies is that they go out and buy all of this stuff at first before they really have any income to support the stuff. I was very selective in terms of where I spent my money, in business as well as my personal life.

Other entrepreneurs had sought outside funding. Debra Rust recalled her initial experience:

> I had wonderful personal credit. I had worked for my former company for many, many years. I owned a house. I had a business plan that was 2 inches thick. I went to my personal bank to get a collateral loan, a line of credit, on my house. It wasn't much, but it was going to help move things along. They said, "Well, you are self-employed, we can't give you any money on a loan." I said, "Well wait, I have had a bank account here for many, many years, been a customer." They said, "No, come back in 2 or 3 years." That was the most shocking thing I had experienced. I said, "If I had come in here the day before I left to go into business would you have given me a loan?" They said, "Yes, but now you aren't working for them anymore."

Said Eileen Duignan-Woods, owner of E.D.W. Associates, Inc., a Chicago and North Carolina engineers and construction consultants firm, "Money is a real sore subject, a real problem. The tragedy of it is that between the [shortage of] money and the bank, I can never grow."

Do Banks Discriminate Against Women Entrepreneurs?

The evidence on this issue is mixed. In a study of bank loan officers' perceptions, Buttner and Rosen (1988a) found that bankers perceive men to be higher on the characteristics associated with successful entrepreneurship than women. In a follow-up study of bankers' recommendations for start-up loans, however, there were no differences in recommendations as a function of entrepreneurial gender (Buttner & Rosen, 1989). Riding and Swift (1990) examined funding decisions made by bankers in Canada and found that, overall, financial decisions appeared to favor male entrepreneurs. The women surveyed paid a higher interest rate on loans, had to put up more collateral, were less likely to have a line of credit, and were more likely to have been required to have a spouse cosign a loan. The women's businesses, however, also were smaller, younger, slower-growing, and more likely to be in the service sector, attributes that made them less attractive loan candidates from a banker's perspective. When Riding and Swift (1990) controlled for age, growth rate, and size and type of business, one gender-related difference remained: For women, the collateral requirement for a line of credit was higher. The difference in treatment is notable because small businesses often need a line of credit to finance growth. More recently, Fabowale, Orser, and Riding (1995) found that although women small business owners felt less satisfied with their banking experiences, there were no differences in rejection rates or terms of credit for Canadian male and female small business applicants.

Establishing Credibility

A fourth theme that emerged in the focus group discussions of transition issues was establishing credibility with potential clients, customers, and vendors during the start-up phase. This concern, too, is consistent with previous research. Participants in Hisrich and O'Brien's (1982) study complained about the difficulty in establishing credibility with bankers in obtaining loans. Similarly, Goffee and Scase (1983) reported that the female entrepreneurs in their interviews attributed the difficulties they had in their businesses to the fact that they are perceived as lacking credibility. According to Goffee and Scase, "Creditors, customers, employees, and husbands do not grant women the esteem and competence they accord to men" (p. 640).

These studies are somewhat dated, however, and women have made significant progress in the management ranks of U.S. corporations, in politics, and in other avenues of society. We examined the data to determine whether a lack of credibility emerged as an issue in the discussion of start-up and operating problems for these female entrepreneurs. Results indicate that establishing credibility was a challenge primarily for women entering a new field or starting a business in a male-dominated industry. Remarks on such issues constituted 9% of the transition comments. Thinking back, Mary Louise Stott reflected on the start-up of her insurance business, in a field in which she had little prior experience:

> Would I start my business in the same way again? No. Because I had no business contacts. I had no credibility. My friends were thinking, "Well, my wife wouldn't be a very good financial consultant. Why should I use this person?" Building credibility was very, very difficult. I slowly got to know other business women and that was really my first foot in the door.

For women starting businesses in traditionally male-dominated industries, gaining acceptance posed an additional hurdle. Gail Withers explains how it worked for her.

> I had name recognition. I took that with me when I left and pursued the construction industry on my own, thinking that the name recognition would help me a lot. I did not realize that I was going into the "Old Boy Network" that one, resented women and, second, very much resented a black woman coming into their industry. I spent a lot of time knocking on doors, being left sitting in lobbies for 3 and 4 hours while the guy I was supposed to talk with walked back and forth and just looked out the window like, "I couldn't be bothered with her." But I'm used to that. And I stuck it out. I started with five workers and the company zoomed in 3 years to 100 workers on a daily basis. And for the construction industry that's great.

Deborah Stange, president and founder of West Fuels, Inc., in Westchester, Illinois, observed of her industry:

They're not used to seeing women in their environment. I was at a garage shop making a sales call. I was all dressed up when I walked in there. Men there were whistling all the way across the garage. They were laughing and asking, "Who is she?" It was terrible. I had more success on the phone than in person because it was so male-dominated. You can't go in there with an attitude like, I am not a woman, but on the other hand you can't flaunt it. There is a delicate balance.

Support Versus Isolation

In organizations, reinforcement, support, and expertise can be taken for granted. "There's something to be said about being able to walk and find someone to share the small frustrations with," remembers Lorena Blonsky, a Chicago entrepreneur. "In a small business," points out Gloriann Harris, C.P.A., owner of her own accounting firm in Northbrook, Illinois, "There is no such thing as having easy access to an expert or someone immediately to consult with on some small technical detail, whether a marketing, technical or regulation change issue."

Having the support of family and close friends is an important factor in women's choice to start their businesses (Stevenson, 1986). Lack of support can be a major obstacle in the start-up process (Humphreys & McClung, 1981). In the present study, 17% of the comments about entrepreneurial challenges in the interviews pertained to support from family, friends, business partners, and others in the business community. For some, support was a positive (35%); family and friends had encouraged entrepreneurial aspirations and expressed confidence in the entrepreneurs' ideas and efforts. Other entrepreneurs talked about the discouragement that important others in their lives conveyed (65%). One entrepreneur reported her experiences as follows.

I felt very isolated and alone. Aside from my husband, my family didn't understand what I was doing. I am not sure people beyond my husband and children yet understand what I do in the way I would like them to. I experienced a lot of alienation with a sister I had been very close to because she felt I was rejecting my children when I started my business. And that is something that has never been quite rectified. But it was a choice between that relationship and me. I felt that I needed to choose myself first.

The entrepreneurs also talked about the professional isolation, an experience that affected 56 of our entrepreneurs (43%). Thirty-three (26%) rated isolation as most important in their role as entrepreneurs, and 23 (18%) rated it as the second most important item. Isolation as an entrepreneur could be very trying. In the words of one Cincinnati businesswoman, "I remember being involved with people in neighborhood functions and not fitting in with the moms who were talking about kindergarten car pools. I couldn't hang out with the guys. I felt very isolated and alone." Said a Dallas entrepreneur: "I found the first few years in business to be difficult because they were lonely and that was probably the hardest transition for me to overcome, that sense of 'I'm in this all by myself.' " "I am more of a loner, so working by myself has suited me," said Bert Gose, an Atlanta entrepreneur, "but I tend to get too isolated. I had to work very hard to get out and network and back on things, it's real easy to sort of let that go and just get a little weird." Another entrepreneur said, "If I had a marketing issue or a technical issue there is no expert down the hall to talk it over with. Now I am just by myself." An entrepreneur who started a catering business found the transition from a corporate environment in which she was surrounded by colleagues to an entrepreneurial venture an eye-opening experience.

When I stopped working for corporate America, it was a Friday and the following Monday I decided, "I'm in business." I had planned it 6 months before. I was used to being around all these people. I had my own little cubbyhole but I could always walk across the hall and chat with someone and when you're working out of your home, all of a sudden you have nothing. The phone didn't start ringing that Monday morning with orders coming in.

The isolation extended beyond the loss of people to socialize with. Entrepreneurs also found they lacked the opportunity to solve problems and troubleshoot with colleagues. "Working alone and not having anyone to discuss issues with is the hardest part about starting a business. And you're afraid to ask; you are afraid someone will think you are dumb and they will wonder, Well why did you start a business if you don't know all these things?" says one entrepreneur. The solution to isolation seems to be making a concerted effort to network on a consistent basis with other businesspeople. As Deborah Stange, who owns a fuel distribution business, explained, "I go out almost every day to see people and to get out of the isolated environment. Networking is very important."

Conclusion

Although the women talked at length about the transition issues they faced, most are now very satisfied with their ventures, as described in Chapter 7. The transition was not easy. These women business initiators had approached the challenges of their transition from the corporate world to entrepreneurship with grit and determination.

5

Interactive Leadership—
The Hub Effect

Interactive Leadership

Leadership plays a key role in the survival and success of entrepreneurial ventures. The focus in small firms is on the entrepreneur, who is called on to build an organizational culture (Schein, 1983), develop a strategic vision (Westley & Mintzberg, 1988), and discover and take advantage of opportunities and resources in the firm's environment (Chandler & Hanks, 1994). There is a scarcity of research on how female entrepreneurs approach this leadership role (Brush, 1992). In the past, male-oriented leadership models were used to study women as leaders or managers (Konek & Kitch, 1994; Powell, 1993). Today, researchers are introducing new models, specifically the interactive (Rosener, 1990) and web approaches (Belenky, Clinchy, Goldberger, & Tarule, 1986; Helgesen, 1990). This chapter examines leadership styles of the entrepreneurs in this study and explores how these approaches are related to the teamwork, power, and decision-making dimensions of managing their businesses.

Leadership Styles

The literature, culture, and socialization processes relating to leadership and management theories in corporate America are predominantly male-oriented (Helgesen, 1990). Konek and Kitch (1994) found that more than 85% of the women they surveyed viewed the American workplace as male-oriented. Citing their sample and other surveys, they show that a majority of women believe that they should be prepared to "compete on the same terms as men" and appear "as much like men as possible" (Konek & Kitch, 1994, p. 49).

Current literature on leadership (Kouzes & Posner, 1987; Sashkin & Burke, 1990) builds on discussions of the transactional and transformational leadership styles. The transactional leader focuses on short-term goals and stability, offering rewards for performance. The transformational leader articulates a vision of the firm that can be shared by peers and subordinates, empowers and encourages subordinates, models effective behavior, shows respect for individual differences among subordinates, and prefers effectiveness over efficiency. For the transformational leader, quality is more important than speed and outcomes are more important than following a specific process to achieve them (Bass, 1985, 1990). Recent research has promoted the transformational leader as the more successful model for leadership (Kouzes & Posner, 1987). Sashkin and Burke (1990) further develop Schein's (1983) long-term vision of the leader's role in organizational culture and expand on the role of vision as used by Parsons (1960) to focus transformational leadership on supporting the central functions and core competencies of the business. Inherent in this model is the need for leaders to act as role models, motivating and empowering followers to become leaders (Kelly, 1991; Kouzes & Posner, 1987; Powell, 1993). Recent studies also suggest that female leaders more than males tend to utilize transformational behaviors (Bycio, Hackett, & Allen, 1995; Bass, Avolio, & Atwater, 1996; Druskat, 1994).

Helgesen (1990, 1995) describes a female leadership style termed the web approach. In her 1990 study, she found differences in how women executives operated compared to a group of male executives observed by Mintzberg (1973). Her findings indicated that women leaders tended to place greater value on their relationships, with emphasis on cultivation and nurturance. Women move toward an integration of personal and professional dimensions of their lives, as contrasted with the compartmentalization found by Mintzberg. Eschewing the traditional perquisites and privileges, which separate leaders from others in their organizations, female leaders also construct a tie to each individual (Yammarino, Dubinsky, Comer, & Jolson, 1997).

According to Rosener (1990), women often did not have the same access to formal power and, therefore, had to rely on personal power and influence, teamwork, and a nontraditional style of leadership to get work accomplished. She termed this style "interactive." Women using this style were characterized as encouraging participation, sharing power and information, enhancing others' self-worth, and getting others excited about their work. Appelbaum and Shapiro (1993) elaborated on the interactive leadership style by adding that it includes a cooperative stance, horizontal and egalitarian structure, intuitive and subjective decision making, low emphasis on control, and an empathetic culture. Shipper (1994) found that the women he studied used interactive skills more frequently than did men. In a study of female entrepreneurs, Vokins (1993) found the most frequently described leadership style matched the characteristics of the interactive mode.

Past research suggests that men and women employ different approaches to leadership. Eagley and Johnson (1990), in a meta-analysis of the leadership literature, found that women behaved more democratically and men more autocratically in leadership situations. Coppolina and Seath (1987) and Korabik (1981, 1982, 1990) found that women placed greater emphasis on maintaining effective working relationships at work. Women may approach leadership differently because of socialization (Hennig & Jardim, 1977). According to Chodorow (1974, 1978), women value cooperation and being responsible to others. Gilligan (1982), in her analysis of the responses of females and males to moral dilemmas, found that the females exhibited a concern for achieving outcomes that addressed the concerns of all parties involved, which Gilligan termed "an ethic of care." Other research findings are consistent with Gilligan's thesis that women's sense of responsibility influence their values and leadership style (Desjardins, 1989; Fagenson, 1986, 1993; Families and Work Institute, 1995).

From this review of the literature, we propose two research questions in an area where little is known about how women entrepreneurs lead their organizations. First, we propose that the interactional style of leadership incorporates the tenets of the transformational, role model/visionary, and web approaches. We should, therefore, find high correlations in the scales for each of these styles, which would suggest they measure a central construct. Our second research question builds from the first. Given a measure of interactive leaders through the three leadership scales, we propose that those scoring as highly interactive leaders will have a greater appreciation of interpersonal and human resource management skills, be more concerned about the welfare of their employees, and rate employee satisfaction as a more important measure of their success. Finally, we explored whether there would be differences in the entrepreneurs' operation of their firms as a function of leadership style. Operational dimensions examined include support obtained, satisfaction with their work, perceived managerial self-efficacy, and perceptions about the importance of creativity and innovation in the operation of their businesses.

Findings

Leadership Scale Relationships

The first research question proposed that a measure of the interactive style may be captured through three scales covering transformational, role model/visionary, and web approaches to leadership. In our follow-up survey, the female entrepreneurs completed the Leader Assessment Inventory developed and revised by Sashkin (1984; Sashkin & Burke, 1990) to measure the extent to which they utilized a transformational approach to leadership (10 items, reliability: alpha coefficient = .68). The extent to which these entrepreneurs articulated a vision for their firm and acted as a role model for members of their company (Role Model/Visionary Scale; alpha = .66) was measured with six items. Each entrepreneur also completed a four-item scale, developed from research by Helgesen (1990), Rosener (1990), and Appelbaum and Shapiro (1993), that measured the extent to which they used a participative, weblike management style (Web Scale; alpha = .69; see Appendix 1 for the items composing this scale).

Our analysis indicated that the three dimensions of interactive leadership were highly intercorrelated. The correlation between the Transformational leadership scale and the Role Model/Visionary scale was .68 ($p < .0001$), between the Transformational Scale and the Web dimension .31 ($p < .007$), and between the Web and Role Model/Visionary Scales .53 ($p < .0001$). We found support for an interactive leadership approach through a number of important commonalities between the transformational scales, the Role Model/Visionary Scale, and the scale to measure the Web dimension. We combine our findings from the quantitative analysis of the follow-up questionnaires and the content analysis to identify the interactive style of leadership supported by Rosener (1990) and Powell (1993) and the web view of leadership proposed by Helgesen (1990). As seen below, these findings are further supported in the themes that emerge in the content analysis in the areas of teamwork and collaboration, value of personal power over hierarchical or institutional sources of power, and the importance of entrepreneurial roles.

Building on the findings from our first question, our second research question explored whether more interactive leaders, as designated by high scores on all three leadership scales, were more likely to appreciate interpersonal and human resource management skills, show concern about the welfare of their employees, and rate employee satisfaction as an important measure of their success.

High intercorrelations among seven human resource skills that had been rated by the entrepreneurs indicated that a composite scale was the most appropriate measure of the human resources dimension (Human Resources Scale; alpha = .86). Separate questions asked the entrepreneurs to indicate the extent to which they were concerned about the welfare of their employees and to rate employee satisfaction as a measure of their success. Nineteen entrepreneurs (25% of the 77 entrepreneurs who completed the follow-up survey) scored above the sample mean on all three leadership scales. For subsequent analysis, these 19 entrepreneurs were aggregated into a subgroup called interactive leaders and then compared to the remaining entrepreneurs. We used t tests to determine whether the interactive leaders differed, on managerial and operational dimensions related to their businesses, from those using other leadership approaches.

As predicted, the interactive entrepreneurs attached significantly greater importance to the welfare of their employees. The interactive business owners rated the Human Resources Skills scale as significantly more important (scale $M = 9.06$, where $1 = highly\ important$ to $5 = unimportant$ for each of the seven items) than did the other entrepreneurs ($M = 12.69$, $t = 2.60$, $p < .01$). Thus, it appears that the interactive leaders had a greater appreciation of the importance of skillfully managing the people in their organizations. In reflecting on their experiences in their prior jobs, the interactive entrepreneurs reported that learning motivational techniques had been significantly more influential ($M = 1.67$) than reported by the other entrepreneurs ($M = 2.49$, $t = 2.14$, $p < .03$). The interactive leaders felt more responsible for their employees' welfare ($M = 1.05$) compared with other entrepreneurs ($M = 1.65$, $t = 2.09$, $p < .05$) and rated employee satisfaction as a more important success measure ($M = 1.10$) than did the other entrepreneurs ($M = 1.93$, $t = 3.00$, $p < .003$). A scale that tapped the extent to which their concern for others was important as a success measure also was rated significantly higher by interactive entrepreneurs ($M = 7.06$, others' $M = 8.82$, $t = 2.23$, $p < .03$).

Exploratory Analysis

Several measures were used in the exploratory analysis to determine whether other operational dimensions differed depending on leadership style. A three-item scale measured the entrepreneurs' satisfaction with their work (alpha = .86; Brophy, 1959). A six-item scale measured self-efficacy perceptions about successfully managing the firm (alpha = .95; Sadri, 1994), and separate items measured the three operational dimensions of the entrepreneurs' business: support obtained from others, the perceived importance of creativity and innovation, and the degree to which the entrepreneurs felt a loss of freedom resulting from business demands.

In the exploratory results, there were significant differences in ratings concerning the operational aspects of managing businesses. Interactive entrepreneurs reported getting more operational support ($M = 1.79$) than did the others ($M = 2.79$, $t = 2.62$, $p < .01$). The interactive entrepreneurs reported higher perceived self-efficacy for their managerial skills ($M = 425.67$ versus 328.90, $t = 2.64$, $p < .01$). Consistent with the visionary aspects of interactive leadership, those entrepreneurs saw creativity and innovation as a more important part of the entrepreneurial role ($M = 1.05$ versus 1.61, $t = 2.46$, $p < .02$). The interactive entrepreneurs were more satisfied with their work ($M = 24.2$ versus 20.1, $t = 3.03$, $p < .003$) and reported that a loss of personal freedom was marginally less of a problem ($M = 3.11$) than for the other business owners ($M = 2.53$, $t = 1.66$, $p < .10$).

The results of the quantitative analysis indicate that those entrepreneurs who reported an interactive leadership style differed from the other entrepreneurs on a number of important management dimensions. The interactive entrepreneurs were more inclined to recognize the importance of their employees, indicate high levels of concern for those individuals, and place greater emphasis on development of skills needed to work effectively with others. They also were more confident of their abilities to successfully run their firms, more satisfied with their work, and marginally less concerned about a loss of freedom.

Focus Interviews

In the focus interviews, we asked the entrepreneurs to tell us how they defined their role in their businesses. Several themes emerged from these discussions. The entrepreneurs frequently raised issues they faced as women in managing their subordinates and talked about their struggles and their success in resolving these issues and about their philosophies and approaches to collaboration in their firms. They frequently discussed the challenges of empowerment of subordinates and clients. A small number of women addressed the importance of their visionary roles in their organizations. A subject often raised was that of integrating themselves, their business, and the rest of their lives into a seamless whole and what this integration meant for them. The business owners talked about managing their multiple roles to be able to "do it all" to successfully lead and manage their firms.

Dominating discussion of the leadership and management of their businesses were themes related to caring, supportive, and empowering approaches to dealing with employees and clients. Thirty-four percent of the comments in the focus sessions related to these themes. Of those entrepreneurs who indicated they used an interactive leadership style in the quantitative analysis, 90% specifically discussed ways they implemented this style in their businesses.

Teamwork and Collaboration

The women entrepreneurs in this study relied extensively on a collaborative approach in working with employees. It is interesting that none of them talked about using their prior corporate experience as a template for managing their own businesses. Instead, they often contrasted their team-oriented approach with the management style that had predominated in their prior organization. Susan Brown depicts how this works.

There were a lot of buzzwords thrown around in the corporate environment. An example of one is a team player. The definition of a "corporate" team player is doing the same thing, looking the same way, using the same language and saying the same answers. My definition of a team is quite different, I think that a team needs to be more than a group of individuals. We don't all have to have soul bonding, but you have to have a common level of purpose.

Getting to the heart of the matter, she continued, "We have to really believe that there is a reason for me to collaborate with you, that if I am open to the knowledge and experience that you have, then we will increase the result that we can get together." Susan Brown had not found that in her corporate experience. Another entrepreneur, rejecting authoritarian management, added that "it is important to understand the kind of team member you need. I am a firm believer that all brains have to be at the table." Ann Angel, the owner of a computer training company, described her method of contributing to the teamwork in her business this way:

> If they have an obstacle, I remove it, or I'll fix it. If they need equipment; if they need me to smooth something through or help them think something through, they come to me. They say, "Help me think this through." And I give them my perception. They are just as competent to make the decision as I am. And they have the power to do it. That's the way I like to run a team.

Caretaking and Support Versus Making the Hard Decisions

Because women have been socialized to be attuned to the needs and concerns of others, they may be able to respond to the needs of other people without perceiving this as a distraction from their sense of identity (Miller, 1986). Women, Miller argues, are more likely to be aware of the pleasure and satisfaction experienced in participating in the growth and development of another person and thus are more likely than men to believe that, ideally, all activity should lead to increased emotional connections. Comments of entrepreneurs in the focus sessions suggested this type of operation. Some spoke of the caring and concern they felt toward their employees and their clients. Some remarked that they saw their role in their business as an extension of their role as mothers. As Patricia Sayre, president of Fiber-Seal, a Cincinnati firm, explained, "I have this concept that this is my child no matter what he does. I can see this transfer to my employees." Suzan Kotler adds:

> I can be very maternal towards the people that work for me partially because I am a woman. When they do something wrong, I tell them. I look out for their interests. I wouldn't say that I am unprofessional, but I perceive that I am there to help, direct and guide. This is more true in women-owned businesses than in male-owned businesses.

Contrasting male and female approaches as being different, Patricia Sayre added:

> I think I get very much more involved with my employees and their lives than any male would do. In the environment where I worked before, they would not have taken all these problems to the attention of the owner or manager. The men would just pat you on the head and say, "That's too bad . . . so when are we going to get this finished?"

An approach different from what is found in most large corporations was the reason for her success, said another entrepreneur:

> One of my employees said, "I see you as my other mother." But what she was saying was that I was an adviser, nurturing in a way that a mother does. My company has grown because I have acted like a mother, along with bringing my professional experience.

Entrepreneurs in the focus groups were more inclined to accept that subordinates have obligations outside work and to work with employees to meet those obligations. Rebecca Carney, an East Coast entrepreneur, described this perception of responsibilities toward her employees, saying:

> I see my primary responsibility as being able to provide some sort of consistent management for people who work here. To create an environment that is healthy, where people feel that it is okay to make a mistake. Where people feel that if they have a question or a problem that they can verbalize it, they don't have to sit on it for a while. Where they don't feel that their personal life is something that I don't care about. And where, if they are sick, they feel that they could stay home. Or if they have an event in the family's life, they don't feel guilty about asking me for time off. I think more than anything it is an open communication. It's an environment where people don't have to spend a lot of their energy trying to figure out what the politics are or what I am thinking or going to do next.

Gilligan (1982) defines the "ethic of care" as according others the respect that a person wishes for oneself. An East Coast Entrepreneur of the Year put it more bluntly: "I want everybody to be treated like I want to be treated. I think women do that more than men."

Gutman (1975) proposed that, with advancing age, women shift from nurturance to agency. In the focus sessions, this shift was reflected in comments the women entrepreneurs made about the difficulty they experienced between being nurturing and supportive and having to make difficult employment decisions in the best interests of the business. Patti Breeze, a charter member and past president of the Lexington chapter of the National Association of Women Business Owners in Kentucky, explained, "I think women have a hard time giving up on those [supportive] roles because women are caretakers." Recounting her struggle, Linda Horn, a financial consultant from the Cincinnati area, said:

> I go the second and third mile and men won't do that. Because I want someone to succeed so much, I often find myself being too lenient. And I have found this to be a serious problem. I recently let an employee go after 2 months. In the past I would have kept him at least 6 months. I consider this a major milestone for me.

A similar hardening of attitude was expressed by a Charleston entrepreneur:

> I am getting tougher as I grow older and cleaning out people who are not doing their jobs. I am sorry about the problems my employees have, but I have a business to run. You simply cannot get bogged down in their problems. You want people who can do the job.

The entrepreneurs also recognized that balance was the key to benefiting their businesses. "With our children," Linda Horn explained, "we have to let them make mistakes and learn to do things on their own. Women are more patient by nature; we are born as less aggressive individuals. I see that women must maintain control over the nurturing concept, not give it up." A number of entrepreneurs had already moved beyond this issue. "We are now to the point where we are having some key people turn over in the organization," said one. "[T]his is very natural and I can see exactly why it has happened. The people who were not able to handle the change and conform to the way we will be in the future have moved on."

Attitudes Toward Power

Excluded from institutional sources of power that historically have been more accessible to men, women tend to pay less attention to formal power and rely more on personal power (Rosener, 1995). Unlike institutional power, which is derived from a position of authority in a hierarchy, personal power depends on a leader's ability to establish trust, mutual respect, credibility, and reliability. Although research has not found any differences in power salience, drive, power anxiety, or power style as a function of gender (see Kelly, 1991, pp. 99-103 for a review), there are differences in terms of ambivalence about holding and exercising power (Kelly, 1991). Women tend to view power as a means to promote change. Men tend to view power as a means of having influence over others (Hale & Kelly, 1989). Men are socialized to seek and hold position power. Having been socialized that this is not feminine, women feel less comfortable being aggressive, preferring to exercise influence by serving as a resource (Gallos, 1989). Socialized for personal power (Kelly, 1991), for women, facilitating change means having and sharing information and empowering others through team building. In this process, one's own power is enhanced (Miller, 1986). This approach is directly opposed to motivation through fear (Fried, 1989).

Because women's culture is often characterized by connection, inclusion, and community, women are more likely to view power as relational, contextual, and consensual, a "power to" or "power with," rather than the hierarchical or structured "power over" (Konek & Kitch, 1994). For women executives, it can be power that derives not from control but from mastery (Hardesty & Jacobs, 1986). A logical inference is that female entrepreneurs probably are socialized as women to be attuned to the needs of others. They may have developed interpersonal skills to compensate for insufficient positional power. With significant business experience, they could be expected, while exercising authority carefully, to try to create an environment that subordinates would find empowering and practice management techniques such as a participative approach in which the rules are made with the involvement and consent of those affected (Martin, 1993).

Empowering Subordinates

Among the entrepreneurs studied here was an owner of an investment advisory firm whose business faced a crossroads with an opportunity to grow significantly in the near future. She said, "In the beginning I set up the goals, but tomorrow we're all going to sit down. I'm going to say, 'We're getting more and more institutional clients. How are we going to do this, do it well, and make sure we meet the clients' needs as well as our own?'" Another woman said:

I see myself as a facilitator of my employees. They know exactly what they're doing. I've trained them. Now they are real good at it. And I'm not about to get in their way. I do call them out in the office about once every week and say, "Okay. I'm going to be boss for about 2 minutes and then I'm going back to my office and let you all do your work." And we just laugh. And that's kind of the camaraderie we have built. Because they don't need me to boss them. They come to me when they have a decision to make.

Another entrepreneur, who owns a clothing design business, defines her role as one of "creating an environment that encourages designers and artists to do something greater than they've ever done before."

Empowering Clients

Ideas for empowering others were not limited to employees. Evelyn Eskin, an entrepreneur who helps design more efficient medical offices, explains it this way:

I view my role as trying to empower other women. We work a lot with medical office managers and people who have never had an opportunity to think of themselves as change agents. So, we do a lot of teaching of the notion that they can change the environment rather than feeling that they are merely reacting to the situation.

Another Philadelphia entrepreneur said:

I tend to have long-term relationships with clients, so I am able to see an organization changing from being very hierarchical to being more team-oriented. People learn more skills about how to make decisions, to work with each other, to work with management and to reduce some of the barriers between the levels of management in the organization.

Role Modeling and Creating a Vision

A recent study of 43 highly successful female executives showed that a style of leadership in which the leader was concerned about subordinates doing their best dominated. Second most common was the style in which the leader acted as a visionary (White, Cox, & Cooper, 1992). Consistent with the quantitative results presented earlier in the chapter, these styles also emerged strongly in the focus group sessions. A challenge for many entrepreneurs, as for Lisa Adkinson, "has been learning to be able to get the big vision communicated and implemented. I am always repeating the same things over and over. You can't move on until you have the last person on the train or you are forced to leave them behind." Renee Peyton added action to go along with her words: "I empowered my employees to do what they need to do. I didn't sit there and say, 'This is what we need you to do; you do it.' I came in on Saturdays and I sat on the floor and counted the bus bills along with them so that we could get caught up. I never asked anybody to do what I wouldn't do myself." Recounted Gail Withers, a North Carolina entrepreneur who runs a construction employment agency:

> I was at the School of Design. We were working up there about a year ago, and I was hanging on top of the air conditioning duct, cleaning it off, and the gal that works for me brought in checks for me to sign. The only thing you could see was my feet. There were several guys up there with me working. She was walking down there and looking at the feet. Finally she came across my work shoes. The guy down there with her said, "Oh, there are only guys up there working." And she said, "Well, one of the 'guys' up here is our boss."

Integration

Miller (1986) defines the issues of integration for women as achieving creativity and cooperativeness, authenticity, self-determination, and the capacity to implement power in serving their and others' needs. Wolfman (1984) summarized many of the dimensions of integration these entrepreneurs described when she said:

> The women who manage multiple roles do so not in a vacuum, but in a context of those who taught them to care and be competent. . . . They have learned to provide for [the needs of others] in a variety of ways while attempting to define their own sense of personhood. Many women . . . act out their own faith and values with a sense of self-confidence and the belief that they can make choices and fulfill their own definition of destiny. (p. 3)

Belenky et al. (1986) found that as women achieved more integrated lives, they became more autonomous and independent in thought. Helgesen (1990) noted that the women executives she observed tended to have lives that were more balanced and integrated than Mintzberg's (1973) male executives. Neugarten (1968) suggested that, in mid-life, people undergo a normal, gradual transition in which they begin to think of time in terms of years left to live rather than time since birth. This shift is accompanied by heightened introspection, stock-taking, and a turn inward.

The fact that 9% of the comments in the focus group sessions concerned ways these entrepreneurs sought or achieved integration across the various spheres of their lives, balanced the competing demands of home and work, and strove to honor and work according to their values—in ways they often had not been able to do in their previous corporate positions—suggests that a number of the entrepreneurs in this study were gaining perspective as they went about integrating the various dimensions of their lives. "I wanted a place where people could be appreciated, people would do the work they were supposed to, where I could rely on them, where everyone could be adult," says Honi Stempler. A woman who does strategic planning for large organizations states, "I was looking for a life that I now call much more seamless. I mean I am working more than I have worked in a long time but it doesn't feel that way. Work felt like an intrusion to me in the corporate world because it was just so different from the way I wanted to use my knowledge and present myself." Marilyn Sifford, the owner of an organizational development business, speaking of her reexamination of priorities, said, "I wanted to have a business that stood for my values." Another entrepreneur said, "I see parallels in growth and direction related to my own growth." "There is some feeling that we want to do this at a pace that feels whole and integrated with us. If we do it too fast, then we feel that we are back doing the same thing we did before" was the way Joan Holliday summarized this issue.

The process of change ran both ways. Values transferred from an individual owner to a firm made working environments different. Experiences of entrepreneurship changed working styles. As one entrepreneur stated:

It inspires me to look a little bit beyond and to stretch and do things that maybe I wouldn't have done before. I'm doing a lot of things now that I never thought I would be doing. Some that are a big stretch for me personally. But I find that the more I do it, the more I enjoy it and the better I get at it. Each one leads to something else.

The entrepreneurs also perceived differences in the need for integration between male and female business owners. One Chicago entrepreneur summed it up saying, "I think that one of the big differences between the traditional male entrepreneur and most of the female entrepreneurs I know is that most women see their careers as interwoven with the rest of their lives and they wouldn't tolerate it otherwise. At least traditionally, men have departmentalized their lives."

Multiple Roles

Focus group comments noted the multiple roles involved in managing a business. The entrepreneurs often described doing many different things to keep their business operational. When asked on the initial survey how she defined her role, one woman wrote, "Owner, president and bathroom cleaner." In the interview, she elaborated, "If you are an entrepreneur, I don't think you can separate yourself from any function in the business." Patricia Sayre explained why she believed women could juggle the varying and sometimes conflicting demands in running their businesses:

Women are accustomed to managing a lot of different things at one time. When we are preparing a meal, we not only have the peas, potatoes, and steak come out at the right time, but probably we have the laundry going and several other things we are synchronizing at the same time. We are more comfortable with managing a lot of different things.

Part of the challenge comes from the fact that customers and clients often want to deal directly with the business owner, reported Eileen Duignan-Woods. "There is a tendency for people to think of you as the business instead of the business as a separate entity. They look upon my business as me. I am expected to do a lot of the work."

Conclusion

There is considerable evidence that the transformational leadership style is quite effective. Korabik (1990) concluded in her review of the leadership literature that the female concern for an equitable outcome, which addresses the concerns of all involved, results in higher subordinate satisfaction. Goodwin and Whittington (1996) found that transformational and inspirational leadership styles were strongly, positively correlated with subordinates' satisfaction with supervision and with their evaluation of the leader's effectiveness. Higgins and Duxbury (1994) found that a supportive leadership style resulted in higher employee job satisfaction, higher organizational commitment, and higher positive expectations about the employees' futures with the company. Luthans (1986) reported that interactive leadership was significantly related to an effective managerial style. In an earlier study, of the relationships between managers and their secretaries, O'Leary and Ickovics (1987) reported that the secretaries who worked for women managers were more satisfied and saw their jobs as more worthwhile than those who worked for men. The researchers hypothesized that this was true because the women bosses expressed concern for their subordinates, treated them with consideration, and encouraged their best efforts. These are attributes commonly reported among interactive leaders. Yammarino and colleagues (1997) conclude "that female leaders form unique one-to-one interpersonal relationships with their male and female subordinates," and that these relationships are independent of one another and group membership (p. 217). The findings suggest that instead of the traditional top-down organizational chart, a graphic of the businesses of these female entrepreneurs would be in the image of a wheel, with the owner at the center, connected directly to each subordinate by a spoke, with the employees linked to one another along the rim.

According to Peters (1990), future leaders will focus on fostering relationships rather than winning at any cost and on the big picture and communicating this vision to employees. They will emphasize sharing rather than withholding information. Kanter (1989) says the "changemasters," those who will master accelerating change in the years to come, will do so with skills such as communicating a vision, working through teams, seeing the big picture, and building coalitions. If the above features describe the leadership style for the 21st century, many of the entrepreneurs in this study seem well positioned.

6

Networks as Vital Links

Entrepreneurial Networks

Entrepreneurs must filter and process a flood of information entering their domain each day. As the global market emerges and technology links businesses worldwide, this information flow increases dramatically, requiring proactive networks to delineate useful from superfluous data (Linn, 1990).

A number of entrepreneurship researchers have examined the positive impact of networks on business start-ups (Birley, 1985; Johannisson, 1986; Leonard-Barton, 1983; Rush, Graham, & Long, 1987). The exchange of information among entrepreneurs and networking activity is considered vital to managerial and entrepreneurial development; without such support systems, ventures are less likely to be successful or even created (Aldrich, Rosen, & Woodward, 1986; Cooper, 1985; Hansen & Wortman, 1989; Hisrich, 1990; Kotkin & Friedman, 1995; Ostgaard & Birley, 1994). Networking has become so important that some contend that the day of the solo entrepreneur may be coming to an end (Hansen & Allen, 1992).

If entrepreneurship begins with extensive connections to others, where and how do entrepreneurs begin to network? Sometimes they acquire networks through contacts in businesses owned by family members, close friends, peers, and former employers. Evidence suggests that men and women benefit similarly from these associations. Most often, however, people forge their

115

first business networks within the companies who employ them. As Harvey and Evans (1995, p. 331) point out, contacts are among the many organizational benefits for the aspiring entrepreneur, along with the identification of potential partners and joint venture possibilities and finding sources of investment. So important are these contacts that Mitton (1984) suggests that the key to successfully starting a business is simply one's movement from entrepreneurial "know-how" to entrepreneurial "know-who."

Networks may be structured or casual. Some research indicates that informal networks are more important than formal ones (Baucus & Human, 1994; Birley, 1985; Brass, 1985; Burt, 1992). Foss (1993) found that the most important kinds of support for starting one's own business were resources obtained through social networks (material support), emotional support for the idea of starting a business (affective support), and advice on finance, production, and other matters (information support). Johannisson (1986) and Baucus and Human (1994) suggest that those who previously have been employed have the advantage of in-place, well-established networks.

Women's Networks

Researchers have pointed out that women in organizations have often been excluded from the formal network structure and that this negatively affected their advancement within the corporate environment and participation on corporate boards (Bilimoria & Piderit, 1994; Haberfeld, 1992; Ohlott, Ruderman, & McCauley, 1994). Similarly, women are often excluded from informal networks and consequently lack access to real-time information via the grapevine (Handley, 1994). Even women who advanced to the top and denied playing politics on the way report that speaking against politically accepted norms often became a career turning point (Mainiero, 1994). Stewart and Gudykunst (1982, p. 586) even suggest that we need separate theories of career development for men and women. Consequently, the authors of this study accept a basic assumption that, for both men and women, status as a beginning entrepreneur may in part be defined by social forces broader than their business experience (Ibarra & Andrews, 1993, p. 279; Salancik & Pfeffer, 1978).

We begin with what we do not know. Researchers know little about the types of female entrepreneur networks, their patterns of interaction, or even how their networks are formed (Ibarra, 1993, 1995). In organizations, it appears that structural factors constrain women, causing the networks they create to differ from those of their white male counterparts (Ibarra, 1993,

p. 56). We have little information on how women entrepreneurs with previous corporate experience use their organizational education to form, transfer, or structure networks. An investigation into how women develop and
sustain networks clearly is at the heart of any study of female entrepreneurship. A key question is, "How did the successful female entrepreneurs who
moved from corporate environments do it?"

Four ideas proposed in Aldrich, Rosen, and Woodward (1987), Birley,
Cromie, and Myers (1991), and Aldrich and colleagues (1991) offer a starting
point: (a) the propensity to network (who connects with others in trade,
professional, and social organizations), (b) network activity (the number of
people with whom the owner/manager discusses business and the time spent
developing and maintaining contacts), (c) network density (the degree to
which the owner/manager reaches out beyond personal friends to discuss
business and the size of their personal networks), and (d) network intensity
(the number of years an owner has known members of the network, the
frequency of interactions, and the quantity of the resources exchanged). We
examine these ideas in the context of a concept proposed by Ostgaard and
Birley (1994, p. 282) that personal networks may be dominant in the formation and implementation of an entrepreneur's strategy. We employ a
fifth construct, that the content of network exchanges can be measured
(Boissevain, 1974, p. 33) to capture their quality and relationship to competitive strategy in marketing and product development. Our approach is
grounded in two assumptions that arise from prior research. The first is that
the development of contacts is important not only to founding a business but
also to firm development (Aldrich et al., 1987, p. 47). The second is that
growth appears to be significantly related to time spent developing contacts
within such strategic interest groups as customers, suppliers, and investors
(Ostgaard & Birley, 1996, p. 47).

Our study of network interactions is based on findings from questionnaire
responses and an ethnographic content analysis of focus interviews. We have
clustered our analysis of the individual and group responses into three broad
areas derived from findings in social network theory. The first area of
analysis focuses on network centrality (Brush, 1992; Ibarra & Andrews,
1993; Larson & Starr, 1993; Salancik & Pfeffer, 1978). In this area, we found
that our entrepreneurs focused on a value-added dimension of belonging to
a network. The dimensions included creating important contacts and finding
the opportunity for teamwork without financial strings. In addition, there was
a trend to associate with those who could enhance their business performance
at a personal or financial level. In the second grouping of items we examine

the references made to developing support systems as defined by Brown (1995) and Foss (1993): constructing sounding boards and idea exchange systems, joining active negotiating groups, and employing networks as sources of training, mechanisms to deal with dominant male environments, and means of access to other resources. The third area, the relationship of personal to strategic networks (Ostgaard & Birley, 1994), identified here as transitions, focused on items identified by the female business owners as important in their pre-entrepreneurial and entrepreneurial pre-adjustment, adjustment, and post-adjustment experiences.

Questionnaire Data and Focus Group Analysis

Questionnaire Responses

Statements from the entrepreneurs in this study offer compelling support for the centrality of personal networks. Of the 129 entrepreneurs who returned questionnaires, 64 (50%) rated establishing networks as their most important contribution to their own success. Another 43 entrepreneurs (33%) rated establishing networks second in importance. To these entrepreneurs, forming cooperative networks was an instrumental entrepreneurial activity: 50 (39%) rated formation of a cooperative network first and another 28 (22%) rated it second in importance. To place all this in perspective, 23 (18%) of the entrepreneurs valued having a cooperative network as an asset more important than making a profit, as an extension of their family role or being the major force in the initiation of their business ventures.

Thirty entrepreneurs (23%) rank ordered networking first as compared to all other skills they took from their incubator environments. Another 23 (18%) ranked it second. Forty-three entrepreneurs (33%) considered the networking in their previous work environment to be the most important influence on the formation of their businesses. Formation of such strategic alliances in prior organizational environments was considered extremely helpful by another 35 (27%) of the entrepreneurs.

In entrepreneurial networking, the opportunity to participate with other entrepreneurs in teams was rated as first in importance by 18 (14%) and second by 36 (28%) of the entrepreneurs. The importance of teamwork to our group of entrepreneurs is also indicated by the fact that 40 (31%) considered it one of the strongest influences in their decision to leave the

TABLE 6.1. Descriptive Statistics of Networking Clusters

Variable	Mean	Valid SD	Minimum	Maximum	N
Network centrality					
Coordinator of relationships	2.50	1.33	1	6	128
Cooperative relationships	2.42	1.53	1	6	128
Interrelated role	1.76	.99	1	6	128
Team building for expertise	2.95	1.32	1	6	128
Altruistic nature of networks	1.94	1.03	1	5	126
Supportive role of networks					
Emotional support	1.67	.93	1	5	129
Help in running business	3.27	1.62	1	6	128
Decision making	3.60	1.72	1	6	127
Financial support	3.88	1.76	1	6	127
Operational functions	3.34	1.57	1	6	128
Financial information	3.12	1.71	1	6	126
Financial sources	3.07	1.78	1	6	127
Transitional functions of networks					
Training aspect of incubator—net	3.42	1.68	1	6	118
Connections/networks—incubator	2.41	1.35	1	6	128
Isolation	2.84	1.47	1	6	128
Follow-up response on networks					
Forming strategic alliances	2.03	1.35	1	5	65

incubator organization and start a business of their own; 23 (18%) considered teamwork second in importance.

In the classification of networking as personal support and operational support for the business, the most important item from a 5-point scale was the value attributed to emotional support received from family, friends, and others. For most of the entrepreneurs, this support came from a spouse ($n = 68$, 53.5%) or significant other ($n = 26$, 20.5%). Support from "others," often people in business, ranked next ($n = 15$, 11.8%). One entrepreneur in this group explained:

> I'd like to say my husband provides the greatest support system, but I have to say it is the other women business owners I know. My husband doesn't understand. He has always worked for large companies and brings a different perspective. He is not entrepreneurial.

Of our respondents, 83% rated the emotional support they received as the most important item ($n = 73$, 57%) or the second most important item

($n = 34, 26\%$) in this category. The scaled items (help in running the business, contributing expertise in operational functions, assistance in making business decisions, and providing financial support) were rated substantially lower (Table 6.1).

Multivariate analysis of variance (MANOVA) tests for significant differences between intentional and corporate climbers in the three networking clusters are reported in Tables 6.2-6.4. Table 6.5 provides further information on networking. In the cluster Network Centrality, we found significant differences at the multivariate level (Hotelling's $F[5,113] = 1.96, p < .089$) outside our 95% confidence interval. At the univariate level, the Interrelated Role of Networking was significant at the .02 level. Here, our research questions focused on the coordinating and integrative role that networks serve. This included an analysis of the questions addressing the entrepreneurial role of coordinating relationship, the cooperative network of relationships, developing interrelated networks, participation with others in teams to build expertise, and the perception of measuring success by helping others.

Multivariate analysis of the supportive role of networks indicates no significant differences between intentional and corporate climbers, $F(7,117) = 3.70$. Two sets of questions were analyzed, regarding (a) supportive relationships and their role in the business and (b) two questions on access to financial information and getting to know potential sources of funding.

For transitional functions of networking, the multivariate analysis reveals significant differences at the .08 level, $F(3,112) = 2.31$ (see Table 6.4). Two standardized discriminant function coefficients explain most of this variance in the two groups: The attribution that forming networks inside the incubator organization was the greatest contribution they took away from the organization and the feeling of isolation once they left the incubator and became involved in their own business ventures. Another item, joining the incubator organization as part of an intensive self-training program, a stage of preparation for establishing a business—thus to be considered as part of a network process in itself—did not contribute to an explanation.

Content Analysis of Focus Group Data

Information was contributed by 102 of the entrepreneurs in the focus sessions on networking. As noted above from the multivariate analyses of the questionnaire data, significant differences do not occur between the intentional and corporate climbers at the 95% confidence interval ($p < .05$).

TABLE 6.2. Multivariate Analysis of Network Centrality

	Intentional Mean	Corporate Mean	Group Mean	Canonical r^a	Correlation With SD on Diagonal					Univariate F	Significance of F
					1	2	3	4	5		
1. Coordinator of relationships	2.59	2.42	2.48	-.20	1.34					.39	.53
2. Cooperative relationships	2.12	2.58	2.42	.48	.07	1.53				2.36	.13
3. Interrelated role	1.44	1.86	1.71	.75	.10	.21	.91			5.68	.02
4. Team building for expertise	3.00	2.92	2.95	-.09	.18	.06	.31	1.33		.09	.77
5. Altruistic nature of networking	2.00	1.91	1.94	-.14	.21	.12	.36	.16	1.06	.19	.66

Multivariate tests of significance (S = 1, M = 1 1/2, N = 55.5)

Pillais: .08, $F = 1.96$, 5/113 df, $p < .089$
Hotelling's: .09, $F = 1.96$, 5/113 df, $p < .089$
Wilks': .92, $F = 1.96$, 5/113 df, $p < .089$

Eigenvalue = .08 (100% variances), canonical correlation = .28.

Standardized discriminant function coefficients

1. Coordinator   -.17
2. Cooperative   .37
3. Interrelated role   .94
4. Team building   -.31
5. Altruistic   -.43

a. Correlations between dependent and canonical variables. Canonical Variable 1, Parameter 2 = -.31. N for intentional entrepreneurs = 41; N for corporate climbers = 78. Responses are scored on a 6-point scale where 1 = *most* to 6 = *least*.

121

TABLE 6.3. Analysis of Supportive Role of Networks

	Intentional Mean	Corporate Mean	Group Mean	Correlation With SD on Diagonal							Univariate Significance	
				1	2	3	4	5	6	7	F	of F
1. Emotional support	1.53	1.68	1.63	.92							.78	.38
2. Help in running business	3.50	3.11	3.24	.20	1.62						1.51	.22
3. Decision making	3.75	3.46	3.56	.12	.35	1.70					.79	.38
4. Financial support	4.08	3.70	3.82	-.00	.36	.18	1.76				1.23	.27
5. Operational functions	3.48	3.24	3.32	.16	.46	.52	.48	1.56			.60	.44
6. Financial information	3.23	3.10	3.14	-.02	.14	-.02	.18	.06	1.70		.14	.71
7. Financial sources	3.35	2.95	3.08	.02	.16	.04	.21	.07	.81	1.77	1.36	.25

NOTE: Multivariate tests and univariate tests do not support statistically significant differences in the two groups on this support dimension. Eigenvalue = .05 (100% of variances), canonical correlation = .21. N for intentional entrepreneurs = 40; N for corporate climbers = 79. No significant differences at [F(max) criterion = 3.70 with (7,117) df]. Responses are scored on 6-point scales where 1 = *most* to 6 = *least*.

TABLE 6.4. Multivariate Analysis of Transitional Functions of Networking

	Intentional Mean	Corporate Mean	Group Mean	Canonical r^a	Correlation With SD on Diagonal			Univariate F	Significance of F
					1	*2*	*3*		
1. Training aspect of incubator—A net	3.41	3.48	3.46	.08	1.68			.05	.83
2. Role of developing cooperative nets	2.23	2.48	2.40	.35	.02	1.36		.87	.35
3. Network to avoid isolation	2.36	3.09	2.85	.95	.13	.05	1.47	6.39	.01

Standardized discriminant function coefficients

Function number

Variable	1
1. Training	−.05167
2. External nets	.30210
3. Isolation	.94270

Multivariate tests of significance (S = 1, M = 1/2, N = 55)

Pillais: .06, F = 2.31, 3/112 df, p < .08
Hotelling's: .06, F = 2.31, 3/112 df, p < .08
Wilks': .94, F = 2.31, 3/112 df, p < .08

Eigenvalue = .06 (100% variances), canonical correlation = .24.

NOTE: a. Correlations between dependent and canonical variables. Canonical Variable 1, Parameter 2 = −.26. N for intentional entrepreneurs = 39; N for corporate climbers = 56. Responses are scored on a 6-point scale where 1 = *most* to 6 = *least*.

123

TABLE 6.5. Multivariate Analysis of Entrepreneurial Role of Networking

	Intentional Mean	Corporate Mean	Group Mean	Correlation With SD on Diagonal							Univariate F	Significance of F
				1	2	3	4	5	6	7		
1. External aspects of networks	2.15	2.57	2.42	1.54							1.90	.17
2. Internal networks (coordinator)	2.53	2.40	2.44	.07	1.34						.25	.62
3. Teamwork for expertise	3.00	2.93	2.96	.06	.19	1.35					.06	.80
4. Team building	2.85	2.88	2.87	.11	.30	.22	1.70				.01	.93
5. Power	2.23	2.05	2.11	.15	.29	-.00	.03	1.26			.49	.49
6. Developing interrelated nets	1.43	1.87	1.72	.22	.11	.31	.04	.36	.92		6.09	.02
7. Altruistic nature of business development—a network link	1.93	1.90	1.91	.12	.16	.16	.00	.20	.39	1.0	2.02	.88

Multivariate tests of significance ($S = 1$, $M = 2 \ 1/2$, $N = 53$)

Pillais: .10, $F = 1.74$, $7/108 \ df$, $p < .108$

Hotelling's: .11, $F = 1.74$, $7/108 \ df$, $p < .108$

Wilks':   .90, $F = 1.74$, $7/108 \ df$, $p < .108$

Eigenvalue $= .11$ (100% variances), canonical correlation $= .32$.

NOTE: N for intentional entrepreneurs $= 40$; N for corporate climbers $= 76$. Responses are scored on a 6-point scale where $1 = most$ to $6 = least$. Note that canonical correlations have not been included because there are no functions significant at level alpha ($< .10$); as a result, the canonical discriminant or correlation analysis was not reported here.

Our content analysis therefore examines the group of entrepreneurs as a whole. The three topics referenced most in the content analysis were the importance of networks for acquiring support ($n = 81, 63\%$), the value-added dimension of networks ($n = 74, 57\%$), and the survival skills the networks contributed ($n = 68, 53\%$). Other items that emerged as important to the entrepreneurs included networking associations related to venture performance ($n = 61, 47\%$), the development of networks that went beyond personal friends and family ($n = 58, 45\%$), and networks as a tool to acquire resources ($n = 56, 43\%$).

Network Centrality

Four data clusters from the content analysis specifically addressed network centrality. The first cluster consisted of references from 63 (49%) of our entrepreneurs to items that may be broadly classified as establishing contacts in their or other fields of business or in related areas. The grouping includes references to teams, teamwork, and establishing credibility. Within this dimension, establishing credibility as an entrepreneur was referenced by 34 (26%) of the entrepreneurs. Thirty-two entrepreneurs (25%) addressed teamwork in terms of how they linked their ventures with other entrepreneurs. The second centrality cluster focused on the attraction of membership in a network that leads to improved business conditions, more customers, and better performance in general. This was referenced by 61 (47%) of our entrepreneurs. The third cluster, value added, was referenced by 74 (57%) of our respondents, most frequently in terms of the value of information that was exchanged. The final cluster addressed the importance of developing ways to continue cooperative and integrative networking. Fifty entrepreneurs (39%) considered the cooperative and integrative aspects of belonging to a network the most important part of their entrepreneurial role. Another 28 entrepreneurs (22%) rated this second in importance. Direct references were made to this aspect of entrepreneurship by 50 respondents (39%) in the focus interviews. This effect of networking is also closely related to socialization, a concept that was addressed by 53 (41%) of our respondents.

Kilduff and Krackhardt (1994) suggest that an individual's reputation within an organization for performance depends on both the actual performance and one's association with prominent friends. The finding is supported by many of the entrepreneurs in this study who value their networks for just this reason.

Tjosvold and Weicker (1993) found that cooperative goals and interaction contribute substantially to successful networking. For entrepreneurs, the absence of formal linkages across organizations can make networking even more compelling. Among our 129 entrepreneurs, 78 (60%) viewed their work and life as a central point connected to an overlapping series of network relationships that included family, business, and society.

In a sample of mature firms, Brown and Butler (1995) found an important relationship of higher growth in sales to building stakeholder and competitor network activities that enabled one to gain strategic advantages over larger, more established competitors. Fifty-nine of the 77 entrepreneurs in our follow-up study (77%) valued the forming of these types of strategic alliances. Elizabeth Morris of Dallas offered a compelling illustration of how this had worked for her:

> Some of my clients went to the Northeast, some of them went to the Midwest, some of them went north, west, and south. So, we tracked them down. And all of a sudden, inside of a year's time, I had a national company. They had liked the quality of our work so they took us with them as preferred subcontractors to their new companies.

Contacts, Teams, Teamwork, and Credibility

Dynamic networks, whereby entrepreneurs position their firms for competitive advantage, are crucial to operating efficient and effective organizations (Miles & Snow, 1984). As a Chicago entrepreneur noted, "Without the personality, networking, connections and the ability to put the pieces all together, one can't do well." Said another entrepreneur, "The more people who know you directly, the more difference there is in the choice of your products." "Business is built on the basis of quality," said another. "It's not cold calls. It's the contacts and referrals."

Although they acquired them, some entrepreneurs did not consciously set out to establish their networks. Patricia Droppelman, president of Pediatric Nursing Care, Inc., in Cincinnati, initially had received little encouragement to start her firm. She networked outward by doing what to her seemed logical and familiar.

> You had to run a house, you had to pay the bills and you couldn't pay any more than you had in your pocket unless you wanted to go into debt. Unknowingly I had established a relationship with a banker and he knew

me when I needed money. My accountant really believed in my company. I didn't know these areas but I could count on them in the areas where I needed the advice. It always worked out in the way I wanted to do it. After a couple of years I found a law firm that believed in what I was doing.

Another entrepreneur found market support by networking. "When I started my business, it was some women executives and some real estate firms who made sure that some business was thrown my way."

Other entrepreneurs had constructed their networks deliberately. A Louisiana entrepreneur used her high-level access to acquire business contacts:

At one time I sat on seven boards. At my first board meeting, my husband said, "They will make you secretary because of being a woman." Well, I am a secretary. And I am going to be president of the board in 3 years. I showed my capability this way. Involvement is important and the networking is important.

Entrepreneurs crafted networks to suit themselves. One designs her networks to support other women. When she started her business, she sought out a female attorney, a female CPA, and a female travel agent to try to use her dollars to support women. She continues this policy to this day. Patty M. Breeze, another entrepreneur from Kentucky, took a different approach.

I took the advice from one of the people in the business to stay away from family and personal friends but instead go to outer circles—to use acquaintances. As I have progressed in my career, I have become very aware of networking with other professional women, women who own their own businesses, who are employees, who are attorneys, CPAs, executive directors, bankers. I always try to pass business on to clients of mine.

Clearly, there are no hard-and-fast rules. Network contact possibilities are nearly endless, with ties ranging from memberships on corporate boards, bank boards, and hospital boards to trustee memberships and a host of social interactions and contacts. Being where the action occurs is extremely important.

Networks are groups of people with some common links. An entrepreneurial team of two or more owners with equity interest in a firm is in effect a network for business strategy (Kamm, Shuman, Seeger, & Nurick,

1990). Beyond one's own business, networks tend to be larger and have more variety. Olson (1994) has found that the most frequently referenced and perhaps ideal number of people in a network (the network density) is six to eight. Ostgaard and Birley (1996, p. 48) find that successful entrepreneurs have denser networks in terms of a "percentage of strangers," that is, people whose presence strongly relates in some way to performance measures. The real secret may be in how many distinct and unique networks each member maintains. As noted by Harding (1996), "A network with two people has but one possible match, one with four people has six, and one with six people has 15. A network base of 50 has potential matches of 1,225 people" (p. 82). The mathematics apply in real life. A common theme regarding networks is expressed by an Atlanta entrepreneur: "The best thing I have done in years was to join the women's network. The opportunity for interaction with so many really terrific women was great. The contacts I have made and the opportunity to peddle my products have really astounded me."

Networks have led women entrepreneurs in many directions. By contracting out segments of work, it has been possible for entrepreneurs to operate with reduced staffs, to gain the expertise from others, and to move into new areas. Reports Pam Pizel, founder of Pizel & Associates Commercial Real Estate in Dallas:

> I think there's a real opportunity for women, if we're smart, to build alliances and networks and build off of each other. For example, I contract independently for some of my work. We all get together once a month with "What are you doing? How are you doing? What are the issues?" And we go from there. You don't have a lot of start-up cost to make that happen.

Networks were essential to establishing their credibility, said our women business owners. Sherie Conrad, a Louisiana entrepreneur who has coined the term *Megalowomanitis,* opened her business when there were no women's networks groups. She immediately set about creating them. She started with a round table, each month inviting 12 women to talk about ideas. She set up her board of directors by choosing 12 people from corporations she respected. When problems such as growing to the next business stage arose,

> I could go to them and say this is where I am now, and in your company when something happened like this what would you advise? What do you think we should do? Where should we go? If I have a problem

chances are I am going to solve it and learn more from calling five other women who have businesses bigger in size and who have reached that point than by calling in a consultant who is going to sit down and study my business and forget what the problem is all about.

Key to networking strategy, say the entrepreneurs, is to keep focused and constantly update the network. "I don't go to networks to talk the woman across the table into hiring people from my company," says Sherie Conrad, "that's my salesman's job. My job is to identify that person, to understand about their business and their perspective, so that I can promote that woman-owned business as I go through and meet other people. And to create another person in my network for information." Another entrepreneur provides still a different approach.

There is a communications guy in my company who can keep his eyes open for me. There is a young woman who knows the business and personnel and she and I have things in common. There is a marketing woman and a graphics artist and printer and those people all have things in common plus they can work with each other. This gives me the opportunity to get out and meet some other people and it works. You get to know these people on a personal basis. You can pick up information from the large group; the small group gives you the opportunity to sit down and talk, one on one.

Not all the entrepreneurs came into networking through the same door, and not all turned to other women when constructing networks. Nancy Smerz, president of Air Comfort Corporation in Broadview, Illinois, took over a family business and totally revitalized and revamped it after her husband's tragic death. She found herself in a male-dominated business environment. She made it clear that, to her, only one thing was important—workmanship. She finessed the gender problems, operating under the theory that, while it didn't matter whether her firm's CEO was male or female; if the workmanship was shoddy her firm was not going to be invited back, and if the workmanship was good she had an account for life. "I don't want to play golf on Saturday morning anyway," she says. "There are ways around these things. You aren't necessarily frozen out because you have these disadvantages. You adjust." Darlene Drake, president of Fitness Pro Health & Exercise Equipment in Lexington, Kentucky, deals with fitness equipment in markets that are predominantly male and where networking is the cornerstone of business. She similarly adapted. Her problem was to convince large organizations to install a fitness center. Because most of her corporate contacts were men, she developed a predominantly male sales staff and trained them carefully to deal with potential clients. She stated, "When you are talking about weight lifting equipment and things like that, customers are just more comfortable. They think men know more about these things. So I send them out to the field."

Network Association and Perceptions of Performance

Kilduff and Krackhardt (1994) suggest that an individual's performance reputation in an organization is the dual function of that person's performance and association with prominent friends. That something similar happens to owners of small businesses is supported by many of the entrepreneurs in this study. An entrepreneur's reputation for performance is vital, says a Dallas entrepreneur: "I knew that to gain the recognition I needed in my field it was more of a matter of who you know than what you know—it opens doors. I just know a lot of people and I am at every luncheon, every women's organization, every club. The more involvement, the more business." A North Carolina entrepreneur similarly described how performance-based networking benefited her:

> I set up my business to approach the big businesses. Of course the networks were already there. I had been working with those people before. One of the biggest things I gained from that job was personal credibility. I can go into a big company and say, I've done this. And then they listen.

For those without networks in place, networking can be a learned skill that, interestingly, may require a network to teach it. Remembers another North Carolina entrepreneur:

> I didn't have a clue when I came out of there how I was going to reach these people in their businesses. While I knew I could get in the front door of the insurance companies that I knew, whether I could sell them on me or not and what I could do was a different thing. It took a network to help me develop that kind of skill.

Value Added

Researchers commonly agree that networks are most vital when people value them without expecting benefits (Sonnenberg, 1990, p. 61). Any apparent contradiction disappears with the explanation by Suzan Kotler, a Cincinnati entrepreneur, that "you have to put out more than what you expect to get back and it will usually come back to you more than one hundred fold. If you don't do it that way you usually end up with zip." As Patricia Droppelman adds, "success" consists of "blending the needs of all those you service, hitting the network of people because you have something to offer them."

The entrepreneurs learned the values of networking in different ways. Ruth Ann Menutis, who served as president of the French Market Corporation for 8 years and is the recipient of the Chamber of Commerce Person of the Year award in New Orleans, was introduced to networking's value-added dimension by being excluded

> while working for my godfather who owned a radio and television station. He was a real slave driver. The women in the business did all the work and the men did all the networking. I learned early that networking was important. When all the guys would leave, all the women in the office did all their work. They just piled it on our desks and went out to lunch. When they came back we'd always hear their conversation, "Hey, you know Joe had a great idea, maybe we ought to get into this or get into that." And I remember thinking, I'd like to be on the other side of the table discussing what I could get into.

For several entrepreneurs, the value-added dimension of networking extends beyond their businesses into a changing society. Says Karen Kline:

> I think the biggest damage that was done to women of our generation and previous generations was giving us the idea that we would be taken care of by fathers and husbands. It didn't work out that way for lots of people. I think the voice that I hear—I hear myself saying it in lots of ways to my daughter and her friends and my son's friends—is that being an adult, whether man or woman, means that you can take care of yourself and other people. To expect someone else to take care of you polarizes your position. You are attaching yourself to someone who decides to take care of you. If you can take care of yourself, then you

can find someone else or another group of people who can join forces so that you can work together. That is the ideal situation. This whole idea of young women being cowed and brought up to be presented to somebody who is going to take care of them, that's the poison . . . that's the poison . . .

Networking as a Cooperative-Integrative Strategy

Tjosvold and Weicker (1993) have said that cooperative goals and inter-action contribute substantially to successful networking. Among our 129 entrepreneurs, 78 (60%) saw their role as an entrepreneur as a major part of a cooperative network of relationships that included family, society, personal, and business relationships. This attribute was highly valued. Lorena Blonsky described how this works.

I have two associates and we each have our own businesses but we share the same clients and candidates. I don't manage them and they don't manage me. We have a working relationship, no formal agreement, no partnership but it gives us more exposure to more people. In that sense, getting that contact initially and setting up that loose affiliation was key for me. I was still breast-feeding when I started and I didn't know how I was going to go out and get clients. But I had an immediate way to start a business on my own by having these other two individuals help me. Now we have our own candidates and clients. Whoever makes the match gets the fee, the transaction. The networks are absolutely essential.

Fifty-nine of the 77 entrepreneurs (77% in our follow-up study) and 46% of all the respondents valued the forming of strategic alliances as an important experience in managing a business. As illustrated by a Boston entrepreneur, the strategy works especially well when the competitor is much larger and disinterested in developing smaller clients, which then can be turned over to a smaller firm.

We only have one direct competitor in our area. And they're friendly. They actually refer money management clients to us that are too small for them by saying "They do a good job." The business is employee owned and founded by a woman.

Network associations are not all beneficial or even benign. A number of entrepreneurs referred to the in-house development of future competitors. "The competitor to fear," says one entrepreneur, "is not the one who opens up a business next to yours that you don't know, but the [future] competitor who is now in your business who will take your network." Adds a California entrepreneur, "The dangers can creep up on you while you are so deeply immersed in your business. The last person who left me sold my list of clients and is now a major competitor in my business." Sherie Conrad, a New Orleans entrepreneur, describes how she learned this lesson the hard way after opening her first business in 1974 and within a few years becoming very successful. Crediting her seven-member staff, she picked up the tab for an elaborate New Orleans dinner to reward them for handling things during an absence and also to show they had her full confidence. "I had no idea that while I sat there, treating my employees to this dinner, that five of them had plotted to quit immediately after my wedding and their intention was to band together to open a business (which soon failed) to compete with mine." Sherie shared this story to alert women who have the same kind of ethical background that she was brought up with:

> I was raised in a relatively large family with a strong work ethic and moral foundation. The foundation I received in my home life was the basis I used in the business to create the "team" or "business family." But the foundation I received did not prepare me well to deal with the situations I would face in the business world. The integrity that was bred into me did not allow for me to understand or even at times be able to comprehend the ability others had to defraud me and deceive me in business dealings. I believe that women operate and manage on a different level with psychodynamics that are relative to a natural instinct we have to "take care of" employees, and so a family-oriented atmosphere fosters itself early in the employment relationship.

The evidence, amply documented in empirical studies, makes clear that society's institutions tend to shape men's and women's expectations differently. In the business arena, although the playing field may not be even, the expectations for successful operation require a competitive strategy and a professional orientation that allows personal relationships to not cloud business judgments and a certain awareness of the vulnerability of business ownership.

Networks as Inclusion

In describing an entrepreneur as "a whole person, a socioeconomic actor with a personal history and private concerns as well as economic interests," Larson and Starr (1993, p. 11) view networks collectively. The networks described by many of the entrepreneurs in this study fit this definition. As Marie Clesi, owner of a State Farm Insurance Agency in Kenner, Louisiana, says, "I have learned to join women's associations, not just women in my field but women in many other fields. I have two women bankers I feel comfortable talking to. I go to a woman gynecologist. I am using the associations to help me." The network descriptions also resemble the spider-like construction defined by Helgesen (1990) as a web of inclusion, as well as ideas proposed by Brush (1992), who said that women see their businesses as cooperative networks of integrated relationships rather than as separate economic units.

One can think of the overlapping, inclusive networks in the image of a wheel, with the entrepreneur at the hub and others in the network at the ends of the spokes, connected along the rim. The image clearly conveys that a centrally located actor will have greater control over relevant resources and enjoy benefits and opportunities not always available to those on the periphery of the network (Brass, 1992; Burt, 1982; Ibarra, 1993). Terri Parker-Halpin, cofounder of the Cincinnati chapter of the National ISO 9000 User Support Group, found her business niche in this fashion.

> I was in an employment referral for a technical communicators organization and had been a past president. It was my best networking effort ever. I saw that a firm was looking for someone to document an entire computerized transportation management system. I looked at that opportunity and thought, "Why not me?"

Ostgaard and Birley (1994) note that the formulation and implementation of the firm's strategy depend heavily on the personal network of the owner-manager. The personal networks also are an important and cost-effective marketing tool, and they offer access to resources critical to the firm's survival and growth (Brown, 1995). From the hub of one of her networks, Hattie Hill, CEO of Hattie Hill Enterprises, a Dallas-based company, found business opportunities that thrust her into some 70 different countries.

I've been doing international work for about 7 years. I'm being thrust into the international market through the corporations I work with. That's where the business is going. And you go where the business is going.

An Atlanta entrepreneur developed a unique approach to building her network by offering training programs to firms that eventually formed a customer base. "I normally train about 20 people," she says, "and whatever they're doing out there, they're always going to be your customer, because none of them do what we do." As observed by this Boston entrepreneur, the networks one enters may be many, wide, and varied. "A network of business- and arts-affiliated women owners provided a nice support group and client base. Other networks of great value were the professional associations. I think the women's groups were particularly helpful. Then there are my alumni friends. I join—I'm a groupie."

Networks as Extension

A number of the female entrepreneurs in this study tended to look at their businesses as interrelated parts of themselves. Says one, "Networking is an absolute must for all people, and I think women do it much better than men. We wear our hearts on our sleeves and I think that is to our benefit." Adds a New York entrepreneur, "I go out and network all the time and I sell myself. I think I am my business." "My husband gets upset when he finds me at a cocktail party handing out my business card," says a Cincinnati entrepreneur. "You know, you can't miss opportunities, and as long as you are not interfering with what is going on you have to advance your business all the time." The lines between personal life and business get blurred. "Even when I am in church," notes Fran (Raglin) Johnson, "I have had people tap me on the shoulder and ask me to arrange flights for them to Las Vegas or elsewhere."

Networks as Support Mechanisms

Questionnaire Data

This part of the analysis draws from two data sets, the personal network system and resource availability.

Having a personal network support system composed of spouses, significant others, family members, and acquaintances is very important to the female entrepreneurs. The broader the range of network relationships, the greater the access to support systems. Sixty-eight (53%) of the entrepreneurs consider their spouse the primary source of support, 26 (20%) put a significant other in this role, and 15 (12%) turn to others. Item ratings (see mean analysis in Table 6.1) from most important to least important are emotional support, considered most important by 73 of the entrepreneurs (57%) and second most important by another 34 (26%). Types of operational support, although valued, rated lower. Support in making business decisions was considered either first or second in importance by 30% of the entrepreneurs ($n = 39$), but 20% (25 entrepreneurs) said the item did not apply to them. Two items, support in running the business and contributions such as financial, marketing, and/or human resource expertise ranked third. Least sought as a personal network resource was financial support.

The availability of business resources made up the second component of the major support system. Here we found three items directly relevant to networking strategies (see data and analysis methodology in Appendix 1): (a) developing an effective selling package to generate business funds, (b) learning about and making contact with potential sources of funding, and (c) access to information on the availability of financing.

Using resources is as important as learning about them. A Dallas entrepreneur in business for 14 years noted that the paperwork was so formidable that only in the last year had she registered as a woman-owned business.

For 13 years we have gone cold up against the market. Part of it was because we didn't have time to pull all these documents together. It is ridiculous. It took us almost a year and a half to get everything together that we needed to file. It took the local agency almost 18 months to process our forms. But in this year it's doubled my business. For the most part, it hasn't been the "women-owned business" credentials, but the help of women clients that has been the most important help to me as an entrepreneur.

An Orlando entrepreneur had faced similar problems with the formidable paperwork.

The entrepreneurs were not in agreement about mixing the two support systems. Some perceived a high value in integrating their personal and business lives. Others saw a definite distinction between the two. Many felt that becoming actively involved in business networks would be possible only at the expense of their personal life. "I don't really network in my business— it would be great to go out to dinner with this one or that one but I don't because I like having my own life," says a New York entrepreneur, who is also sure that her business would be even better if she did more business networking. Another New York entrepreneur identified a different conflict. "If I schmoozed more and went to a lot more parties—all that kind of stuff, I might be a lot more successful, but that would be selling myself and I want to sell my product, my service, and remain ethical about it." A number of the entrepreneurs recognized that receiving value from networking required a willingness to invest time and energy, personal properties that were limited. "Any place that I have the opportunity to spend my time and money must have some payback to my business or my professionalism," says a Winston-Salem entrepreneur,

> otherwise I am just throwing the time and money in the wind. Belonging to everything doesn't necessarily mean that it'll make your business grow. If you're not in my industry, I support you morally and perspectively, but the name of the game is business—I'm here to make money.

Content Analysis

We found more descriptive data in the content analysis. Eighty-one (79%) of our 102 respondents (those who specifically addressed network issues in the focus session) and 63% of our respondents overall referred to the importance of networks as a key support system in their business operations. Fifty-eight (45%) referred to personal networks beyond their family and close friends. Components that made up the support cluster include building relationships to access information ($n = 43$, 33%), finding needed resources ($n = 56$, 43%), establishing joint relationships with partners or other businesses or associations ($n = 32$, 25%), teamwork with cooperative and competitive entrepreneurs for larger market shares ($n = 32$, 25%), developing sounding boards ($n = 30$, 23%), sanity checks ($n = 30$, 23%), forming strong negotiation groups to influence legislation and for venture growth ($n = 29$, 22%), and ways of providing or accessing various organizational training programs ($n = 13$, 10%).

Sounding Boards

Networks composed of trusted advisers serve women entrepreneurs as confidential sounding boards for voicing concerns and sharing solutions. Boards made up of other women who own businesses appear especially valuable. Says a Southern entrepreneur:

I have some girlfriends who own companies and I draw a lot of strength from them. We go to lunch. It is a sounding board, it's a release, it has been a network for me. There are so few women entrepreneurs out there that you can go to lunch with and talk about problems, or just talk. You could talk about adding new phone lines, health benefits, and other issues. You need that whether you have 5 or 65 employees. You can't talk with your average next door neighbor about these issues.

The absence of a sounding board can be keenly felt. "I don't have a group of people with whom I have a lot in common to talk with about dreams, ambitions, and implementation strategies," says a Northern entrepreneur. "You know, getting support if something doesn't work out, and encouragement to try something new." As evidenced by the comments of Andrea Coates, a Massachusetts business owner, sounding boards combine information, a sanity check, and release:

A lot of times we talk about how we're doing with our energy, how we're able to balance the diverse demands and the rest of our life and how we're managing the customer relations and the paperwork. And it's more about—I think, more about time management, new techniques, and new research and how we are surviving as people in our businesses.

Smart (1991) states that because effective networks evolve over time, the soundest advice is to build a network and have it well in place before you need to use it for assistance. In like fashion, the entrepreneurs in the focus group interviews warn that it is important not to make the error of developing superficial networks with targeted benefits in mind. An Atlanta entrepreneur likened her network creation to a personal training program that offered the opportunity to create mutual loyalties: "The positiveness and the creative force is going to come back," she says. "When I talk like that, most people don't understand. But the network really gives broad-based support." The networks serve an important function because these female entrepreneurs are comfortable talking to other women. "I don't know why, but women talk differently about the issues," says Susan Weiner of West Newton, Massachusetts, editor of the leading weekly trade publication on the mutual fund business. "Each of us has the opportunity to take turns sharing an issue about our own businesses." Ethel Cook, also a New England entrepreneur, defines one of her networks as a strong support system. "We meet on the phone once a month for an hour with a definite agenda and we Rah! Rah! each other for the successes. It provides a fresh viewpoint." As another notes, "It provides the opportunity to have someone be a 'witness to your triumphs.' " "It is like having a staff meeting," says still another.

Sanity Check

"I need a strong support group," says a Dallas entrepreneur, to help "when you feel that there's nothing there, to get you built back up so you can go back out and face everything." At moments like these, the focus group entrepreneurs say, it is important to have a network of other business owners with whom you can talk freely about the ups and downs of running a business. "We have just this kind of inside network," says a Chicago entrepreneur, "the Women's Information Support Group, consisting of women who have been in business for at least 7 years and are affiliated with the National Association of Women Business Owners. We have the opportunity to throw our problems on the table—expansion, bankruptcy, confidential stuff." In Cincinnati, the Women's Business Development Center provides a similar function. "You need a good support group," says one member. "Something bad happens and it bothers you. Until I came to the Center I had really no support group in a business sense. Just working alone and not having anyone to discuss these issues with is the hardest part about starting a business."

Resource Access

Informal network contacts form the basis for access to formal sources of capital (Olm, Carsrud, & Alvey, 1988). The scope of resources available through networks may vary depending on a number of factors. This can be especially true for young firms attempting to acquire resources (Zhao & Aram, 1995). As one entrepreneur indicates, networks provided an important source of acquiring credit: "You have to know people to get credit and I have some companies who give me unsecured credit. If I had not known these people in the beginning, I couldn't have gotten started."

Transition Strategies

The third cluster of our analysis focused on the networking and transition strategies businesswomen used as they prepared and then moved from corporate environments into entrepreneurship. In this section, we examine networking in two contexts: first, in the context of establishing the business, and second, in the context of dealing with the isolation inherent in being the boss.

Twenty-three (23%) of our entrepreneurs who returned the follow-up questionnaire had hit the ground running because they had contacts and a well-established network already in place when they opened their businesses. Across all respondents, this group represented 18% of the entrepreneurs. Thirty-two (25%) of our respondents said that while working in the incubator organization they had moonlighted in the same business that they later started. Another 25 (19%) said that they had been moonlighting in other types of businesses. Some entrepreneurs moved business directly from their incubator environment to the firm they created. Sometimes this direct transfer took place with the full blessings of the parent organization, as in the case with Gale Wise, a clinical social worker with the Center for Change in New Orleans.

> I would say 90% of my clientele comes from the organization that I left, so the networking link is very important. . . . [C]ontracts and clientele received are because of the familiarity with our work, so it is very important. We have established many good contacts over the past years.

We next examined whether or not these businesswomen had networks in place when they opened their firms. Thirty-one entrepreneurs (30%) said that prior to leaving the incubator organization they had established either internal ($n = 11$, 11%) or external ($n = 21$, 20%) networks. Another 14 (14%) had not yet established their networks.

The third analysis area dealt with differences between corporate and entrepreneurial networks. Twenty (20%) of the entrepreneurs reported specific differences between the value of networks inside the incubator organization and those they established as entrepreneurs. Fourth, we examined the assessment of the effectiveness of using networks and the level of control in one's environment that can be gained through network access. Forty-three of our entrepreneurs (42%) referred to this dimension of networking in the focus interviews. Finally, we addressed networking in areas where 27 of our entrepreneurs (26%) perceived that gender had made a difference. These differences ranged across a wide spectrum, including lack of access to networks, denial of contracts because they were women, or other types of special treatment, while inside the organizational incubator, in transition, or once established in their own businesses. Regarding their old organizational ties, as entrepreneurs, the owners in this study were now either completely outside their former organizational networks or dealt with them in a changed relationship.

The Corporate/Entrepreneurial Difference

Prior to leaving their organizational incubators, entrepreneurs often prepare for the separation from the organizational support systems on which they had come to depend. On average, when starting a business, they have 4.9 network contacts inside the organization and 2.8 outside (Burke, Rothstein, & Bristor, 1995). No matter how many networks and where they are, the differences between the two environments are noticed immediately. For some, the drawback in the corporate environment had been the lack of tolerance for creativity and different operating styles. Now they were experiencing the drawbacks of going it alone. "I keep finding out how much I don't know about being an entrepreneur. So most of my education in that field has been stepping in holes and then climbing out of them. The financial part, the managing people, all those things, it has been a long learning curve," says a Dallas entrepreneur. Recalls a California entrepreneur, looking back on her corporate life:

I was fascinated with my colleagues. There was a creative side of exchange that I loved. The feedback was wonderful. Every once in a while I get a call and the company is asking me to come back. I was making six figures and I miss talking to all the smart people. You leave the structure that allows you to communicate with smart people. I miss the people who are interacting on a higher level. It was only that I am so excited about the business I have created that allows me not to notice the difference in my life.

Moving into a small business also changed status. "As an executive in a large company doing business," says a Chicago entrepreneur, you are able to present a glamorous and prestigious image. You have the name of the company on your card and everyone wants to talk to you. If it is your name on the card and no one knows who you are, then they don't care because they get 5 to 10 calls a day. You end up having 5 to 10 seconds. It isn't a matter of how smart you are, how much more professional, but can you get that strategic window.

I'm in the people business and I take people out to lunch almost every day. And if I don't do that I am in a lot of professional groups that fulfill the same needs whether they're professional organizations or political or social welfare kinds of things. I discovered early on that the affiliations had to be part of my professional life.

For some entrepreneurs, networking initially was not a solution to the problem of not being accepted because they faced the hurdle of being accepted into the network. In the words of a New York businesswoman:

Because you're not schmoozing, you're not networking. In my industry, if you are not multistate, you're a little guy. The national people say that since we can only help them in New York we can't really offer them anything in return. We go back and forth about this, but nobody wants to network with you. You start feeling like you're the littlest guy in the world.

Minuses, Limits, and Pluses

Women professionals left their prior organizations for different reasons and sought different things. Not surprisingly, their perceptions of women and women's networks vary. Much of this variance depends on the type of business they started. For some, like this Boston entrepreneur, it was important to stay in touch.

I really feel that being a part of women's groups and being involved in women's studies and research, and getting women to look at themselves and study themselves and take an interest in learning about themselves is important for self-esteem.

Others, particularly those who competed in fields that remain predominantly male, like this licensed professional engineer in five states who has owned and operated both a design firm and a construction services firm, viewed women's networks with a more skeptical eye:

> I think it is because women compete with one another for men. It's quite primitive. They look on anything worthwhile out there as something that we compete for. We don't have much regard for other women either because we don't think about them as strong. We think about them as vulnerable or beaten up. Every time we do that, they will not get the proper respect and we lose.

Many female business owners were positive that networking among women did not guarantee that women would see eye to eye. In the words of a New York entrepreneur (whose comments indicate sharp disagreement with theories that women automatically network better than men):

> I think there are invisible barriers that women put up between each other. We're just not as good at networking and I think part of it is that women want to go and have our other life, too. We want to strike that balance. But I think that there are a lot of women out there, you know, the receptionist and the secretary and in various clerical levels who don't understand what we're trying to do.

In addition to the possible absence of common ground among female entrepreneurs, perspectives differ because these women business owners found themselves cast in all sorts of different roles. Says one female business owner, "I think it's interesting that in this mostly male group I'm in, they do expect to pay for things." Several entrepreneurs with a similar experience referred to this as a "social reservation." Entrepreneurs recalled memberships in all-female groups where the members took "pro bono work" without as much as a thank-you note. The mentality of "This is a women's network, they're gonna take care of me" must be replaced, an Atlanta entrepreneur pointed out, with a more businesslike approach: "I am only willing to do so much. Yes, I will do X amount of pro bono work, but after that I expect you to pay." Said a Chicago entrepreneur speaking to the same issue:

> There comes a point in your life when you don't have a life with women and find you are more comfortable with men. I tend to observe women at a distance in organizations. I have observed that many want to destroy one another. It is very difficult to find someone to talk to. No one [in

women's organizations] even understands what I do. You identify with men. But could it be that you are more like men than women because of the kinds of things that you are doing? Because you share more in common with men because of the kind of work you are doing?

Several entrepreneurs found other types of women's networks less than supportive.

I don't get business from these women organizations. And the areas I really do need to get into I can't. Because I can't go to their country club. It is limited in membership. There are certain clubs that they belong to and I am not going to be accepted in those clubs. So, it's really rough. But I think there are plenty of women's organizations and we probably need fewer of them.

Such experiences—a number of entrepreneurs in the focus groups had them—lead to being more selective in deciding which networks to join. Says Linda Horn, a Cincinnati area entrepreneur:

I first refused to join women's organizations. I found women's organizations to be dreadful. I just would not go. They sat around deciding whether to do pink napkins versus yellow napkins, square card tables versus round tables and it made me totally crazy. And I left a wreck.

Later convinced by the president that WEI would be different, this entrepreneur gave it a try and found the network to be a tremendous resource, adding literally thousands of dollars to her volume. Her business is now ranked among the top 5% among her competitors nationwide.

Stories of struggles to find the right women's network were repeated in focus sessions around the country. When good networks were found, the benefits were clear.

I found that one of the best things I have done in the past 2 years is really getting involved in women's networking organizations, right now with the National Association of Women Business Owners (NAWBO) but prior to that the Women's Business Development Center. I was one of their first clients and they are marvelous. So it's finding that we can do for each other what the boys have done for years. Knowing that you do a good job and put out a good product and keep your word. And you build a good reputation. I've been allowed to do that without constraints.

A Midwestern entrepreneur suggested simply, "I think the biggest problem is that we have the wrong networks. We all network with women. It is really hard to get into the right network, which is the one with those who are making it in the field."

In networks, as elsewhere, leadership makes a difference. A number of the entrepreneurs confirmed the importance of not only participating in leadership roles in key networks but also of changing the focus of groups and the orientation of boards by placing entrepreneurs in charge instead of managers or executives. An Atlanta entrepreneur points out, "There is a difference in the leadership style of corporate types and entrepreneurs. It is our responsibility as entrepreneurs to be in charge of the groups that we participate in."

The Gender Difference?

Although a number of women indicated that they were kept out of opportunities because of the male dominance in the markets in which they operated, reaction varied among the business owners about the role they could play in changing the system for the better. Quite often, women remembered being blocked out of a number of civic organizations. This had been part of the history of the Dallas-Fort Worth area, but that situation is now being replaced by a perception of more openness. In the view of one Dallas entrepreneur: "I think the 'good ole boy' network has opened up a little bit more here and it's accepting finally, much more than when we started our businesses—they appear to be taking us much more seriously during the last 10 years." Despite perceptions that things had changed and there were now more opportunities for women, there was a feeling that somehow men could do a lot of things more easily and had the real advantages in networking. As an entrepreneur who came from Charleston says, tongue in cheek, "I really owe males a lot because of this enormous wall that I had to leap over. It freed me up from thinking only of the local market focus and gave me the entire country to focus on."

Black female entrepreneurs faced even more difficult barriers because many networks as well as sources of funding were closed to them. When Fran (Raglin) Johnson, a Cincinnati entrepreneur, started her business, she was told there was no history of a minority agency in the line of business she wanted to open, so she would have to prove herself before obtaining a

loan—Catch-22. Gail Withers, an entrepreneur in the Piedmont region of
North Carolina, gained a reputation for competence from contacts in her
previous environment and on the basis of the quality of her work once she
became an entrepreneur. Because of the nature of her work, however, most
of her clients did not know she was black. Although many were shocked
when they discovered that the company they did business with was owned
by a black woman, they remained clients.

Does gender make a difference? Is it a fact that, irrespective of how many
seals you crack, how many boards you sit on, there will always be valuable
information or resources to which females do not have access but males do?
A New York entrepreneur who is a member of a well-established group of
entrepreneurs contends, "There are many things women have never been
exposed to growing up and one of the main areas I see with most entrepreneurs is the financial. They seem to be afraid of anything to do with numbers.
I think that is a reflection of early schooling that says girls and math don't
go together." Others disagree. Access to knowledge is very important
whether it is in financial expertise, political access, or in acquiring needed
insider information. Fran (Raglin) Johnson believes that women need better
access to the same kinds of financial information that men readily have in
their associations on leading boards and through other forms of social
interactions not yet widely available to women:

> I would be willing to bet that those fellows on the board get together on
> some things that are not shared with the few women who serve on the
> same boards. Irrespective of how shrewd or clever the woman is, she
> will still not have access to the well-kept information that is saved for
> the good old boys. As women, we are just now learning how to get some
> of that information from them. But believe me, they network with one
> another, which women are doing, and they talk to the point that they
> say, "Go in and see my banker" and I'll call him for you. They call the
> banker and say "Help him out." When the person gets there, the banker
> says, "Well, I'll give you a 30-day loan and then you can turn it over
> and you can do this and that." That is information that women have not
> been privy to. But most of all, we have not been in those board rooms
> with men learning how to do things. It's something new for women of
> all colors.

Obviously, while this is not learned by sitting in a board room, the
access to the information is created by that membership. Where you

learn it is after you meet that person in the boardroom and you are standing and chatting and working the crowd.

The trick is to break into male-dominated networks when you have no ties other than through business associations because much of the information, while related to business, is considered personal. The key to the problem that women entrepreneurs confront may lie in something they are not discussing. It is deeply embedded in the relative absence of women on the boards of directors of Fortune 500 firms ("Spotlight on Women Directors," 1992) and reports of sex bias, even though "female directors were as qualified as, if not better qualified than, their male counterparts on most characteristics examined" (Bilimoria & Piderit, 1994, p. 1469). It is equally embedded in the culture. Around the country, women refer to increased access into a number of professional clubs and associations that previously were closed to them. At the same time, men are "preferred for membership in compensation, executive, and finance committees and women for membership in public affairs committees" (Bilimoria & Piderit, 1994, p. 1453).

Networks to Make a Difference

Questionnaire data reveal that a number of women entrepreneurs have a personal goal to help other women succeed in business. Among items in its group, this was rated most important by 55 entrepreneurs (43%) and second most important by 37 (29%). The two totals represent 72% of the ratings for the item group. Says one entrepreneur:

I want to be in a position to encourage other women who are coming out of engineering programs to hire them and give them similar opportunities. My goal is to get the good quality projects and then spend a lot of time networking with women who are considering careers that are nontraditional because there should be an opportunity for those careers.

Another entrepreneur adds, "I think it is up to all of us to be visible, to share our goals and to share our time to help people and give back to our business." Entrepreneurs also reach out to assist former female corporate executives, women who have been downsized, rightsized, or laid off. One Chicago entrepreneur's development of an Awareness and Matching Program came about 3 or 4 years ago when she learned about the need for niche networking in her age group for women who formerly were top executives.

Summary

This chapter has examined how former corporate women who have become entrepreneurs network for survival, to achieve goals, or to gain an edge. We looked at what entrepreneurs said about the connections that contributed to successful network use and strategies. Despite the lack of sufficient information to do a formal methodological study, we can nevertheless draw some conclusions from the comments of these entrepreneurs in the focus group interviews and the answers they gave on the follow-up questionnaires.

There is general agreement that all aspects of forming networks are important. Networking to form strategic alliances was considered more important than the formation of teams. The entrepreneurs consider personal and emotional support, which mostly comes from the spouse or significant others, far more important than financial, operational, or other types of assistance in running their businesses. We found compelling support for the importance of personal network strategies as an interrelated part of centrality, of support, and in organizational transitions. We also note from the conversations feelings of a lack of support for women within the previous corporate structures.

Our findings support the proposal of Stewart and Gudykunst (1982) that a separate theory of women's careers is needed. Nothing we uncovered contradicts the findings of Haberfeld (1992), Ohlott, Ruderman, and McCauley (1994), and Handley (1994) that women were excluded from many of the formal and informal networks, both in organizations and as entrepreneurs. Although researchers such as Ostgaard and Birley (1994) have said that entrepreneurs focus on the strategic dimensions of networking, we did not find that here. In large part, this may be due to the fact that the context of the networking we see here appears to differ for women, an idea that previously has been proposed by Ibarra (1993, 1995).

It appears from our data that one of the chief reasons that women became involved in networking was to overcome a number of organizational contextual factors they had witnessed, both inside organizations and later as business owners. This is suggested by the fact that most of our entrepreneurs went through similar, distinct phases in forming networks. First, there were limited transfers of networks from the prior corporate environment. Once in business, the businesswomen were reluctant to be involved in networking. Then, over time, convinced of the values of networking, they began to participate.

The data provide clear evidence that women understand the importance of assimilating a large amount of information in the "creation corridor," as referenced by Hansen and Allen (1992). Data also suggest that they understand the importance of the exchange of information at later stages in the development of their businesses, as proposed by Hansen and Wortman (1989), and that the marketplace exchange is a key driving force for membership in the networks (Kotkin & Friedman, 1995). Although many of the entrepreneurs took a proactive role in networks (Linn, 1990), this was not the adoptive mode for this group.

Rich illustrations support the findings of Aldrich (1989) about how women assimilate contacts and update them and reach out to weaker ties. These contacts represent a wide spectrum of associations with experts in an array of fields, as proposed by van de Ven, Hudson, and Schroeder (1984). Whereas 53 women in our respondent group considered network transfers one of the most important tools from the prior organization, only 14 said they had firmly established networks when they started their own businesses. This may represent a different pattern for women than the one identified by Cooper (1985), Ostgaard and Birley (1994), and Hisrich (1990), who found the forming of networks inside the previous organizational environment crucial to entrepreneurial development and success. Perhaps because the majority of our entrepreneurs formed networks after they became owners, they placed greater value on support issues.

Many of the women entrepreneurs here sought business partners, most often out of feelings of isolation and for sounding boards. A number of the women, but not the majority, had gone into joint ventures and were up to date on how to invest. In support of the findings of Harvey and Evans (1995), we found that a number of entrepreneurs had developed their own strategies to create support networks and to identify key people to serve on boards. Part of their ability to do this came from being good negotiators and networkers.

Our findings support the work of Birley (1985) regarding the value of informal networks compared to formal ones, and those of Ostgaard and Birley (1994, 1996), who found personal networks to be vital mechanisms for access to critical resources. We do not find the strategic references and the usage of networks for acquiring critical resources to be similar. In the content analysis of the focus sessions, we identified a cluster of relationships used in the Ostgaard and Birley (1994) model, but they were referenced in a very different way by our group of entrepreneurs. The component in their network model titled Content of Network Exchanges was used to tap the relationship to competitive strategy in marketing and product development. In the content of network exchanges, the comments of our entrepreneurs were more focused in the global terms of resource availability, sanity checks, sounding boards, and a value-added dimension. Instead of referring to product and service development, our entrepreneurs referred to the context of association and performance.

Although special strategic windows for resource acquisition are available to women, not until very recently have women had major support networks in which they felt comfortable. It is clear that the women in this group had not benefited from incentive plans or programs that could be considered special or conferring benefits that male colleagues might consider special. Instead, there was a spirit of "I am going to prove I can do this all alone." Further, unlike in the findings of Foss (1993), we did not find the acquisition of material resources through social networks to be perceived as the most important kind of support for starting one's own business. We did find emotional support for ideas in conducting business, once the venture had started, to be a major contribution. This was attributed to network affiliations and was deeply embedded in centrality and support issues. Again, our findings may differ because of the timing of network development of the women in our groups: In most cases, the social networks were not set up when the women started their businesses.

The socialization aspects of networks were extremely important to the female entrepreneurs. Their value appears to lie more in terms of sounding boards, rather than in resource gathering. Perhaps this is because many of the women's networks are at the initial stage of formation as compared to the more seasoned networks referenced for men. Whether the formation of the types of activities are unique to women and different from men is worth further testing. The rich scenarios in this chapter clearly indicate how very different the composition and characteristics of their relationships with network members appear to be.

Major underlying network themes emerge from our analysis of the questionnaire data and focus interviews. First, it is obvious that, when many of these women started their businesses, useful networks were not available. Strong supportive women's networks have just begun to emerge, with the National Association of Women Business Owners being a key player. Second, these women did not bring extensive networks with them from their prior corporate environment or elsewhere; many deliberately avoided doing business with friends just to test the waters, to see if they could cut it alone. Most entrepreneurs also felt that they did not fit into either the male networks or the traditionally female networks, which left them isolated at the top of their firms. Third, women are hungry for the rich experiences produced by the strong and supportive networks they have recently constructed. From the peer network interactions, they build survival skills and strategies for success, are able to find and act as mentors, and construct a foundation on which others can build.

7

Success:
Fulfilling the Dream

Fulfilling the Dream:
Definitions of Success

As reported in Chapter 2, the women entrepreneurs said they left their prior corporate positions because of disappointment about slow career advancement, experiences with hostile organizational cultures, and frustration that large companies measured success and distributed rewards in ways that were inconsistent with their values and aspirations. Now in business for themselves, how do these entrepreneurs measure success? Do the reasons they left their corporate positions influence the ways they define success in their own companies? As we have seen, in this study, most entrepreneurs indicated that having more flexibility to manage work and family was a relatively unimportant reason for beginning a business. Is it also a lesser concern when they report the ways they measure success? In a related vein, does the "ethic of care" (Gilligan, 1982), evident in the entrepreneurs' management of their employees and their networks, play a role in the women's definitions of success?

Understanding the answers to these questions is important for several reasons. Although business reporters and widely read magazines such as

Fortune, Forbes, and others measure and report success in terms of business size, as measured by sales and growth rates, these economic measures may not be consistent with the ways women entrepreneurs measure their success, as Larwood and Gattiker (1989) report.

The Women Entrepreneurs' Measures of Success

Survey and Focus Group Findings

On the survey instrument, we asked our respondents to indicate how they rated nine success measures on a scale from 1 (*most important*) to 6 (*least important*). The results show that the women entrepreneurs' most important measures of success are self-fulfillment and effectivness, followed by profits, goal achievement, and employee satisfaction. Helping others was rated sixth in importance and balancing family was rated seventh. Business growth and making a social contribution were rated eighth and ninth, as shown in Table 7.1. A factor analysis of the nine success measures employed to explore themes yielded three factors: Self-Actualization, composed of the items self-fulfillment and achievement of goals; Business Performance, consisting of profits and business growth; and a Web Effect that included employee satisfaction, helping others, balancing family and work, and social contributions. The research question of whether or not women entrepreneurs measure their business successes as self-fulfillment, along with business profits and growth, is supported.

Departure Factors and Success Measures

The most influential factors for leaving their prior organizations were related to the entrepreneurs' measures of success. The results are shown in Table 7.2. To remove the effect of demographic and business influences, the entrepreneur's age, marital status, number of children, education level, size of the firm (as measured by the previous year's sales), number of employees, and years in business were partialed out of the correlations. The first departure factor, Challenge, as reported in Chapter 2, was significantly and positively related to the entrepreneurs' highest ranked success measures, self-fulfillment, profits, and goal achievement. These entrepreneurs also rated as important in their departure decisions overcoming career barriers,

TABLE 7.1. Mean Ratings and Factor Scores of Women Entrepreneurs' Ratings of Success Criteria

Success Measure	Mean	SD	Factor 1	Factor 2	Factor 3
Self-fulfillment	1.31	.59	**.81**	−.22	.20
Effectiveness	1.48	.82	.15	−.61	.34
Profits	1.53	.80	.32	**.65**	.22
Goal achievement	1.71	.87	**.81**	.17	−.11
Employee satisfaction	1.80	1.13	−.12	−.21	**.63**
Help others	1.94	1.03	.21	.07	**.76**
Balance family and work	2.15	1.27	.03	.18	**.49**
Business growth	2.22	1.17	−.07	**.74**	.04
Social contribution	2.57	1.22	.02	−.09	**.72**
Eigenvalues			2.13	1.56	1.27
Percentage of variance explained			.23	.17	.14

SOURCE: Buttner, E. H. & Moore, D. P. (1996). How do they measure success? Former corporate women entrepreneurs' responses. In M. Schnake (Ed.), *Southern Management Association Proceedings, New Orleans* (pp. 318-322). University, MS: Mississippi State University.

getting better treatment, and achieving self-esteem. Collectively, the reasons suggest emphasis on the intangible personal development benefits of entrepreneurship including self-fulfillment. The reasons also are consistent with Noble's (1986) finding that women see their decision to start a business not as a career but as a life strategy.

Making Money

Entrepreneurs who rated profit as an important measure of success also rated several considerations important in their decision to leave their prior organizational positions. These included making more money, controlling their time, and achieving a better life. The other entrepreneurs also understood that a profitable operation was essential to long-term survival. As one recounted in a focus group interview:

Today I would have to judge my success on my profits. I didn't always. I thought other things were more important, but in the past 2 weeks I've had two clients, small ones, but they both went out of business. I look at them going under and I think, "That could happen to me," I would lose everything that I've invested and not get to fulfill my lifelong dream.

TABLE 7.2. Correlations of Entrepreneurs' Reasons for Leaving Prior Organization With Measures of Success, Partialing Out the Effects of Demographic Characteristics

Success Measure	Mean	Reasons for Leaving Prior Position					
		Organizational Dynamics	Blocks to Advancement	Challenge	Self-Determination	Family
Self-fulfillment	1.31	06	07	48***	04	18
Goal achievement	1.71	09	−14	21*	−04	−03
Profit	1.98	−13	08	31***	06	23**
Growth	2.43	14	01	−00	22*	−08
Balance family and work	2.53	−28***	−08	10	14	31***
Social contribution	2.72	02	20*	−03	−08	29***

SOURCE: Buttner, E. H. & Moore, D. P. (1997). Women's organizational exodus to entrepreneurship: Self-reported motivations and correlates with success. *Journal of Small Business Management, 35*(1), 34-46. Used with permission.
NOTE: The effects of the entrepreneur's age, marital status, number of children, level of education, size of the firm (as measured by sales in the year before the study), number of full-time employees, and years in business were partialed out. Decimal points are omitted from the correlations.
*$p < .10$; **$p < .05$; ***$p < .01$.

The focus group comments about profits also implicitly recognized the instrumental nature of money. Twenty percent of the entrepreneurs talked about money for the purposes of ensuring personal and family security, steady employment for employees, and contributing to society. While acknowledging the importance of profits, however, the entrepreneurs also pointed out how other concerns were critical. Said Rebecca Carney:

> I'm sole supporter of myself, have been all my life. I need a certain amount of money to be comfortable. So I think that's my primary criterion. Coupled with that is being able to feel fulfilled in what I do and in liking the fact that I am able to bring my own values to the environment. I feel a sense of accomplishment particularly from one of my employees who has just grown enormously. I know that's a reflection of my work with her as well as her own ability. Those things also make me feel successful.

Other departure influences that correlated with profit as a success measure were the desire for more respect and recognition, to be in charge, and to regain excitement about work. As Dallas entrepreneur Joanne Pratt explained, "I'm not particularly interested in the money per se. What really excites me is getting somebody to pay me to either get from here to there or solve problems. And I like to help people."

Stability Rather Than Growth

Research has indicated that many entrepreneurs, both male and female, place an emphasis on control of the business rather than its growth (Davidson, 1989; National Foundation for Women Business Owners [NFWBO], 1994). In the present sample of entrepreneurs, only 2% said they measured success in terms of business growth. Some clearly felt that growth could lead to challenges and unwanted difficulties. Said one, "All you do is exchange one kind of problems with another kind of problems. And just tack on a couple more zeros. Some of that never changes. You're just moving more money around." Other entrepreneurs saw a trade-off between sales volume and the quality of the product or service they deliver. A North Carolina respondent said:

> I have a strong need for my business to be a high-quality business. If that means I give up a little profit to have a better quality service business, then so be it. I don't believe, and I absolutely believe this to

my core, that success is measured in dollars earned or bottom line profits. It is in the satisfaction of that client relationship. Certainly we have to make a profit in order for us to have business. We have to have good business relationships in order for me to continue to employ these people that I do. That's very important for me that they have a sense of security and well-being in their job. So, all of it ties together.

An entrepreneur cognizant of the risks of overextending the business in an attempt to increase its size said, "You can grow your company way too quickly and find out that you can put yourself out of business and you are not doing anything wrong." Another woman business owner was concerned about replicating the environment she had left: "Once you have more than three pages in the policy manual you are a bureaucracy. The bigger we get the less personal the care becomes." Still another entrepreneur saw other outcomes:

What is important? Growing the business? I don't think so. If I can have a good job and create a good job for the people who work for me, a good work ethic, and a good lifestyle, that to me is success. Professional achievement, yes, but it is not three condos in Palm Beach. I don't measure success that way. Because there are too many people who have all of that who are not successful.

Self-Fulfillment

Hardesty and Jacobs (1986) stated that corporate women sought personal growth, development, and challenge, which they expected to fulfill through their work. Brenner and Tomkiewicz (1979) found that women preferred work that furthered their development of knowledge and skills, was intellectually stimulating, and provided congenial colleagues. In a study comparing entrepreneurs and managers of large companies, entrepreneurs gave greater weight to being capable and to feeling a sense of accomplishment about their work than did the managers (Fagenson, 1993). In another study of female entrepreneurs, the women indicated that they wanted to be doing something worthwhile from which they could derive fulfillment (NFWBO, 1994). Values related to measures of women's career success including intellectual stimulation, continued development of skills, and feelings of accomplishment were reported by Beutell and Brenner (1986) and Bigoness (1988). White et al. (1992) reported that women's measures of success include interesting jobs with variety and challenge. Astin (1984) considered the sense of accomplishment derived from the process of performing and successfully completing tasks to be an important motivator for women.

In the focus groups, the women entrepreneurs spoke of how these aspirations had not been fulfilled in their incubator environments. Twenty-nine percent talked about entrepreneurship in terms of their desire for self-fulfillment, personal and professional growth, recognition for their contributions at work, and the importance of their reputation. Marilyn Sifford, an entrepreneur who often worked with employees in larger corporations, said success was "actually having an impact on people's lives. A part of it that is important to me is continually growing. The kind of work I am doing now is very challenging. It is work that I know I can grow doing for quite some time."

Another dimension of personal growth includes the search for opportunities to stretch one's capabilities and talents. Hardesty and Jacobs (1986) wrote about the "Myth of the Unlimited Potential," the belief of women that the key to success lies within themselves and that through hard work they can accomplish anything. Two entrepreneurs talked about their desire to stretch themselves. Said one, "Success begins the minute that you decide to do something. You can look at yourself as successful just by stepping out of your comfort zone and feeling good about what you are doing. Stepping out and doing it is the measure of success." Sherie Conrad explained:

Success to me means competence perfectly fulfilled. What I do is something that involves my mind and all of the resources that I have. I enjoy every day intensely, competing with and outmaneuvering my competitors, and what I do is a battle of wits, and I have a fierce pride in matching my rivals and being the person to identify the needle in the haystack that nobody else can find.

Such comments are consistent with research by Burke, Belcourt, and Lee-Gosselin (1989), who found that being an entrepreneur had significantly changed the self-concept, self-esteem, and assessments of professional competence for their female participants.

Hardesty and Jacobs (1986) described women's expectations, based on their experiences in school and college where individual achievement is recognized and rewarded, that achievement will be recognized and rewarded at work. The belief fails to account for the political nature inherent in bureaucracies or for difficulties in identifying individual contributions among interdependent employees. Recognition of one's achievements is important, however, and many of the women entrepreneurs noted this, as demonstrated by the comprehensive statement of Evelyn Eskin.

> I certainly feel that success is one standard. That standard is, "Am I doing the best that I possibly can, given what I have to work with, given my own resources?" I also love being recognized as somebody who is an expert in the field. I like it when people come to ask me for advice about career changes, but it's only a derivative because I feel that I got there by doing the best job I could possibly do. And that's what was missing in the corporate environment. The notion that if you did the best job you could possibly do, somebody would notice and reward you— whether it was money or an office or a secretary or whatever. That notion was missing.

Recognition as an important indicator of success was discussed by 15% of the entrepreneurs, and 21% talked about having a good reputation and/or getting referrals. Bert Gose summed up her most important measure of success this way: "I think that what I enjoy is the reputation that I have and doing a job and knowing I've done it very well, and that people appreciate that and then refer me to other people."

The Internal Measure

Some entrepreneurs indicated that they were more focused on the process in their work and enjoying it than they were on the outcomes. Success for them appears to be an internal rather than an external standard or measure. In describing success for herself, Honi Stempler, an Atlanta company owner, said, "It is something inside of me as a woman. Success is a feeling in your heart. And it's about what you do every day, and whether you enjoy what you do. We could get into this power stuff but I have never been into power." Susan Brown, the owner of a strategic consulting company, reflected about success:

> I think of that as a very linear male thing. Right now for me, the thing that drives me is finding a way to be happy, whatever that means. And having a life that is congruent. I don't really know how to define that. In some ways I hope I don't define that because part of what has been wrong for me and part of what I really fed into in the corporate world was that it was always about getting there, wherever "there" was, and

not enjoying the journey. So right now I'm much more oriented toward learning to enjoy the journey. And I don't know how I'll define success. Although there is a lot of pride when I remember that my son, who is 8, was asked what I did, and he said, "Well, my mommy gives advice and helps people." I thought that was really great. If my children can understand what I do and they think that that's neat, that's a big thing for me now. That's a big part of what is my success. So, I am in a more altruistic, self-actualizing phase of my life right now and I like that. And I know it will change. I am not into lifetime commitments anymore in terms of being one thing.

Important to another entrepreneur was "having set goals and objectives and knowing that I have done what I could to realize them. Success is in the process as well as the outcome." Yet another woman business owner, Joan Holliday, described success as "Living out one's core values in the most authentic way possible, while making a contribution to the greater whole— receiving a sustained response for one's work."

Freedom and Autonomy

A less frequently mentioned theme in focus group interviews (6% of the comments) was gaining freedom and autonomy, not having to deal with annoying clients, and having control over the business and hence one's destiny. Anne Sadovsky, a Dallas entrepreneur and the author of *101 Thoughts to Make You Think* (1991) and *101 Thoughts for Becoming the Real You* (Sadovsky & Rice, 1991), which can be found in bookstores nationally, described success as:

Having what I want when I want it. Doing what I want when I want to while at the same time meeting all my responsibilities and obligations and growing to my full potential as a human being, as a businessperson, as a mother, a spouse, a friend, a daughter. And at the same time helping other people do the same.

The Ethic of Care

Research suggests that female ethical concerns revolve around issues of relationship and understanding and that relationships often take precedence over achievement (Chodorow, 1978; Grusec & Lytton, 1988; Kelly, 1991).

This applies as well in the workplace (McKeen & Burke, 1992). In the entrepreneurial context, female respondents in a study of values indicated they gave a greater weight to equality than did their male counterparts (Fagenson, 1993).

Entrepreneurs deal with multiple constituencies: employees, customers, family, and community. Brush (1992) and Thompson and Hood (1991) theorize that women entrepreneurs view these relationships as an interdependent web. As noted already, Gilligan (1982) describes this approach in terms of an "ethic of care" in which women are concerned with achieving a solution that best fits the needs of all individuals involved. The NFWBO and Dun & Bradstreet Information Services (1995) study of women entrepreneurs indicated that they were concerned about building relationships as a measure of their success.

Our study also investigated the overlapping relationships as women entrepreneurs defined success. Of the comments on measurements of success, 28% addressed the concerns of the entrepreneur's network or "web." One important group in the entrepreneur's web was the clients or customers served by her business. Client "satisfaction" for these entrepreneurs was broadly defined. Rather than seeing the work with clients and customers as a transactional relationship, the entrepreneurs saw it as a more transformational relationship, in which they invested and felt a sense of accomplishment when they had helped their client grow and develop. A Cincinnati entrepreneur explained her view:

> The success of your clients is your success. This is something that I identify with very heavily. Being a facilitator, being a catalyst, being a liaison, having clients who were pioneers with a two million dollar business and now they have a 14 million dollar business. I helped them grow. It's not just a measure of my business success but also a measure of the client's business success.

Being able to influence clients' lives by enhancing their appreciation for beauty was important to Pauline Yeats, a designer of "home couture" and interiors whose collection of furniture and fabrics is sold at the Pauline Yeats' Interior Design Shop in New York and through architects and designers nationwide and internationally. As she said, "I want to get my vision over to people. And offer a way for them to see their environment, their surroundings, and their life in terms of beauty, identity, and self-reflection. How that can impact their lives and make them better." Another way of enacting the transformational relationship was through empowering the client to do something new. Says Renee Peyton, an Atlanta entrepreneur, "I like being able to empower other people, and I do that with my clients, and I have had them tell me, 'Thank you for allowing me to do that.' Pure success to me is having that client keep coming back. As long as they're coming back, I know they're happy."

Entrepreneurs in the focus group interviews also spoke about empowering employees, another essential group in their "web." Carol Hecht, CLA, is president of BarriCorp, Inc., in Dallas. As she explained, "I like to stretch my employees to their limit—push them to use everything that they are so that they can feel that they have achieved something other than just doing the same mundane task-oriented things. That's a feeling of success; it's a feeling of growth." Nancy Smerz talked about the priority she placed on employee retention: "I feel tremendous success because I measure it by the people who stay there and who choose to do their work there. Nobody quit that I really wanted to keep. It is a source of tremendous success to me. It's a very friendly, very cordial, very caring kind of relationship. To me that is success. To me success is keeping good people there." Other entrepreneurs worked hard to create a positive working environment as a means of achieving success. One participant defined success as "Creating a company where people are encouraged to be creative and where people are listened to and are involved, where people work in responsible ways, and to create a financially healthy company. Here the people I work with grow professionally and personally."

Work and Family

The number of entrepreneurs who left their prior corporate positions in search of a better balance between work and family responsibilities was small, as noted in Chapter 2. The family concerns departure factor was significantly and positively related to balancing family and work, social contribution, and profit as measures of the entrepreneurs' success. Accordingly, those entrepreneurs who left in search of a better work and family balance measured success by how well they had achieved it. The results suggest that, in general, these women had learned to integrate family and work concerns, and the issue was not a major determinant in their current business. Although the percentage of women entrepreneurs in the study with children under 18 who ranked balancing work and family as important is higher than those without children (18% versus 10%) and the rankings are in the expected direction, chi-square analysis does not reveal a significant difference in the ranking (chi square = .83, $df = 1$, n.s.). Note, however, that the average age of the study participants was 43 years, so many had passed the primary childbearing years. The issue thus may not be as salient for these women as for those in their twenties or thirties. Powell and Mainiero (1992) propose that family and relationship concerns assume relatively greater importance when children are young, and work assumes greater importance when family responsibilities are decreasing or absent.

The correlation between the family concerns motivation factor and profits suggests that one way these women ensured the financial security of their families was to make the profitable operation of their businesses a priority. Although balancing family and work are important concerns for 3% of the women, this was not an overriding issue for most women in either their entrepreneurial motivation or their measures of success. Rather, the entrepreneurs seemed more concerned about achieving a sense of balance in their lives in general.

Multiple Definitions of Success

Although the survey results indicate their priorities, the entrepreneurs often explained in the interviews that success was defined in several ways and that they had to find a balance among those various criteria. One entrepreneur explained it this way:

> I think it's a twofold question. I think being successful in business is being successful on the bottom line. That allows you to survive and to keep going. I think doing certain projects and seeing them succeed is absolutely exciting. Or coming up with a new program or a new idea. It's very, very exciting. That feels good because you've made a decision and it works and it continues to make your business successful. When I hire somebody and they are the right fit for the job and I teach them the job and then they start doing it, I get very excited.

An entrepreneur concerned about both revenues and her ability to sleep at night said,

> I measure my success through my billings and through repeat customers and the fact that customers are so satisfied with what I'm doing that they would refer other organizations to me. The other thing that's very important to me is my peace of mind and my mental health. Because if

I don't have peace of mind then everything else goes out the window. So, it's important that I find a satisfaction in what I'm doing, and that I also feel fluid, that the work is fluid, that it's not confining for me.

Another entrepreneur explained the multiple dimensions of success as "Loving what I do, earning a good living at it, and feeling that I have wisely used my talents, treated others better than fairly, and that every day was well spent."

In open-ended responses on the survey, entrepreneurs wrote about their priorities in measuring success. Bert Gerla, a Cincinnati attorney-at-law, demonstrated the priorities of others as well as herself: "self-respect, improving the community, helping employees to grow, and financial rewards."

Fourteen entrepreneurs mentioned a concern for achieving balance in their lives as an important determinant of their success. Seeking harmony between the personal and professional aspects of her life, Marie Clesi said, "I set annual goals in terms of production and personal goals. I think it is important to set personal goals because, if not, they will be in conflict with the business goals and the two must be integrated." Another entrepreneur was clear about her priorities in her business and personal life: "I have a strong need for the business not to run me. For me to set some limits on that business's impact in my personal life, in my health, and every other way. I want to have a balance of time and lifestyle that allows me to have that fullness. I'm not willing to give that up for the sake of the almighty dollar." Continued the Philadelphia strategic consultant:

The word "success" for me conjures up a very linear scene about continuing to go up in a straight line. But I don't really think that life is about straight lines. What's important to me is the combination of things and how those things get balanced. I know that balance, that equation is going to change over time. The ability to change and the ability to recognize, that is part of how I would know that I was successful in my life. I am more concerned with being successful in my life, not just with work. I don't see them as two separate things anymore. That is a big change for me. It took me a long time to get that.

The Interplay of Size and Success Measures

Although there are a few companies that have grown quite large—Mary Kay Cosmetics and the Body Shop, for example—many women-owned

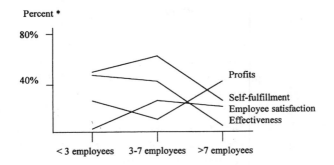

Figure 7.1. Women Entrepreneurs' Success Measures as a Function of Number of Employees

SOURCE: Buttner, E. H. & Moore, D. P. (1996). How do they measure success? Former corporate women entrepreneurs' responses. In M. Schnake (Ed.), *Southern Management Association Proceedings, New Orleans* (pp. 318- 322). University, MS: Mississippi State University.
*Percentage of entrepreneurs within each size category who ranked the success measure as important.

businesses remain relatively small in sales and number of employees. One possible explanation for the size difference may be women's differing success criteria. Some women may prefer to keep their businesses small because they value self-fulfillment, control over their lives, and employee satisfaction. Other women who grow their businesses may place a greater value on growth and profits. Although a number of explanations have been given for success in women-owned businesses (Aldrich, 1989; Cuba et al., 1983), this research has been based on measuring success in terms of traditional economic measures of size, such as the number of employees, and has ignored other measures of success such as self-fulfillment. Chi-square analysis of the ratings of the success measures by size of the business (as measured by number of employees) indicates significant relationships for three success measures: self-fulfillment (chi-square = 7.49, $df = 2$, $p < .02$), effectiveness (chi-square = 12.85, $df = 2$, $p < .002$), and employee satisfaction (chi-square = 8.13, $df = 2$, $p < .02$). Marginal significance was shown for the relationship with profits (chi-square = 5.56, $df = 2$, $p < .06$). The rating of each measure's importance as a function of business size is presented in Figure 7.1. The growth measure of success did not vary significantly as business size changed. Overall, the number of women who ranked growth as an important success measure was small (12%). The results suggest that the female entrepreneurs grow their businesses to varying degrees, depending on how they measure their success.

Conclusions

Those entrepreneurs who left for the highest rated "pull" reason, seeking challenge, measured success primarily in terms of self-fulfillment and secondarily in terms of profit and goal achievement. The results also suggest that although profits are important to these modern female entrepreneurs, self-fulfillment is the most important measure of success. This finding sheds additional insight into the concerns and aspirations of modern women entrepreneurs. Success seems to be measured internally in terms of personal growth, professional development, and improving one's skills, rather than measured externally in profits or business growth. Money, then, is a means and not an end.

Women business owners historically have been clustered in the retail and service segments of the U.S. economy. This sample was no different. These segments tend to be slower-growth, labor-intensive businesses. The findings here are that most of these female entrepreneurs measure their success in terms of self-fulfillment and achievement of their goals, followed by the traditional performance measures of profits and business growth. One explanation, which requires further research, might be that, as cited in the chapters above, growth opportunities in terms of available bank capital and venture financing historically have limited female entrepreneurs. The ways women lead their businesses to achieve the success they desire, then, may combine with the more limited growth opportunities they have experienced. As a result, use of traditional success measures including growth in sales or employees would present a one-sided view of female entrepreneurs' success. Other criteria, such as stability of employment, duration of the business, and the entrepreneurs' satisfaction with her work, also could be important success dimensions for women business owners.

8

Summary and Advice

Summary

This study has examined the role of previous incubator organizations on the career progression of successful female entrepreneurs. In the main, we find that many of the activities that these entrepreneurs consider important in terms of leadership, networking, and measures of success are not necessarily those defined in previous studies.

Corporate Exit

We find support for the relationship of incubator experience and entrepreneurship to be stronger for those who have always intended to start a business (see Shapero, 1982). We also find support for the work of Katz (1994) that entrepreneurial intentions need not be long range. In particular, the corporate climbers here exhibited shorter-range intentions to become entrepreneurs, possibly because they were in the position described by Greenberger and Sexton (1988) and Bird (1988) that a decision results from the interaction of potential and the situation. Study results here also support the use of entrepreneurial career anchors as proposed by Schein (1978, 1990). Two of Schein's eight distinct career anchor categories, general managerial competence and entrepreneurial creativity, appear to have special relevance:

(a) The person with the real entrepreneurial intention may serve in a number of roles, including managerial, until the creative opportunity emerges (Schein, 1990, p. 29) and (b), as in the case of the corporate climbers here, one's career anchors can change (see Schein, 1990, p. 34).

As predicted, both the intentional entrepreneurs and the corporate climbers valued in a similar way expertise in finance and networking activities acquired while working in incubator organizations. This bears out the research of Hansen and Wortman (1989), who stressed the importance of the exchange of information among entrepreneurs and of forming networks while inside the organization (Cooper, 1985; Hisrich, 1990; Ostgaard & Birley, 1994).

Primary differences between corporate climbers and intentional entrepreneurs appear to be centered in the self-determination of intentional entrepreneurs and their desire to start their own businesses. The items compare to the two career anchors previously identified by Schein (1990) as autonomy/independence and the creation of something new. Included are the motivations to overcome obstacles, run risks, and develop personal prominence in whatever is accomplished. The findings support the thesis of Katz and Gartner (1988) and Cromie and Hayes (1991) that, because intentional entrepreneurs have the goal of starting their own business and a higher propensity and drive to do so than corporate climbers, this is the most important reason why they leave corporate environments.

Fagenson (1993) stated that managers and entrepreneurs had very different characteristics, but we did not find this among the entrepreneurs in this study. At our point of analysis, however, both the intentional entrepreneurs and the corporate climbers had made the decision to operate a business. As postulated by Fagenson (1993), findings here suggest that once the female manager leaves the organization, she adopts entrepreneurial characteristics quickly and gives up any managerial characteristics that earlier differentiated the two groups.

We found that, irrespective of whether a woman was an intentional or a corporate climber, the areas of autonomy, freedom, and control were important dimensions of the reasons why she left her previous organization. Autonomy, operationalized here as the desire to make it on one's own, freedom, and self-esteem (Capowski, 1992; Cromie & Hayes, 1991; Scott, 1986; Shane et al., 1991) accounted for most of the variance. This finding supports the hypothesis of Schein (1990) that the important stable career anchor of autonomy/independence emerges from work experience. The entrepreneurs in this study associate organizational climate with both a desire to create an environment to fit their personal value system and their reaction to the bureaucratic environment. They associate control with time, the potential to regain excitement, and the desire to be in charge. The finding supports the concept of the stable anchor of entrepreneurial creativity, as proposed by Schein (1990) and Katz (1994). Research here also supports Brodsky (1993), who said that entrepreneurs seek to define their own work environments and parameters. There were no significant differences between these ratings for those who had always intended to be entrepreneurs and those who had more latent intentions of becoming an entrepreneur.

Survey and interview data both indicate that women's motivations to leave organizations are influenced by negative organizational factors and by personal aspirations. The reasons for leaving ranked as most important were to advance and to create a more value-consistent work environment. Data also show conflict between these women's entrepreneurial values of freedom, autonomy, and personal responsibility and the bureaucratic requirements for conformity. Women in this study were caught between the stereotypical expectations that they be compliant and nurturing and their job requirements to be assertive and decisive. Dependency occurs in large organizations because of the limited access to power and resources. This leads people to rely on organizational politics as a means to get things done. Such unwritten organizational rules clearly had frustrated many of these entrepreneurs. Entrepreneurs searched for authenticity, as shown in their conversations about an internal journey to rediscover aspects of themselves or to acknowledge and nurture personal dimensions not yet developed.

Discrimination and work/family balance issues emerged as important concerns for these women, but these did not exert nearly the influence on the women's departure decisions as the items self-determination and organizational blocks to advancement. The stereotypical perception that women leave large organizations to address family needs did not apply to this group of expatriates.

Transition

The issues women found in making the transition from a large organization to entrepreneurship appear to have changed little in the past 10 years. Finding competent employees who will take the initiative and make a valuable contribution to the business continues to be a challenge. The entrepreneurs walk a tightrope between giving up control to allow subordinates enough autonomy to exercise initiative and trusting that employees will follow through. One of the major reasons that the women started their own businesses, to have greater control, may also inhibit the growth and development of both subordinates and the businesses. Some of the entrepreneurs have learned how to empower employees effectively; others are still struggling in the journey.

Financing the business through external sources, especially banks, continues to be a challenge for women entrepreneurs, including this study's participants. The increasingly competitive financial marketplace, with institutions of other types beginning to offer services to small business, may open alternative sources of financing. Some women may still be somewhat uninformed about the way banks operate and the criteria they consider in funding decisions. Women entrepreneurs can serve themselves well by participating in opportunities for education by bank officers about the loan application process and funding criteria (Klinkerman, 1996; Maltby, 1995). In addition, American Express, Sears' credit operations, and other nonbank institutions are beginning to target entrepreneurs as a potential new market segment, offering small business credit cards with credit lines, new credit options, and financial management services (Dugan, 1996).

Incubators

The experiences of these women demonstrate that entrepreneurship need not be the first career choice. In spite of the frustration experienced, their tenure with their prior employers provided several benefits. These women had time to develop and hone their managerial, leadership, and technical skills and to develop strong professional networks that yielded valuable contacts during business start-up. Perhaps most important, they had time to develop their competence and self-confidence, a sense of purpose about their career, and clarity about their professional and personal priorities.

Leadership

We find considerable evidence of an interactive leadership style characteristic of female entrepreneurs. This conclusion is consistent with the work of Goodwin and Whittington (1996), Higgins and Duxbury (1994), Korabik (1990), Luthans (1986), O'Leary and Ickovics (1987), and Yammarino and colleagues (1997). Although not all the entrepreneurs in the present study used an interactive style, according to the quantitative findings, many talked about aspects of their leadership in terms of empowerment, personal influence, collaboration, and collegiality. All of these are dimensions of the interactive leadership style and appear common among the study participants. Findings here and also in the research cited immediately above suggest that entrepreneurs currently using a more traditional leadership style can enhance their effectiveness by integrating a more interactive approach into their management of subordinates.

There is a considerable literature on the differences in leadership styles between men and women. Because we did not include males in our sample of entrepreneurs, we do not address this question. Although we do conclude that the entrepreneurs here employed an interactive leadership style, we do not automatically assume that this is because they are female. The size of the businesses, among other factors, could encourage substantial interaction with employees at all levels.

Networking Opportunities

Three major underlying themes emerge from our analysis of the questionnaire data and focus interviews regarding networking. First and foremost, women's strong supportive networks have just begun to emerge, with the National Association of Women Business Owners being a key player. Second, women did not bring extensive networks with them from their prior corporate environment or elsewhere; in fact, many women deliberately had avoided doing business with friends and acquaintances just to test the waters to see if they could make it alone. Also, most of the women here felt that they did not fit into male networks or the traditional networks of housewives or society clubs. Third, isolated at the top of their businesses, these women were hungry for the rich experiences produced by the strong and supportive networks they later created or discovered.

Success

Findings here suggest that most of these female entrepreneurs measure their success foremost in terms of self-fulfillment and achievement of their goals, followed by the traditional performance measures of profits and business growth. Success seems to be measured internally in terms of personal growth, professional development, and improving one's skills, rather than externally in quantitative measures. A much smaller group of women entrepreneurs in the study are motivated primarily by the desire for more income through growth of the business and subsequent profits. This finding in no way suggests that these entrepreneurs do not understand the importance of running profitable operations.

Implications

Starting a Business

We find support for a suggestion of Baucus and Human (1994) that corporate acculturation in management and technical skill are important entrepreneurial benefits. For people in business who are contemplating entrepreneurship, we offer a caution: The results here suggest a tendency among the latent entrepreneurs to underestimate the importance of technical expertise in areas such as marketing and for intentional entrepreneurs to underestimate the importance of managerial experience. These are important dimensions for entrepreneurial success. Awareness of the importance of these differing areas of expertise may encourage those starting out to balance their management team or seek advice from others with experience in areas where they are deficient.

Further Investigation

Our sample distribution did not permit the opportunity to subdivide the corporate climbers and intentional entrepreneurs into firm size to examine managerially oriented goals; to relate firm type, as reported for entrepreneurs in the studies of Cooper et al. (1989) and Dyke et al. (1992); or to examine level of professional and administrative experience as noted by Hambrick and Crozier (1985). These all are worth further investigation in future studies of how entrepreneurs use the incubator experience. At the univariate level, there appear to be differences between the groups on the importance of the similarity of the incubator industry to the new business, with the intentionals valuing this more than do corporate climbers.

In the post hoc analysis of data collected in a follow-up study, significant differences were not found at the multivariate level in the perceptions of specific areas of managerial experience that contributed most to running a business. Across both groups of entrepreneurs, support was found for the findings of Cooper et al. (1989), Duchesneau and Gartner (1990), Stuart and Abetti (1990), and Vesper (1990), who suggest that organizational and management experiences relevant to the new business are especially important. Factors found here include gaining experience dealing with challenges involved in facing major setbacks and successes, supervisory experience, and the similarity of the organizational and industry type, product, service, customer, competitors, technology, and size to the entrepreneurial venture. Although our findings support those of Fischer et al. (1993) that gaining expertise in a particular sector or industry and start-up exposure are perceived as important components in successful venture operation, it is important to note that experience in facing challenges and setbacks and in supervision were perceived as more important. This is worth further investigation, as there is much to be learned from the transfer of managerial experience from the corporate environment to private ownership. The measure developed by Barrett and Christie (1994) needs to be validated to quantify this experience.

For this study, we compiled the research from the work of Appelbaum and Shapiro (1993), Helgesen (1990), Mintzberg (1973), and Peters (1990) and from a cursory review of the leadership literature to develop a questionnaire to tap three of the dimensions of interactive leadership. We also used Sashkin (1984) and Sashkin and Burke's (1990) Leadership Assessment Instrument for the transformational dimension. We pretested the three dimensions we developed in a trial run, but the instrument needs further development and testing. We recommend that future researchers continue to develop this instrument to measure women entrepreneurs' leadership styles.

As predicted, intentional entrepreneurs placed a higher value on expertise gained in marketing and technical areas than did corporate climbers. This supports the research findings of Morgan and Hunt (1994) regarding the importance of the perception of the market niche advantages acquired while still in the incubator organization among those who intended to start businesses. Also supported here are the research findings of Cooper (1985, 1986) of the importance of marketing and supplier expertise for those who have long-range intentions of creating their own businesses. One of the key competitive advantages of entrepreneurial firms competing with much larger rivals is the ability to identify and serve a specific market niche in a superior fashion. The results of this study indicate that intentional entrepreneurs appreciate the importance of this strategic advantage. Latent entrepreneurs may be less aware of the importance of this critical competitive competence and therefore less sensitive of and responsive to shifts in the marketplace. This could have implications for firm survival.

Organizational Dimensions

Findings here suggest three areas into which large corporations might inquire profitably. First, there is a suggestion that as organizations downsize or re-engineer, a careful analysis is needed of the impact this has on who stays and who goes. Generally, those in charge of these decisions may not be cognizant that among their more talented employees exist two groups of potential entrepreneurs, those who always intended to go into business for themselves and those who have become frustrated for a variety of reasons with the present organization. An organization has a vested interest in not losing some of the more talented and productive members of this second group. Employee retention thus requires a better understanding of career anchors of managers at all organizational levels.

Second, results from this study strongly suggest that intentional entrepreneurs will not remain in an organization irrespective of the compensation package, autonomy, or level of organizational satisfaction. The intentional entrepreneur was never the dedicated corporate type, and this is a critical factor in their launching a business (Bird, 1988, 1992; Bird & Jelinek, 1988; Hansen & Wortman, 1989; Learned, 1992). Organizations may wish to develop a strategy to meet the entrepreneurial expectations of this group to avoid ending up with them as competitors, perhaps by developing the new firms as outsourcers.

Third, for would-be entrepreneurs, the natural strategy suggested in this study is to join an organization with a strong training program, a favorable nurturing environment, and opportunities to acquire marketing, financial, new technology, and management experience. The education gained clearly is a portable commodity in the transition to entrepreneurship.

Advice

Making a Difference

A number of the entrepreneurs in this study have a personal goal of making their fields more accessible to the women who will come after. Clear from our questionnaire data is the driving, burning need to make a difference by helping others. This personal measure of success was rated as the most important by 55 entrepreneurs (44%) and second most important by 37

(29%). The total represents 73% of the ratings. As a Cincinnati entrepreneur says:

> I think it is up to all of us to be visible to share our goals and to share our time to help people and give back to our business. It takes a lot of commitment. I am committed to making a difference.

Contacts and Influence

For small business owners, establishing one's performance credibility a step at a time can be laborious. Many of the entrepreneurs in this study had been selected by their cities and states as elected delegates to the White House Conferences for Small Business. One of these women pointed out how this association has become an important voice for all women entrepreneurs. The association may also offer the opportunity for entry into formerly exclusive groups and clubs, for impressing people in the field, and to bring entrepreneurial interests to the attention of politicians. The suggestion is that women entrepreneurs need to have high visibility at these meetings.

Such associations confer another benefit. Andre (1995) says that women entrepreneurs can demonstrate an active voice by participating in influential organizations geared to economic development. Diane Hanson, a Philadelphia entrepreneur, started an organization designed to open doors for women entrepreneurs. Called the "Women's Referral of Chester County," the organization now has more than 100 members, offers scholarships to female entrepreneurs, and has a World Wide Web page. Existing networks such as the National Association of Women Business Owners and professional women's groups also provide active ways to gain access. Entrepreneurs from Atlanta, Chicago, Cincinnati, and New Orleans succeeded in local organizations that worked to influence legislation to positively affect minority and female entrepreneurs. Says an Atlanta entrepreneur, "It is all about getting included so you can educate and influence."

Making It Happen

The women in this study spoke most strongly about the need for planning, realism, knowledge, and support. Said Suzan Kotler, an entrepreneur in Cincinnati, "You have to really want to do it. You should know about the business you are in. You have to know your market and have to know yourself. You need to know the business plan, how you are going to do it, the expenses. You need to do a lot of research. You have to develop realistic expectations."

Having a Personal Plan

The entrepreneurs believed that those contemplating an independent business should carefully study themselves. The personal planning should precede any business planning. "I am suspicious when people say I want to be my own boss—I don't want anyone telling me what to do," said Nancy Smerz, a Chicago entrepreneur:

When you are the boss you have a lot of people telling you what to do. You have to live up to the expectations of every employee, the customers, suppliers, the union, the OSHA, the EPA—you have all kinds of people telling you what to do. If you want to be the boss, forget it! Control is a very illusive commodity when you own the company because you are controlled by an awful lot of forces that you didn't know about when you started out. Anybody who thinks they are going to have their own business and loll around at home while somebody else makes money for them is unrealistic.

Pick a business for the right reasons, said Gee Tucker, a New Orleans business owner. "Whatever you get into, be sure it is something you like. Never get into a business because you think you are going to get rich, or that there is a silver-lined rainbow." "Pick something that you love," said Hattie Hill in Dallas. "When you are in a small business, you may be there by yourself forever and you better have the discipline and the talent for it. Because if not, it will die." Select something you understand, said Pamela Pizel, another Dallas businesswoman.

Don't just start into something you've never done before. I see people all the time—"I want to start up a sandwich shop"—6 months later they're sick of it. And they've invested in equipment. They've got a lease. They've got all kinds of things. Really know that you want to be married to that business for a long period of time.

Understand, Pamela continued, that "you've got to be very self-sufficient. You've got to be resilient and be able to bounce back when the tough times come." "It is important to know what you don't know," another Dallas entrepreneur added:

> I did not identify my strengths and weaknesses. I didn't realize that I didn't have the financial background to run the business. Position yourself with people who have the strengths you don't. If you're a good people manager, that's what you need to be doing and find other people to do your financial things, and be learning them so that you end up with an overall knowledge of all phases of the business.

"You must have a real passion for the idea," said Gail Wise, a New Orleans entrepreneur. "It is important to have the proper knowledge and skills. It is important to establish resources and a networking base, get financial backing, get supports, and get others excited." "What are you willing to live without?" asked Mary Tanner, a Cincinnati entrepreneur. She continued:

> I went from AT&T where I had it all. The top of the line copy systems, I had anything that I could have possibly wanted. Now I have a place that is very humble. We think twice before we buy anything. We haven't bought new office furniture because we are trying to keep our overhead as low as possible. We don't have customers coming to us and it is not as though we have to impress with our surroundings. I think that people in large corporations don't understand some of the things that they are not going to have.

In the same vein, Linda Sahagian advises:

> If you want to be an entrepreneur, you had better have strong shoulders, know what you are talking about, do your homework, and stand up for your rights. Understand that things may be difficult. Don't be afraid of fighting, or overly concerned with gaining enemies. Sometimes that comes with visibility and success. Go for it. It's your life. You have nothing to lose.

Understand too, noted a Kentucky entrepreneur, that this still "is a chauvinistic society. It will change, but with difficulty. In the South, many women are still encouraged to get up and identify with their husbands. They are not encouraged to be aggressive." Indeed, several entrepreneurs had encountered unexpected gender effects. Said Eileen Duignan-Woods, a Chicago entrepreneur:

> I found that clients expected to see an office. They hired men working out of their homes but did not hire women. I was forced to go out and get an office and spend money to furnish it and take out a lease and get everything that went with it. And naturally then I had to increase my rates. I still find myself competing with men who work out of their basements.

How does one know if she is right for a business venture? "I call it my three Knows," answers Mary Hopple, a Cincinnati entrepreneur. "Know yourself. Know if you have enough energy to do it. Know your customer. If you can't assess any of those three, then a business is not for you."

Realism

The entrepreneurs repeatedly cautioned those interested in beginning businesses not to be mesmerized by a dream. "Knowing which road to go down is important," said Joanne Pratt, a Texas entrepreneur. "You get opportunities you didn't expect and some of them may be golden. The challenge is to separate the golden ones from the lead ones." You must "go out and talk to people who started their own business and get a realistic view," a Cincinnati entrepreneur advised. Marie Clesi finds that "people will take time to talk to you about potential problem areas." Repeating the importance of getting complete information before launching a venture, Sherie Conrad of New Orleans adds, "Make sure that you understand what you are getting into. Opening a business should depend on a well-thought-out plan with a marketing strategy in advance."

Realistic expectations are important because it is easy to be misled. People could find themselves facing real financial hardship. Said Terri Parker-Halpin, a Cincinnati entrepreneur, "When starting a business you hear of all these great programs that are out there to help you in financing, but the money is not there, unless you have collateral to put up." She recommends that you "prepare by having 2 or 3 years income set aside in advance." "Money is the big thing," agreed Debra Rust, a Chicago area entrepreneur.

> Most of the people I know who have gone into business for themselves, whether male or female, are married and their spouse has a regular

income coming in. If nothing else, you have enough to live on. But by yourself or when the husband and wife are part of the business, you are very dependent. It gets very scary sometimes wondering where the next salary is coming from.

"Plan for it to cost more to start up your business than you ever thought and it's going to take you longer to make money than you ever thought," said Hattie Hill of Dallas. To be successful, said Saralyn Levine, an Atlanta businesswoman, "Figure it's gonna take two to three times longer than you planned."

The entrepreneurs felt that people considering a business venture should understand that things are changing rapidly. "I don't think you can emphasize too much the importance of doing your homework," said Dallas business owner Laurie Moore-Moore. Continuing, she said, "Today's marketplace is changing quickly and a key success factor in business is the ability to define the viable opportunities. That was less true 10 years ago than it is today. It's amazing how a business opportunity which was there 2 years ago and looked great might not be a valid opportunity now." Eileen Duignan-Woods offered a market-based caution:

I think I would tell them to give it a great deal of thought. A great deal of thought. I am not sure the advantages in this economy outweigh the disadvantages. This is not an economy that is always expanding. You are always in a situation where you are competing with people who are out of work and who will try their own businesses and will fail in a year. And every year you have a new crop who will come along and try to undercut you and that is a very difficult situation. We would all be a lot better off in a healthier economy.

Business ownership involves trade-offs, the entrepreneurs warned. "Wait until your children grow up. You can't avoid the long hours when you are working in your own business," said a Lexington entrepreneur. Suggested Darlene Drake of Lexington, Kentucky, "I would never tell a mother who has a family to go into business." A New Orleans entrepreneur added:

I have a lot of guilt about not spending the amount of time I should have had with my children. I want my grandkids to become teenagers before their mothers go into business. They are enjoying some things that I missed. I have three kids who have never seen anything but career women in their lives.

"Be wary of saving face to stay in something when it is not working out the way you envisioned," said a New Orleans businesswoman talking about the possibility of not succeeding. "Be able to walk away. This is not a failure."

Advice was also available for a more positive business outcome. "Hey, try it, if you really want to do this. You can always go back. If it doesn't work you can always go to something else," said Pat Sayre, a Cincinnati entrepreneur.

The Business Plan

The entrepreneurs were emphatic that no one should even think of going into business without having a well-prepared business plan. "It is critical to determine what the customer wants and needs and make sure that you have that for them," an Atlanta entrepreneur advises. "Find your niche," says Debra, a Chicago entrepreneur.

Do some research, figure out what you want to do, have some direction, find out where you want to go. Find out who your competition is, find out who your customers are going to be, find out who they buy from now. Find out what your competitors are offering the customers, their strong and weak points, and do a comparison. Then, at least you have some road to follow, at least you won't go in blindfolded.

It is important to have such a business plan, added Suzan Kotler, a Cincinnati entrepreneur, "Not the one you take to the bank but the one you are going to use to operate." She continued:

You need to do a lot of research. If you are in this type of industry that lends itself to it, you can do the research on the side before you go ahead and do the business full time. While you will never understand the full magnitude of the problems before you are in it, at least you will have some idea of what it might be like.

The planning should be explicit. "Go talk to customers, whoever those customers are going to be," says Shirley Schwaller, a Dallas entrepreneur, "and make sure that they really are going to do business with you." "Make sure you have contracts, clients or customers, that you have some kind of firm commitments," echoes a Chicago businesswoman.

Entrepreneurs should be prepared to weather some tough times at the beginning. Says an entrepreneur in the deep South, "They should be able to support themselves and their business for at least 12 months and develop networks of support. There are at least 100 things that you've never thought of before that come up." A Chicago entrepreneur advises a longer perspective: "I would make sure that I had enough income from all resources to survive for at least 2 years. If you have to make money during those 2 years starting out on your own you probably are not going to make it." The reasons for such advice are clear, Suzan Kotler says. "There is a big difference between knowing what you do and running a business. You need resources for those days when you are not making any money. You must be able to survive."

How does one begin? "Take advantage of opportunities. Plan, organize, design, listen, respond, change," says an East Coast businesswoman. Relates another:

> I took an entrepreneurship class when my partner and I decided to start a business. At that first session, I'll never forget, they said there are three kinds of businesses: sole proprietorships, partnerships, and corporations. We looked at each other and, "Geez, we're beginners." So I knew zero. By having a rather formal class, that gave me a checklist of questions to ask and what I needed to answer. I had the confidence to know that I had, sort of, covered the bases.

Those looking for a shortcut might consider Laurie Moore-Moore's suggestion to "Try to find an existing business and buy it." Catherine Marrs, another Dallas business owner, adds that "Whether it's buying an existing business or whether it's starting one from scratch, do as much research and develop as much knowledge about what you're doing as possible. Then step out the door with white knuckles." Adds a Florida entrepreneur, "It does help having some experience working with men."

Spouse and Support

Entrepreneurs agreed, as Darlene Drake says, that "An emotional support system, whether it is family or not, is important. You need other people to reaffirm for you that you have not lost your mind." For most entrepreneurs in this study, support came from a spouse or significant other. It is important to know that person, advises Carol Hecht, because:

> If your spouse is not 100% behind you and is not entrepreneurial, it creates some problems. Your spouse needs to understand and be supportive. You need to be able to discuss things without pushing the panic button, particularly when the times are difficult and finances come into play, because their name may be on the line next to yours, but their control is not day to day.

Prudence in Developing and Using Support Systems

Sherie Conrad, an entrepreneur from New Orleans, says, "Make it a motto to disengage personal friendships from business working relationships. The friendships that you can afford when you are the owner must remain part of a sound business strategy and are to be held at arm's length because you cannot succeed if you become involved emotionally." She then relates how "blind trust" in a long-term personal friend led her astray. In taking on a personal female friend's fiancé as a client, she says, she discovered that, in addition to manipulating her, his firm was engaged in fraudulent activities that he had no intention to straighten out. Responding to pleas to help correct the existing situation and adjust the business structure to operate in a legal manner, she sacrificed her personal integrity by investing good-faith time, money, and her personal health, only to learn that she had been deliberately deceived by her long-term friend and her friend's fiancé. "The lessons I have learned are invaluable," she says, "but I wish I had been better educated about the dynamics of men and women in the workplace at a much earlier stage of my career to understand and recognize behavior that indicated danger, deception, and a need to remove the caring cloak and put on the one emphasizing prudence."

Selling Oneself

One of the most important pieces of advice related to having people understand that you do no business until people know you are there. As Anne Sadovsky cautions, "You can build a better mousetrap, but if you don't have a way to let people know about it you're going to starve to death." Said a Midwestern entrepreneur, "I have worked with a lot of start-ups. When you start talking about selling they say, 'What do you mean about selling? All I want to do is do the work.' If you don't want to sell yourself, then go work for somebody. The biggest thing we do is the marketing." Added another entrepreneur, "No one told me everything about business goes back to sales. It is difficult to hire someone to sell you until you can sell yourself. I assume that anyone who owns their own business must be able to sell. The ability to build the business is important." Several of the entrepreneurs in this study found that having to establish their business by selling customers on it was their most difficult hurdle. Catherine Marrs of Dallas said:

> I came out of a bureaucratic background and a salaried position. I knew not one thing about sales. I didn't know a prospect list from a contract. I didn't know whether I was identifying someone who could buy services from me. The first year I went through $30,000. It took me 15 months before I started generating anything at all because I had to learn how to sell.

Other entrepreneurs were better prepared or more fortunate. Said a Dallas businesswoman, "With my background, I did so many presentations, saw so many presentations, that when I found this opportunity, getting the money was the easiest thing. I put a package together and I showed it to three people. And in 24 hours all three wanted to do it. I picked the person who I wanted to do business with."

Being the Boss and Operating the Business

Entrepreneurs in this study were equally insistent that people should understand that, once in business, the owner had all the responsibility. As a Georgia entrepreneur says, "Basically the buck stops here. Anything that anybody falls down on, ultimately it's my liability, my name. I have to deal with the problem effectively, or somebody is disgruntled."

You cannot do it alone, the entrepreneurs advised. "In the areas where you do not have expertise, get outside help," a Charleston businesswoman advised, "preferably a well-recommended consultant who knows your business and can come in to talk to you who has no ax to grind and you can trust. If he doesn't give good advice, fire him. It is useless to pay someone for something that is not working for you." "I'm not afraid to hire professionals to help me," Hattie Hill of Dallas adds. "As Red Adair (an expert in extinguishing oil and gas well fires) said, if you think it's expensive to hire an expert, just wait and see how expensive it is to hire an amateur." Carol

Hecht suggested the business should "have a board of directors that has some outside people who bring a new perspective, aren't emotionally involved, and can be objective. A sounding board is terribly, terribly important." Added another Dallas businesswoman, "You need to have somebody you can bounce things off of." Substance is always important. Says Joanne Pratt, "What you need in addition is good market research."

There were some minor practical suggestions as well. "I finally learned that you put a Dictaphone by the side of your bed so that you don't have to turn on the light when you wake up at 3 o'clock in the morning with a thought," said Catherine Marrs of Dallas.

Employees

The entrepreneurs said that having good employees was important. Notes an Atlanta entrepreneur, "You have to have people with you who support your vision for the company, or at least have the responsibility of doing the job." Says Terri Parker-Halpin, a Cincinnati businesswoman, "You need to surround yourself with people who have knowledge and experience in areas that you don't. We as entrepreneurs are less threatened in our own house than anyone, but if you do not fill your house with talented people you can't move up to the next level."

"I am nothing without all the people who work for me," says Lisa Adkinson, a Midwestern entrepreneur. What this meant for many entrepreneurs was that one had to build customer confidence in the staff. A Cincinnati businesswoman relates, "When the customer has a question, although you may have the answer, you want to start turning the reins over to somebody who is going to handle that account day to day." To Julie Thomas, an architect, this means that "You must absolutely hire people who are better than you are."

Among other things, such an emphasis on employees means that these businesses do not tolerate poor work. Said a Charleston entrepreneur, "You cannot let the deadbeats in your business stay, because they are bad for the morale of the whole organization."

Getting Away From It All

The study entrepreneurs emphasized that operating a business took more than 100% of their time. They also understood the importance of getting away. "You want to try, when you leave the office, to not discuss business anymore. Sometimes you can't help it, but it is really important to have a personal life," an Atlanta entrepreneur says. Suggests Hattie Hill, a Dallas business owner, "Take care of yourself physically because of the energy that's required to keep you going." A Lexington entrepreneur advises to put things in perspective. "I worked 7 days a week, most times 20 hours a day since I became a business owner. You put all you can into your business. You still must realize that if you take a day off it is going to be there."

Personal Networks

Context

Many of our entrepreneurs have joined women's associations. The networks they describe resemble a design much like a spiderweb, wherein "women see their businesses as cooperative networks of integrated relationships rather than as separate economic units" (Brush, 1992, p. 16). Helgesen (1990, 1995) called this the web of inclusion. From the advice offered here, we would more nearly define this as a "hub effect." There is little doubt that those who are centrally located within the network acquire the most control of resources and develop the support so essential to survival as a successful entrepreneur, as has been found by other researchers (Brass, 1992; Burt, 1982; Ibarra, 1993; Larson & Starr, 1993).

There is no magical solution to establishing networks or to achieve the most effective results from networking. Network membership is expensive in terms of valuable time, energy, and resources. Every entrepreneur needs to be able to target a network small enough and comprehensive enough to provide a value-added dimension. The best advice is to begin by taking inventory of one's useful contacts; attend trade, professional, civic, cultural, and social events; utilize methods of increasing visibility and network opportunities; and ruthlessly discard network systems that do not pay off.

There is a general agreement among this group of entrepreneurs that the most useful networks or mentor groups are composed of six to eight people. A strategy that appears to be worthwhile is to join groups large and powerful enough for one to identify the special subgroup with which to join forces. Once found, with work the networks may prosper because of mutual interests and a common desire to associate without any expectation of gain.

Acquiring New Channels

Information is needed. It is available from many sources, including government at all levels, colleges and universities, and business owners. The increasing flow of information available through electronic networks can make it possible for small businesses to operate with all the power and information of large-scale enterprises. Creative avenues also are being used for network accessibility. Cravens, Shipp, and Cravens (1994) suggest that the new evolving model is a network of corporate units, independent organizations, and entrepreneurs.

Networking for nonprofit operations among entrepreneurs often leads to expanded business opportunities. Marilyn Sifford, a Philadelphia entrepreneur involved in such a project, explains it this way:

> I helped to start a group of consultants who were doing some work with the local guru of our field, who uses a process that's called a "future search conference" that involves stakeholders inside and outside of the organization. He agreed to mentor us to learn this process. We all agreed to give our time to conduct a conference for a nonprofit organization. We are now doing a second round with a new group of consultants. It has evolved into a little nonprofit organization called Search Net. These are starting up in Boston, Toronto, and Chicago, and on the West Coast.

To gain strength, entrepreneurs may use networks to address important policy issues that affect all female entrepreneurs. Some of these policy issues to address are the development and implementation of standards for financial and banking institutions. As noted by a former White House representative who participated in this study:

> Women entrepreneurs can become the movers and shakers in lobbies in Washington to develop legislation that makes it illegal for businessmen and others to "redline" women owners who want to borrow money, rent or lease property or equipment, purchase insurance and other services and goods, and obtain public services such as utilities, and to gain entry to the formerly exclusive clubs open to men only.

Entrepreneurial awareness of changes in services offered by the federal government and the ease in getting on line to receive these services will open new doors. A number of our entrepreneurs mentioned the large volume of paperwork previously required. This process has changed:

> One of the most important changes in the purchasing system for the federal government has been brought about by the Federal Acquisition Streamlining Act. This encourages agencies to buy off-the-shelf goods rather than items made to detailed specifications. The law also establishes a simpler process for entrepreneurs to bid on many smaller contracts. The federal government will stop communicating with vendors on paper, going on line instead on a system called FACNET (Federal Acquisition Computer Network). (Litvan, 1995)

An array of additional exchanges are also available to small business owners. For example, International Business Exchange (Ibex) was launched by a consortium led by the U.S. Chamber of Commerce in Washington, D.C., to "allow nontechnical users with modest budgets to find buyers, sellers, or investment opportunities with a $250 software package, PC, and modem. So far, 37 state and local chambers of commerce and national business organizations in 34 countries have agreed to market Ibex" (Anthes, 1995).

Other vital resources have been established through the combination of university and private alliances of entrepreneurs, scientists, venture capitalists, and the new interests expressed by banking institutions and other retail operations. These alliances make resources available that were only dreamed about in the past. Assistance is provided in all areas of information needed to successfully operate a business. More recent packages have been developed for accessing capital resources through databases such as the ones at MIT, the University of California, and Baylor University.

Summing Up

As we said at the outset, we sought talented, successful entrepreneurs nationwide to participate in this study. Some had always wanted to own and operate their own business. Others chose entrepreneurship as a new career. All had substantial experience in large organizations before launching out on their own. Each is a unique individual. Collectively, they enable us to construct a profile.

The successful female entrepreneur strongly values her autonomy and freedom. She has high self-esteem. At some point in her earlier career, she felt the stifling effects of a bureaucratic environment. She was competent but did not always fit well into the organization. Although she did not necessarily experience discrimination at work, she concluded early on that gender made a difference in the endless game of organizational politics.

She sought to run her own business because she wanted to be excited about her work again, as well as finding other rewards. Confident of her abilities and apprehensive about the future, she left her prior organization with more skills and savvy than she perhaps realized at the time. The knowledge she had acquired in the organizational incubator more than made up for her lack of expertise in areas she soon discovered were important.

Things were not easy at first. She had doubts in the early days, yet she persevered. She reached out for assistance, beginning the process of establishing the networks she would later value so much. Having sought good leadership in her corporate incubator, and also having endured bad bosses, she managed people more wisely than she had been managed. Genuinely concerned about the welfare of her employees, she built a strong, employee-centered business. Her concern with others carried over to her customers.

She was successful. Her business made money. Although closely related, the two are not the same thing to her, for she measures success in a new way. She is one of many in the fastest growing sector of the American economy. She is going to be around a long time. And there are going to be a lot more like her.

Appendix 1

Methodology

Study Overview

Funding for this study came from The Citadel Development Foundation, the Berkley Center for Entrepreneurial Studies at New York University, and the University of North Carolina at Greensboro. The research findings are based on in-depth questionnaires and videotaped focus interviews. Focus sessions addressed entrepreneurial intentions, corporate strategies, and how the previous organization was used as an incubator for launching a successful business. Conference facilities at all the major research locations were generously furnished by entrepreneurial centers, private businesses, universities, and colleges. A special acknowledgment to each of these contributors to the research project is included in Appendix 3.

Selection Criteria

Prospective participants were identified with the aid of the various chapters of the National Association of Women Business Owners, various governors' offices, small business development centers, chamber of commerce groups, women's entrepreneurial groups, civic groups, and small business owners. Many who participated in the study had achieved recognition such as being named the Entrepreneur of the Year in their city or state. The criteria for selection as a participant included such dimensions as organizational, professional, or managerial experience prior to launching a business, being established in business longer than a year, initiating a business, ownership of at least 50% of the business, and present service in a major managerial role. Each of the organizations we contacted was requested to help us identify women entrepreneurs who worked in managerial or professional capacities in corporate environments before leaving to start businesses of their own. From this list, we constructed a representative sample of willing participants from different geographic regions.

Focus groups of female entrepreneurs were interviewed in cities where, according to the National Foundation for Women Business Owners (1992), the density of women-owned businesses is greatest. To develop the broadest possible spectrum and also to avoid regional bias, we conducted additional focus group sessions in five other small and medium-sized cities. The focus group interviews were conducted in Atlanta, Boston, Charleston, Chicago, Cincinnati, Dallas, Lexington, New Orleans, New York, Orlando, Philadelphia, Winston-Salem, and San Francisco. Although male control groups also were used in three of these major locations, the data from those groups are not part of this study.

Focus Session Format

The focus sessions were divided into two segments. Each respondent first completed a questionnaire, which took approximately 30 minutes, before joining a videotaped focus group discussion with two to seven other entrepreneurs. The average number in a group session was five.

Given the exploratory nature of our study, our sample may be classified as a judgment sample, in that it was selected to meet specific criteria (Emory & Cooper, 1991; Kerlinger, 1986). First, it was necessary for us to identify among successful women entrepreneurs those who had worked in prior corporate environments and then left. We then asked these entrepreneurs to participate in a research session. In addition to filling out a detailed questionnaire, participants spent at least an hour and a half with their group. In all, our participants had to commit about 3 hours of their time plus any travel.

Contact Protocol

Each entrepreneur was contacted by one of the researchers by phone and invited to participate voluntarily in a focus session in her city. In the calls, we made a personal introduction, identified the sponsors of the research, and provided information about the study, topics to be discussed at the focus session (see Table A1.1 for the format used in the focus interview sessions), and other data. Each contact was told the criteria for her selection as a potential participant. Of the 148 entrepreneurs contacted by telephone, 129 later participated in the research project, a response rate of 87.2%.

Prior to the focus group meetings, each entrepreneur received a letter confirming the place, time, and date of the meeting; biographical data on each of the researchers; a statement of the purpose of the study; focal topics for discussion; data analysis procedures; probable research outlets; and assurances regarding the confidentiality of individual information. Each respondent was also informed in advance that the focus sessions would be videotaped. (See Appendix 2, which provides the confidentiality statement.) Specifically, the introductory letter read:

TABLE A1.1. Focus Format for Sessions

  I. WELCOME TO FOCUS SESSION
 II. BRIEF PERSONAL INTRODUCTION
III. ANSWERS ON ENTREPRENEURIAL PHASE ASSESSMENT QUESTIONNAIRE
     This should take about 30 minutes.
     A. CODE OF ETHICS AND CONFIDENTIALITY
     B. HANDLING OF INFORMATION ACROSS FOCUS GROUPS
     C. RESPONSES SHOULD BE BASED ON FIRST REACTION TO QUESTION
 IV. COLLECT QUESTIONNAIRES
  V. PERSONAL INTRODUCTIONS AND BRIEF STATEMENT FROM EACH "E" ON
     INITIATION OF BUSINESS
 VI. FOCUS AREAS FOR DISCUSSION
     A. TRANSITION FROM PREVIOUS ORGANIZATIONAL ENVIRONMENT
        1. Drive for leaving
        2. Retention would have depended on
        3. Importance of networks in leaving organization
        4. Decisions to start own business based on
        5. Transitions I went through in starting the program
     B. PRIMARY ROLE AS OWNER AND MANAGER
     C. DEFINING SUCCESS AND MEASURING IT
        1. Feelings about success
        2. Power
     D. GOALS OF AN ENTREPRENEUR
     E. MANAGEMENT OF PERSONAL AND BUSINESS ASPECTS OF ROLE
     F. ADVICE FOR THOSE LEAVING ORGANIZATIONS TO START BUSINESSES
     G. FUTURE INTERNATIONAL INVOLVEMENT FOR WOMEN ENTREPRENEURS
     H. FUTURE OF ENTREPRENEURS IN _____ AREA

Managers have been dropping out of organizational environments to start their own businesses in unprecedented numbers. Equipped with more education and management experience, and holding clear objectives, these entrepreneurs bring corporate backgrounds, experiences, and business contacts to their ventures. This study is designed to identify and explore organizational and individual factors contributing to the success of entrepreneurs who have had corporate managerial experience. The objectives of this study are to identify successful entrepreneurial strategies and develop programs to assist potential entrepreneurs as they make the transition from the corporate environment. The group discussions will center on the important transitional points in the life of an entrepreneur as she moves from the corporate environment to private ownership.

Focus session topics included entrepreneurial intentions, transition strategies, leadership styles, networking strategies, success measures, and how the previous organization was used as an incubator. The participants were not told the hypotheses of the study.

Respondent Profile

Respondents in this study were on average 44 years old, white, college educated, and married with at least one child at the time of the interviews. An average entrepreneur had operated an incorporated service business with sales in the $250,000-499,999 range for 7 years. The entrepreneur defined her role as CEO, president, or owner. She worked an average of 52 hours a week in her company and earned most of her income from the business. She earned at least as much and probably more than she did in her former corporate position, where she had worked for 6 years. The entrepreneur was 37 years old at the time of business start-up and had young children in elementary school at that time (see Table A1.2).

Instrumentation

Original information in the study is based on the responses of the 129 female entrepreneurs to an eight-page survey instrument, formatted intensive focus interviews, and a follow-up survey. Instruments are included in Appendix 2.

Pilot Test of Instrument

The initial survey questionnaire and focus group items were drawn from a careful review of the literature on entrepreneurship and women in management. Two initial focus groups of two and seven women entrepreneurs were used to pretest the questionnaire. Items not included in the survey that were mentioned frequently by members of these focus groups were added. The survey was then pilot tested on three additional groups of women entrepreneurs. From the three-group pilot results, questions were honed and clarified to measure the focal areas of interest in women's transitions from the corporate environment to establishing and operating successful businesses.

Methods

Measures

Organizational Exit

Two sets of literature were used to develop questions on why entrepreneurs leave their prior organizations to start businesses of their own. Thirty-two items were rated

TABLE A1.2. Demographic Profile of the Female Entrepreneur Participants

	n	*Mean*	*S.D.*
Age		44	7.9
Age at start-up		37	
Children's age		12	
Children's age at start-up		5	
Years in business		7.4	4.7
Number of employees		15.1	37.6
Percentage of business ownership		83.3	26.4
Percentage of income from business		83.1	33.0
Hours worked per week		52	14.3
Hours worked per week in prior job		46	12.3
Length of tenure in prior position		6.1	5.38
Annual sales			
Up to $49,999	15		
$50,000–$99,999	16		
$100,000–249,999	17		
$250,000–499,999	19		
$500,000–1,000,000	15		
$1,000,001–4,999,999	22		
$5,000,000–9,999,999	8		
$10,000,000+	7		

	Percentage
Entrepreneurs with children	7
Education	
High school	6
College	53
Master's	36
Doctorate	6
Operational role in the business	
Owner, president, CEO	87
Other (e.g., CFO, vice president)	13
Industry type	
Service and retail trade	81
Finance, insurance, and real estate	6
Construction	4
Manufacturing	4
Transportation and communication	4
Wholesale trade	1
Business organization	
Sole proprietorship	36
Partnership	6
Corporation	58
Percentage of women who earned at least as much as in their previous corporate position	88

on a 6-point scale, 1 (*most important*) to 6 (*least important*). Questions developed on the basis of research of Brodsky (1993), Capowski (1992), Fagenson (1993), Gabor (1994), and Shane and colleagues (1991) addressed autonomy (making it on my own, freedom, and self-esteem), organizational culture issues (values different from those of corporate culture, desire to create an environment to fit one's own values, reaction to bureaucracy and lack of autonomy, desire for a better organizational climate), and control (a desire to be in charge of one's time, regain excitement about life, and be in authority). Reasons for leaving organizations identified in the research of Birley and Westhead (1994), Cooper and Dunkelberg (1981), Denison and Alexander (1986), Dubini (1988), Scheinberg and MacMillan (1988), and Shane and colleagues (1991) made up the remaining questions. Two write-in blanks were provided to allow participants to list additional reasons. The comprehensive list of questions is provided in Appendix 2.

Grouping Variable for Incubator Analysis

Assignment of entrepreneurs into the designated analytical groups of intentionals and corporate climbers was based on self-reported data from each of the respondents. Questions addressed intentions to start a business or to rise in the corporate ranks within previous organizational environments. The grouping variable for intentionals and corporate climbers was based on responses to two items with the stem "I worked in the last organization prior to launching out on my own" as (a) an incubator period for the business I always intended to create or (b) going up the corporate or organizational ladder. The stems were attached to 6-point scales from 1 (*most important*) to 6 (*least important*). To be considered significant on this measure, the score had to be 1 or 2. The consistency of the grouping variable was confirmed with this question: "Which of the following sentences best describes your prior organizational experiences before starting your business: (a) I had intended to be an entrepreneur and used the organization as a training ground to gain experience; (b) I had intended to work in a large corporation as a career; or (c) other (please explain)." This division of entrepreneurs into corporate climbers and intentionals was further confirmed by the analysis of the content data from the focus interviews.

Two sets of questions examined the direct impact of the previous organizational environment. Ratings on the first set of 5-item scales were 1 (*most influence*) to 6 (*least influence*) for organizational skills acquired in the areas of technical, marketing, financial, networking, managerial, or motivational techniques. The second set of scales, used as part of a follow-up study, incorporated 12 items of a questionnaire developed by Barrett and Christie (1994) with 5-point scales, 1 (*extremely useful*) to 5 (*not useful at all*) to ask about entrepreneurial perceptions of the organization as an incubator. Items included being in the same industry, facing major setbacks, successes, supervision of managers or workers, forming strategic alliances, similar products or services, customers, suppliers, competitors, technology, and starting a previous firm. Prior to the time we administered this questionnaire, no scales had been developed to measure incubator effects.

Transition Problems and Strategies

The entrepreneurship literature on transition problems and challenges was reviewed, and questions for inclusion on the first survey were developed based on the work of Alpander and colleagues (1990), Hisrich and Brush (1984), Humphreys and McClung (1981), Kuratko and Hodgetts (1989), and Terpstra and Olson (1993).

Leadership

Three instruments were used to measure leadership styles on the second survey. The Leader Assessment Inventory developed and revised by Sashkin (1984) and Sashkin and Burke (1990) was used to measure the extent to which entrepreneurs utilized a transformational approach to leadership (10 items: Q3, Q5, Q7, Q8, Q14, Q15, Q17, Q19, Q20, Q25, reliability: alpha coefficient = .68). The Role Model/Visionary Scale was used to assess the degree to which entrepreneurs articulated a vision for their firm and acted as a role model (6 items: Q28, Q32, Q39, Q40, Q43, Q44, reliability: alpha = .66). A scale composed from the work of Appelbaum and Shapiro (1993), Helgesen (1990), and Rosener (1990) was used to assess the participative, interactive dimension of leadership (4 items: Q30, Q33, Q34, Q37, reliability: alpha = .69). The questions used in the leadership dimensions are contained in the second (follow-up) questionnaire in the Management/Leadership Style Inventory in Appendix 2. This section also contains the Self-Efficacy Scale adopted from the work of Robertson and Sadri (1993).

Networks

Our measurements of network activities were largely based on a cluster analysis of items appearing most frequently in the Ethnograph Content Analysis in the focus group discussions. From the questionnaire data, Part III A, we had a direct measure of the effect of the previous organizational environment on network formation (Q1, d). In Phase II, My Role as an Entrepreneur, we asked each entrepreneur to assess the degree they participate with others in teams to gain expertise (Q1, o) and to assess their support system (Q4, a-f). We also included a global measure of networking and a measure of the training impact of the incubator for network affiliation. See other items that we analyzed with regard to networking in Table 6.5.

Success

A number of success measures were used on the questionnaire. Traditional measures of success have been economic in focus, including profits and growth in sales and employees. Our initial interviews and research cited in Chapter 7, however, suggested that women may seek other outcomes. Thus, we based our questions on this initial feedback and on the literature about women's development. See Phase II, My Role as an Entrepreneur, and Phase III, Processes for Success, on the questionnaire. Also see items listed in Tables 7.1 and 7.2 and in Figure 7.1.

Data Analysis

Questionnaire

Analytical techniques varied across the chapters. For Chapters 2, 3, and 7, in addition to means, frequency, and rank order analyses, factor analyses were completed to examine the underlying dimensions. The split-half alpha reliability procedure was used to examine scales in Chapters 3 and 5, and Cronbach's alpha was used to measure reliability in Chapter 7. One-way ANOVA analysis, chi-square, and t tests were used throughout the study where appropriate. Two-group multivariate analysis of variance with the discriminant function was employed as the primary method of data analysis for Chapters 3 and 6 (see Tabachnick & Fidell, 1996). This procedure involved a computation of the means for the intentional entrepreneurs, the corporate climbers, and the entire sample from which confidence intervals were calculated. Within-cell correlations with standard deviations on the diagonal and within-cell correlations with the Bartlett test of sphericity were used. The procedure computes a discriminant function only when the multivariate level of significance meets the cutoff alpha level. Univariate F tests were used to further examine the data, as were the correlations between dependent and canonical variables.

The ranking and rating of female entrepreneurs' reasons for leaving were analyzed in several ways. The six reasons most frequently ranked as the first or second most influential reason for leaving to initiate a business were tabulated. To determine whether there were distinct themes in the 32-item ratings of entrepreneurs' reasons for leaving, the ratings were factor analyzed with varimax rotation. A scree plot indicated the existence of five factors. Consistent with Ford, MacCallum, and Tait (1986), loadings of .40 or greater were considered meaningful for interpretation. Items were assigned to factors when they had loadings greater than .40 and low or negative loadings on other factors. The means for the five factors and for each factor item were then computed for each group.

Focus Interviews

Nine entrepreneurs completed the questionnaire but because of scheduling conflicts did not participate in the focus group discussions. The content analysis is therefore based on the comments of 120 entrepreneurs. Within this group, 80 are classified as corporate climbers, 35 as intentionals, and 5 as neutrals (those who took the best position available at the time). Where appropriate, information is reported separately for the various groups. The focus of the study, however, is largely on the group of entrepreneurs as a whole.

Corporate Exit and Incubator Experience

The data for the focus interviews were content analyzed with the aid of The Ethnograph (Seidel, Kjolseth, & Seymour, 1988). All preliminary procedures prescribed in the Ethnograph program were used in preparing the data for content analysis. A first step was an intensive examination of the literature in which themes were identified for the classification of comments for the Ethnograph analysis. Two independent raters were used consecutively for data analyzed in Chapters 2, 3, and 6. Many iterations of the Ethnograph program were used to identify clusters of data representing the responses across focus sessions of emerging themes. In addition, data for Chapters 2 and 3 were content analyzed on the basis of the factors identified in the factor analysis procedure as noted above.

The Ethnograph program was used to identify the predominant themes in the incubator experience and in exit decisions. Each of these entrepreneurs contributed in different ways to the focus group discussion. A frequency analysis was taken of key words used to describe their incubator experiences in their previous organizational environments and to equate those experiences to the transfer or value of this information in the organization they now own. Although the frequency obtained from the content analysis provides an understanding of important topics discussed within the focus sessions, it provides only one index of the measure of the relationships. This is the case for several reasons. Because of the limited time within the session, topics shifted on the basis of interests, the dominance and attractiveness of corporate and entrepreneurial transitions (transfer of information), and commonality of interests. The dominant themes in the analysis are used here to supplement the questionnaire data.

The Ethnograph program was used to label the former corporate environment experience and the entrepreneurial venture, as well as to identify the degree that the two environments were similar in terms of direct or indirect transfer between the two. On the basis of the conversations, as many topics as possible were examined as related to the incubator experience. Some of the key areas examined were the number of skills considered to transfer directly from the incubator experience to running one's own business. This provided an index of comparison for the measurement of the perceived effectiveness of the organization as an incubator.

At level one of the incubator analysis, we examined the direct and indirect transfer of skills acquired in the incubator to those skills perceived to be needed in the new business venture. We also examined those skills the entrepreneurs said they had lacked. We examined the direct transfer of specialist skills, generalist skills, and skills acquired from experiences in one's own ventures. For a better understanding of the transfer, we looked at the occurrences of the reference to the development of contacts, professional expertise in the field, business experience in general, technical expertise in equipment operations or as gained through a special degree program, financial expertise, management skills, marketing skills, sales know-how, legal expertise, special training programs, formal education, and the degree to which these skills were perceived to be general or specialist in nature. Just as we examined the skills transferred, we also analyzed the number of occurrences when these skills were considered to be lacking.

At the second level of incubator impact on the entrepreneurial venture, we looked at the degree to which the entrepreneur took away from the organization a sense of heightened awareness of self in the form of excitement about a new venture, self-confidence, creativity, credibility, autonomy, empowerment, and support.

The final level included information on the organizational incubator as a culture in which the entrepreneurs had operated and anything in that culture that may have led them to create a business of their own. We looked at how many of the entrepreneurs left because of a reorganization, downsizing, or outsourcing; a sense of a lack of ethics; the pull of home responsibilities or conflicting career demands of a husband and wife team; politics and bureaucratic policies or a tinge of "the good old boy system"; the feeling of burnout; and reaching a dead end or a career block in the form of discrimination, pay, or harassment.

Transition Problems and Strategies

The focus group interviews were content analyzed using a three-step process (Krippendorff, 1981; Miles & Huberman, 1984). First, the transcripts were reviewed by two independent raters to identify all comments that pertained to transition problems and strategies reported by the entrepreneurs. Comments identified by either or both raters were then collated into a master file. The master file was read independently by three raters to identify common themes, including but not limited to the themes identified in previous research. These themes were then presented in round robin fashion, and those identified by at least two of the raters were retained for step three. The file was again analyzed and comments classified according to the themes identified in step two. Comments for which there was disagreement were reanalyzed. If all three raters agreed that the comment fit in a specific category, it was thus assigned. If there was not unanimous agreement on a category but the raters agreed that the comment concerned a transition problem or strategy, the comment was placed into an "Other" category. Otherwise, it was dropped from the analysis. Interrater reliability was .89.

Leadership

The same three-rater procedure used for analysis of the transition problems and issues was used to content analyze the transcripts for leadership styles and issues. A master file was created using the same two-rater procedure. Two of the three raters in the subsequent analysis were unfamiliar with the leadership literature regarding the interactive or transformational styles of leadership. The three raters nevertheless independently identified dimensions of the interactive leadership as themes among the comments in the second analysis. In the third round of the analysis, the raters shared their sorting of comments into the categories identified in round two. Comments for which there was disagreement were reanalyzed. If all three raters agreed that the comment fit in a specific category, it was thus assigned. If there were no unanimous agreement on a category but the raters agreed that the comment concerned leadership, the comment was placed into an "Other" category. Otherwise, it was dropped from the analysis. Interrater reliability was .82.

Networks

The procedure used for the application of the Ethnograph program to the data on networking followed that prescribed above for the corporate exit and incubator experience. From the Ethnograph analysis, themes emerged in the following areas: survival, resource availability, number of memberships and meetings, the degree to which networks were personal, the degree to which networks went beyond personal acquaintances and friends and family, intensity, and cooperative strategies. We also found themes emerging with regard to how networks were used for sanity checks, sounding boards, negotiation groups, joint relationships, training, teamwork, to control the environment, and resource acquisition. Another cluster identified a value-added dimension for information exchange, association and performance, how networks were used for credibility, the web effect, and socialization. A support cluster also was identified. In addition, themes emerged for gender differences, network savvy, loneliness, and the perception of corporate/entrepreneurial differences in using networks. We also found the presence of the GOBN (Good Old Boy Network). For a complete list of the themes, see Chapter 6 and supporting tables.

Success

The procedure used to content analyze the comments regarding success measures was the same as those for analysis of transition issues and leadership styles, except that only one rater was used. Unlike the other analyses, the data analysis and themes in this area closely paralleled each other. Initial identification of comments regarding success measures was conducted before common themes were identified and comments classified.

Limitations of Study

This focus group field research study of entrepreneurs who previously worked in organizations prior to starting their own businesses, one of the first of its type, was exploratory in nature and based on volunteers from the major metropolitan areas of the United States. We used precedents set in other research in selecting participants for our study. Our overall objective was to select heterogeneous groups of representative entrepreneurs from each of the regions. Similar sampling techniques have been used in a number of entrepreneurial studies because of the complexity and design of the field research (Belcourt, 1991; Birley, 1989; Brodsky, 1993; Brush, 1992; Brush & Hisrich, 1991; Cromie & Hayes, 1991; Fagenson & Marcus, 1991; Kalleberg & Leicht, 1991; Phelps & Mason, 1991).

Although there was a small representation of minority entrepreneurs (nine non-white American women), the number is too small to draw any conclusions regarding the generalizability of the findings of the present study to minority women entrepreneurs. Further study of African Americans, Hispanics, American Indians, Asians, and other minorities would clarify the experiences of those female entrepreneurs.

The qualitative data show that the incubator experience of a previous organizational environment and the comparison of the intentional entrepreneurs with the former corporate climbers merit additional research. For example, understanding the difference in entrepreneurial intentions, long-range versus more latent, may have important contributions to make to understanding of threshold decisions that corporate climbers and intentional entrepreneurs make. Scale development also is needed in this area.

The set of questions derived from the literature used in this study need further development and application in larger samples in a longitudinal nature. The work of Barrett and Christie (1994) on the in-depth factors involved within the incubator process might be used with the questions here to gain additional insight into the role intentions play among those who use the organization as an incubator for career development. The web approach to leadership, developed on the basis of what little information was available, also needs further development.

The question of how widely the results here may be generalized awaits further investigation among women and men who have been successful managers in corporate environments, left those environments, and started businesses of their own.

Questionnaires:
Organizational Incubator Effect
Entrepreneurial Phase Assessment

Organizational Incubator Effect:
A Predictor of Entrepreneurial Success

Protection of Privacy

Public Law 93-579, the Privacy Act of 1974, requires that all individuals be informed of the purposes and uses to be made of the information which is solicited in a research project. The Academy of Management Code of Ethical Conduct in conducting and reporting research, including the treatment of participants and the dissemination of all results,[1] applies here also. The following is furnished to explain why the information is requested and the general uses to which that information may be put.

Authority: The information requested is being collected by Professor E. Holly Buttner, the University of North Carolina at Greensboro, and Professor Dorothy P. Moore, The Citadel. The research is partially supported by grants from the Center for Entrepreneurial Studies, Leonard H. Stern School of Business, New York University, and The Citadel Development Foundation.

Purpose: The function of this research study is to identify and explore organizational and individual factors contributing to the success of entrepreneurs who have had organizational "incubator experiences" prior to becoming an entrepreneur. The

---

[1]Ken Cooper, Ed. (Ohio Northern University), 1992. Academy of Management Code of Ethical Conduct, *Academy of Management Handbook 1992 Edition*, pp. 38-40. (The Academy of Management is the largest professional organization in the field of management. It has approximately 10,000 national and international members.)

purpose of video-taping is to back up shorthand notes to clearly identify focus issues across sessions.

Uses: The results will advance the knowledge in the field of entrepreneurship and be important to would-be entrepreneurs, to our business society, and to those attempting to improve the education of entrepreneurs. The initial and primary outlets for this research will be professional journals of business administration. Additional outlets will be in book manuscripts.

Confidentiality Clause

Questionnaire Data:

Your answers will be kept completely confidential. All information from the questionnaires will be reported only in normative ways (summarized results across the entire sample).

Focus Interviews:

No entrepreneur will be individually identified by name without that person's prior approval. Some of the remarks which an entrepreneur in one focus session makes may be very similar or the same as those made by entrepreneurs in other sessions. Any quotes attributed to a specific entrepreneur or business will be with that entrepreneur's approval. Persons who have given approval for citations will have an opportunity to review and correct written material prior to its publication. We mention this explicitly because in many cases entrepreneurs have asked us to cite their remarks. Examples appear in the book chapter "Stepping Off the Corporate Track," by Professors Moore, Buttner, and Rosen, which appears in *Womanpower, Managing in Times of Demographic Turbulence*, and which explains much of the project's development.

ENTREPRENEURIAL QUESTIONNAIRE

This questionnaire is designed to identify why women establish businesses, the obstacles they encounter, and the challenges they must address. In addition to answering the questions, please feel free to include comments which will give a more complete description of the challenges you face as an entrepreneur.

<u>Demographics</u>:

Age ____   Marital Status [1]____M; [2]____S; [3]____D; [4]____W.   Children____; Ages ____ ____ ____

Educational Level: [1]____Grade School; [2]____High School/GED; [3]____College; [4]____Masters; [5]____Doctorate. Area of Concentration_____.

Special Training Programs_____.

Business Type_____. This is a new business [1]____; family business [2]____; I bought the business from the previous owners [3]____.

My operational role in the business is_____.

PHASE I -- LAUNCHING OUT ON MY OWN

I.   <u>Work History</u>.

Previous and present work environments. If more than one previous environment, describe the one that you feel had the greatest influence on you as an entrepreneur. Please identify that environment; i.e., corporation, partnership, public sector organization, etc.

Sales	Other Firm (Previous)	My Own Firm	Growth of Business	Other Firm (Previous)	My Own Firm
Up to $49,000	[1]____	[1]____	Slow Growth Industry	[1]____	[1]____
$50,000 to $99,999	[2]____	[2]____	Moderate Growth	[2]____	[2]____
$100,000 to $249,999	[3]____	[3]____	High Growth	[3]____	[3]____
$250,000 to $499,999	[4]____	[4]____			
$500,000 to $1 million	[5]____	[5]____	Description of Business		
1 to 4.99 million	[6]____	[6]____	Traditional for women	[1]____	[1]____
5 to 10 million	[7]____	[7]____	New area for women	[2]____	[2]____
over 10 million	[8]____	[8]____			
			Type of Industry		
Type of Business			Agriculture	[1]____	[1]____
Proprietorship	[1]____	[1]____	Mining	[2]____	[2]____
Partnership	[2]____	[2]____	Construction	[3]____	[3]____
Corporation	[3]____	[3]____	Manufacturing	[4]____	[4]____
A publicly held firm	[4]____	[4]____	Transportation,		
Other	[5]____	[5]____	Communication, Utilities	[5]____	[5]____
A privately held firm	[6]____	[6]____	Wholesale Trade	[6]____	[6]____
A government organization	[7]____	[7]____	Finance, Insurance & R.E.	[7]____	[7]____
A university	[8]____	[8]____	Services	[8]____	[8]____
			Public Sector or Government	[9]____	[9]____
Number of Employees			Other [10] _____		
Full-Time	[1]____	[1]____			
Part-Time	[2]____	[2]____			

II.   <u>Work History Continued.</u>

1.   Earnings comparison.

In my own business I make:
- ¹____less than ½ as much as I did in my old job;
- ²____approximately the same as in my corporate job;
- ³____½ more than in my previous job;
- ⁴____double what I made working for someone else;
- ⁵____other_____.

2.   The average weekly hours I spend working in my own business   ¹____;
                                                           in previous position   ²____.

3.   Length of Service in previous organization: ____Yrs

4.   Length of Ownership: ____Yrs
           % of the business I own   ____
           % of my income from business   ____

5.   For the six items below, first read the statement and give your first response by circling the number on the right which most closely resembles your feelings: Most Influence (1) to Least Influence (5). Mark (0) if the reason does not apply. After you have rated each item (a-f), then place your rank order of the importance of the items to you in the space provided on the left. 1 = Most Important to ... 5.

Rank Here	I worked in the last organization prior to launching out on my own:	Most				Least	N/A
	a) an incubator period for the business I always intended to create.	1	2	3	4	5	0
	b) going up the corporate or organizational ladder.	1	2	3	4	5	0
	c) to gain expertise to seek a better position in another organization.	1	2	3	4	5	0
	d) it was the most desirable position at the time.	1	2	3	4	5	0
	e) I am a member of a dual career couple.	1	2	3	4	5	0
	f) other _____						

6.   The gender mix in the organization where I worked just prior to becoming an entrepreneur was: ____% females.

		Circle Whether Answer Given For	
On average, females had been working	____ (# years) and males ____ (# years).	Dept.	Org.
The management hierarchy was composed of	____ (%) females.	Dept.	Org.
The board of the company was filled with	____ (%) females.	Dept.	Org.
Top managerial (executive) positions had	____ (%) females.	Dept.	Org.
Middle level management positions had	____ (%) females.	Dept.	Org.
Supervisory management positions had	____ (%) females.	Dept.	Org.

7.   I would best define my role as an entrepreneur (small business owner) as _____

_____

Rate each item (a - g) on scales to right and then rank the top 5 items, 1 = Most important to ... 5.

Rank Here	I see my role as an entrepreneur (small business owner):	Most				Least	N/A
	a) as an extension of my family role.	1	2	3	4	5	0
	b) as a cooperative network of relationships (i.e., family, society, personal and business.	1	2	3	4	5	0
	c) as a coordinator of relationships.	1	2	3	4	5	0
	d) to make a profit.	1	2	3	4	5	0
	e) as creator of a business (initiator or innovator).	1	2	3	4	5	0
	f) separate from non-business family or personal relationships.	1	2	3	4	5	0
	g) other _____	1	2	3	4	5	0

III.   Circle the response which most closely resembles your feelings:

A.   Effect of My Previous Organizational Environment:

For #1, rate each item (a - g) on the scale: Most influence (1) to Least influence (5). Mark (0) if the effect does not apply. When you have completed the rating of each item (a - g), please return to the left and rank the five most important items; 1 = Most important to ... 5.

Rank Here	1. The most valuable things I took away from my previous work environment:	Influence Level					
		Most				Least	N/A
	a) technical skills	1	2	3	4	5	0
	b) marketing skills	1	2	3	4	5	0
	c) financial skills	1	2	3	4	5	0
	d) making connections or networks	1	2	3	4	5	0
	e) learning managerial or motivational techniques	1	2	3	4	5	0
	f) strengthening areas of expertise where I was weak	1	2	3	4	5	0
	g) Other _____						

For #2, first rate each item on the scale to the right. When you have completed the rating of each item (a - p), please return to the left and rank the five most important items; 1 = Most important to ... 5.

Rank Here	2. I would best describe my reasons for launching my own business:	Influence Level					
		Most				Least	N/A
	a) launching out on my own was the only way to advance myself	1	2	3	4	5	0
	b) left previous business because of bureaucratic environment	1	2	3	4	5	0
	c) left a family business to show I could do it on my own	1	2	3	4	5	0
	d) left a previous business because I experienced discrimination	1	2	3	4	5	0
	e) free of household responsibilities	1	2	3	4	5	0
	f) previous company had massive layoff due to structural change	1	2	3	4	5	0
	g) to make more money	1	2	3	4	5	0
	h) to create a work environment more consistent with my values	1	2	3	4	5	0
	i) I saw entrepreneurship as a method of overcoming barriers	1	2	3	4	5	0
	j) I left because I did not fit into the culture of my previous org.	1	2	3	4	5	0
	k) the lack of shared information deterred the completion of projects	1	2	3	4	5	0
	l) there was no urgency to complete projects	1	2	3	4	5	0
	m) there was little motivation to be productive	1	2	3	4	5	0
	n) quality standards were low	1	2	3	4	5	0
	o) management support was lacking	1	2	3	4	5	0
	p) I saw entrepreneurship as a method to balance family and work	1	2	3	4	5	0
	q) Other _____						

B.   Climate Characteristics in Last Organization:

After rating each item on the right according to how well it describes your previous organization's climate, rank order the items from 1 = Most to ... 5 in the space provided on the left.

Rank Here							N/A
		Most				Least	
	1. All employees were treated equally in the environment.	1	2	3	4	5	0
	2. Success depended on being a team player.	1	2	3	4	5	0
	3. Men got preferential treatment.	1	2	3	4	5	0
	4. Women got preferential treatment.	1	2	3	4	5	0
	5. Irrespective of sex, career advancement was political.	1	2	3	4	5	0
	6. Other _____						

After rating items 1 - 17 in C below on the scale to the right, please rank order the Most Important Items (1 = Most Important to ... 5).

C.   I left the organization to become an entrepreneur:

Rank Here		Most		Influence Level		Least	N/A
	1. to gain more respect from others for my skills and talents.	1	2	3	4	5	0
	2. opportunity to be on the ground floor of a new and exciting business venture in which I am in charge.	1	2	3	4	5	0
	3. to regain the feeling of excitement about my work.	1	2	3	4	5	0
	4. to build a team with the same goals.	1	2	3	4	5	0
	5. to make more money than I could working for someone else.	1	2	3	4	5	0
	6. to gain control over my time.	1	2	3	4	5	0
	7. to get better treatment.	1	2	3	4	5	0
	8. to get recognition.	1	2	3	4	5	0
	9. to get a better life.	1	2	3	4	5	0
	10. my childbearing (rearing) time clock was running out.	1	2	3	4	5	0
	11. others less qualified than me kept getting advanced more rapidly. They were primarily ____female; ____ male.	1	2	3	4	5	0
	12. to develop a more favorable organizational climate.	1	2	3	4	5	0
	13. to have the opportunity to determine if I could make it on my own.	1	2	3	4	5	0
	14. for self-esteem.	1	2	3	4	5	0
	15. to fulfill a life-long goal to become an entrepreneur.	1	2	3	4	5	0
	16. freedom from supervision and rules of bureaucratic organizations.	1	2	3	4	5	0
	17. Other _____						

PHASE II -- MY ROLE AS AN ENTREPRENEUR

All entrepreneurs want to become and remain successful. To establish the concept of success more fully, it is important to identify obstacles, barriers and challenges to building a successful firm. From your perspective, which of the following factors are important?

The rating on the scale is from (1) Most Important to (5) Least Important. 0 indicates no impact in building a successful entrepreneurship. When you have finished rating (a - p) on the right, please rank order the five most important in the spaces provided to the left (1 = Most Important to ... 5).

Rank Here	1. The ability to:	Level of Importance					
		Most				Least	N/A
	a) make and implement a decision.	1	2	3	4	5	0
	b) manage people with understanding and effectiveness.	1	2	3	4	5	0
	c) delegate as necessary for growth.	1	2	3	4	5	0
	d) determine the market niche.	1	2	3	4	5	0
	e) focus on the needs of the consumer.	1	2	3	4	5	0
	f) direct business as a profession.	1	2	3	4	5	0
	g) employ various marketing strategies and sales efforts.	1	2	3	4	5	0
	h) use financial savvy.	1	2	3	4	5	0
	i) obtain managerial experience in organizational settings.	1	2	3	4	5	0
	j) effectively use negotiation skills.	1	2	3	4	5	0
	k) acquire initial capitalization from outside sources.	1	2	3	4	5	0
	l) plan for future growth.	1	2	3	4	5	0
	m) use presentation skills effectively.	1	2	3	4	5	0
	n) supplement technical skills with non-technical skills.	1	2	3	4	5	0
	o) participate with other entrepreneurs in teams to gain expertise.	1	2	3	4	5	0
	p) Other _____						

2. Problems in being an entrepreneur:	Most				Least	N/A
a) life style changes	1	2	3	4	5	0
b) time management	1	2	3	4	5	0
c) not having enough family time	1	2	3	4	5	0
d) managing the stress of making decisions	1	2	3	4	5	0
e) Other _____						

3. I have experienced the following as an owner:	Most				Least	N/A
			Level of Importance			
a) sense of responsibility for the welfare of my employees	1	2	3	4	5	0
b) a feeling of isolation	1	2	3	4	5	0
c) unmet expectations	1	2	3	4	5	0
d) worry that I'm making the right decisions	1	2	3	4	5	0
e) conflicting new roles	1	2	3	4	5	0
f) a lack of personal freedom (work never ends)	1	2	3	4	5	0
g) appreciating the ethical context of business	1	2	3	4	5	0
h) Other _____						

4. I have experienced the impact of my support system (family, friends, etc.) in the following ways:	Most				Least	N/A
a) in providing emotional support	1	2	3	4	5	0
b) providing help in running the business when needed	1	2	3	4	5	0
c) in making business decisions	1	2	3	4	5	0
d) in providing financial support	1	2	3	4	5	0
e) in contributing expertise in operational functions (i.e., finance, marketing, human resource management)	1	2	3	4	5	0
f) Other _____						

5. The primary role support I get comes from [1]____spouse; [2]____mother; [3]____father; [4]____other family member; [5]____significant other; [6]____other_____.

6. I do [1]____ or do not [2]____ plan to become involved in a global economy. The following appear to be reasons or restrictions affecting my choice.

	Most				Least	N/A
a) U.S. and foreign government regulations	1	2	3	4	5	0
b) lack of financial and managerial resources	1	2	3	4	5	0
c) strong sales in U.S.	1	2	3	4	5	0
d) do not want to be dependent on exports	1	2	3	4	5	0
e) unable to find access	1	2	3	4	5	0
f) current weaker value of U.S. $	1	2	3	4	5	0
g) lack of information on how to become involved	1	2	3	4	5	0
h) Other _____						
The market I would most like to get involved in _____						

7. My business performance is best measured by _____
    _____
    _____

Rank the importance on the left after completing the ratings on the right.

Rank Here		Level of Importance					
		Most				Least	N/A
	a) profit.	1	2	3	4	5	0
	b) growth in size.	1	2	3	4	5	0
	c) employee satisfaction.	1	2	3	4	5	0
	d) social contributions.	1	2	3	4	5	0
	e) goal achievement.	1	2	3	4	5	0
	f) effectiveness.	1	2	3	4	5	0
	g) Other _____						

PHASE III -- PROCESSES FOR SUCCESS

Servicing the potential market requires skillful management of resources and well-timed change strategies. As an entrepreneur, please circle the number best representing, 1 = Most important to ... 5 with 0 indicating not applicable, how each item has affected your success.

1. Human resource function	Level of Importance					
	Most				Least	N/A
a) acquiring the right staff	1	2	3	4	5	0
b) managing the staff effectively	1	2	3	4	5	0
c) building and applying an appropriate appraisal system	1	2	3	4	5	0
d) compensating employees equitably	1	2	3	4	5	0
e) developing support systems within staffing function	1	2	3	4	5	0
f) training	1	2	3	4	5	0
g) developing staff	1	2	3	4	5	0

2. Technological innovativeness	Level of Importance					
	Most				Least	N/A
a) long-range planning for technological efficiency	1	2	3	4	5	0
b) updates to systems	1	2	3	4	5	0

3. Developing financial support systems	Most		Level of Importance		Least	N/A
a) planning and selling the business plan	1	2	3	4	5	0
b) access to information on financial availability	1	2	3	4	5	0
c) getting to know potential sources of funding	1	2	3	4	5	0
d) developing an effective package for generating funds	1	2	3	4	5	0

	Most		Level of Importance		Least	N/A
4. Planning and setting priorities	1	2	3	4	5	0

	Most		Level of Importance		Least	N/A
5. Managing change	1	2	3	4	5	0

	Most		Level of Importance		Least	N/A
6. Acquiring and projecting personal power	1	2	3	4	5	0

	Most		Level of Importance		Least	N/A
7. Developing interrelated networks	1	2	3	4	5	0

I would best define success as _____

_____

Rank Here	8. How I measure success: (After rating on the right, rank in order of importance (1 = Most important to ... 5).	Most		Level of Importance		Least	N/A
	a) profits are my hallmark of success	1	2	3	4	5	0
	b) self-fulfillment	1	2	3	4	5	0
	c) achievement of goals	1	2	3	4	5	0
	d) making a difference by helping others	1	2	3	4	5	0
	e) a balance between family and work	1	2	3	4	5	0
	f) growth and expansion of my business	1	2	3	4	5	0
	g) Other _____						

Management/Leadership Style Inventory

Survey Instructions

The following questionnaire takes about 25 minutes to complete. **If you complete the enclosed survey, we will send you personalized feedback about your leadership style.** When you have completed the survey, return it with the enclosed opscan sheet in the post-paid envelope.

Part I

Following are statements about one's beliefs and actions as a manager and a leader. Please respond to each statement by indicating the extent of your own personal agreement or disagreement. The answer form is the enclosed opscan sheet, with five alternative responses indicated for each statement:

>   (A) = Strongly Disagree
>   (B) = Disagree
>   (C) = Neither Agree Nor Disagree
>   (D) = Agree
>   (E) = Strongly Agree

Fill in the circle that represents your own level of agreement (or disagreement)–A, B, C, D, or E– on the opscan sheet. For example, the first statement is:

> My primary mission as a leader involves maintaining stability.

If you agree with this statement you would darken the circle under letter "D" on line 1 of the opscan sheet.

There are really no "right" or "wrong" answers, nor is there any implication intended that agreement or disagreement with any particular statement is "good" or "bad." Some questions ask about your attitude or behavior with employees. Even if you have no subordinates, please respond as you would think or behave if you had employees. Your responses should be based solely on your own personal views, the way you see yourself as a leader and a manager and your own philosophy and action-orientation.

Thank you for your input.

(A) = Strongly Disagree
(B) = Disagree
(C) = Neither Agree Nor Disagree
(D) = Agree
(E) = Strongly Agree

1.	My primary mission as a leader involves maintaining stability.
2.	I am concerned that those who follow my leadership are rewarded equitably for their efforts.
3.	I believe that leadership is a process of changing the conditions of people's lives.
4.	As a leader I enjoy rewarding followers for jobs well done.
5.	Regarding my work as a leader, I have a strong sense of mission.
6.	My requests of followers are limited to what is required according to their expectations.
7.	As a leader I approach problems by examining them in novel and speculative ways.
8.	My destiny as a leader is essentially within my control.
9.	My philosophy as a leader is to be constantly involved in the challenges, concerns, and problems of administering the organization.
10.	As a leader my relations with followers are based on a fair exchange of efforts for outcomes, an equitable arrangement.
11.	As a leader my role is to facilitate activities and events so that the organization operates smoothly.
12.	As a leader a primary task I have is to ensure clarity of responsibilities and roles for my subordinates.
13.	I believe that leadership is a process of exchange between leader and follower.
14.	As a leader I spend considerable energy in arousing hopes, expectations, and aspirations in followers.
15.	As a leader I must represent to followers a set of ethics and a morality of the highest order.
16.	To me leadership should be practical.
17.	When I give followers assignments, I am able to generate enthusiasm.
18.	As a leader I must think in the short range, in terms of what is realistic.
19.	As a leader I enjoy stimulating followers to want to do more.
20.	I typically ask more of followers than they had expected.
21.	As a leader I approach problems by acquiring information about prior, related situations and I proceed accordingly.
22.	The most important aspect of my role as a leader is to provide job and task clarity for followers.
23.	My power to influence others as a leader comes primarily from my status and position.
24.	My philosophy as a leader is to get involved in operational problems and issues only when explicit problems arise that make this necessary.
25.	As a leader my relations with followers are based on deep bonds of understanding between us.
26.	I view unscheduled tasks and encounters as an opportunity to keep key relationships in good repair inside and outside the organization.

(A) = Strongly Disagree
(B) = Disagree
(C) = Neither Agree Nor Disagree
(D) = Agree
(E) = Strongly Agree

27.	It is important that I retain the power to make decisions in my business.
28.	I am a role model in the development of my employees.
29.	Employees are responsible for their own professional development.
30.	I welcome feedback on all facets of the business operation.
31.	Fair solutions are more important than addressing individual needs.
32.	I make a habit of recognizing employees' achievements and successes publicly in my business.
33.	I view my position in the company to be at the center of operations as a facilitator rather than at the top as an authority.
34.	By sharing information, I encourage fuller participation in decisions among employees.
35.	I empathize with the problems of my employees.
36.	As head of my company, I exercise my control over others in assigning their work.
37.	In my organization, rules are made with the input of those who will be affected by them.
38.	Dividing up a task into separate activities and assigning the work to subordinates is the most efficient way to get the job done.
39.	Getting my employees excited about their work is an important part of my job.
40.	I see my organization as part of a larger environment which includes society at large.
41.	I have little control over my employees' level of motivation and effort in their work.
42.	I seek feedback from the widest span of employees and contacts in all decision making.
43.	In my business I make a positive personal difference in the lives of my employees.
44.	Creating and communicating a vision of my company's direction to others is a priority for me in my business.
45.	I see my work as separate and distinct from my private non-work life.
46.	An important part of my job is assigning work to, developing, appraising, and assisting subordinates with work problems.

Part II Background Questions

47.	Did downsizing or restructuring in your prior organization influence your decision to start a business of your own?	
	(A)	Yes
	(B)	No
48.	Prior to leaving your former organization, had you started a business in your spare time?	
	(A)	Yes
	(B)	No
49.	Was this venture in the same field as your current business?	
	(A)	Yes
	(B)	No
	(C)	Not applicable
50.	Your current business status:	
	(A)	I am still in the same business I was in at the time of the entrepreneurial focus group interviews. My business is _____.
	(B)	I have started a new business. This business is _____.
	(C)	I have joined another company.
	(D)	I am not currently working.
	(E)	Other (please describe) _____.
51.	How much do you expect your business to be affected by change or turbulence in your industry as a whole over the next five years?	
	(A)	Very much
	(B)	Moderately
	(C)	Only slightly
	(D)	Not affected at all
	(E)	N/A - no longer in business
52.	Over the next five years do you expect your number of employees to:	
	(A)	Decrease
	(B)	Not change
	(C)	Gradually increase
	(D)	Substantially increase
	(E)	N/A - no longer in business

If you answered "E" to Question 52, please skip questions 53 and 54, go on to Part III.

53.	How did your gross sales for 1993 compare with 1992?	
	(A)	Higher than 1992
	(B)	Lower
	(C)	Same
54.	If higher or lower, by approximately what percentage?	
	(A)	Less than 10%
	(B)	11-35%
	(C)	36-50%
	(D)	51-100%
	(E)	More than 100%

Part III

People have different views about what kinds of experience help most in learning to manage a business. Please indicate how valuable you feel each of the following has been in giving you the skills to manage your current business by darkening the circles for either A, B, C, D, or E on the opscan sheet using the scale below. If you have not had the experience described, please skip the item.

   A = extremely useful
   B = moderately useful
   C = somewhat useful
   D = slightly useful
   E = not useful at all

How useful were these aspects of your experience (as owner or employee) in previous firm(s):

55.	Being in the same industry
56.	Facing major setback(s)
57.	Facing major success(es)
58.	Supervising managers
59.	Supervising workers
60.	Owning or managing the firm
61.	Forming strategic alliances
62.	Similar product or service
63.	Having similar customers
64.	Having similar suppliers
65.	Having similar competitors
66.	Using similar technology
67.	Being in a firm of similar size
68.	Starting a previous firm
69.	Other (please specify) _____
70.	Please select which of the following sentences best describes your prior organizational experiences before starting your business. (A) I had intended to be an entrepreneur and used the organization as a training ground to gain experience. (B) I had intended to work in a large corporation as a career. (C) Other (please explain) _____

Please go on to next page →

Part IV

Please answer the following questions in the space provided below.

For the managerial functions defined below, consider yourself when making your very best effort. Estimate your confidence in performing each activity compared to your peers. Give your estimation of confidence a numerical rating using the scale provided and place your score for each item in the left hand column of the questionnaire.

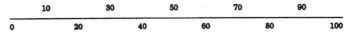

10	30	50	70	90
0	20	40	60	80	100

Now, for the six different managerial functions below consider your relative strengths (i.e., which ones are you better or best at?). Allocate 100 points between these dimensions, giving the highest number of points to the dimension you are best at and so on. (Remember that if you give 40 points to one dimension you are left with a total of 60 to allocate, as you choose, among the other dimensions. Place your score in the right-hand column.

Confidence Level		Managerial Function	Relative Strength
	71.	Assigning work to, developing, appraising, and assisting subordinates with work problems.	
	72.	Working with others (from inside and out) to integrate the work activities of the organization by smoothing, persuading, and negotiating.	
	73.	Gathering, processing, and supplying information from within and without the organization.	
	74.	Analyzing and evaluating laws, problems, programs, work procedures, processes, and reports.	
	75.	Changing the organization structure, tasks, procedures, or the behavior of people.	
	76.	Developing mechanisms to ensure adequate progress toward goals, maintaining appropriate records, and inspecting ongoing activities.	
		TOTAL	**100**

Please rate your satisfaction with your work as an entrepreneur over the past two months:	Very dissatisfied							Very satisfied	
	1	2	3	4	5	6	7	8	9
77. Overall;									
78. In comparison with the satisfaction of other women your age;									
79. In terms of the percentage of time you feel satisfied in your business?									

Thank you for your time and input!

Appendix 3

Acknowledgment and Appreciation

We especially appreciate the assistance of the following centers and individuals.

Resource Conference Centers and Facilitators

Alumnae Resources (AR) of San Francisco is a unique Bay Area career development organization providing career management assistance in a professional and supportive environment. AR offers workshops, counseling, and a comprehensive career library, as well as programs focused on the needs of college-educated women and the diverse workforce, to individuals seeking to begin, advance, or change their careers. Facilitators: Alice Cochran and Linda deMello.

American Women's Economic Development Corporation (AWED), New York, New York, is an association founded in 1976 to train and counsel women who want to grow their own businesses. AWED has served more than 100,000 women entrepreneurs through courses, conferences, seminars, and one-on-one counseling provided by a faculty of expert volunteers. Director, Roseanne Antonucci.

Melinda Duncan facilitated the Lexington focus sessions. She has her own real estate practice in Kentucky and sold more than 80 homes in 1996. Melinda speaks in her community to women starting new businesses. She encourages them to have the courage to begin and advises them on their business plans. Melinda was a cofounder of the National Association of Women Business Owners in Lexington.

Patricia Ann (Patty) Habeeb facilitated focus sessions in New Orleans. Patty is president and owner of Conventions à la Carte, Inc., in New Orleans. She was twice named as the "Woman of the Year" by the New Orleans Business and

Professional Women's Club of New Orleans, served as the Elected Louisiana Delegate to The White House Conference on Small Business in 1986, and in 1995 was named as one of 10 "Women's Voices of Louisiana" and was listed among Who's Who in Leading American Executives and among Global Business leaders. She presently serves as the secretary of the Japan Society of New Orleans.

The National Association of Women Business Owners (NAWBO) propels women entrepreneurs into economic, social, and political spheres of power worldwide. NAWBO offers assistance in securing access to financial opportunities; educational programs, seminars, and leadership training; opportunities to meet and exchange ideas and establish business ventures; chapter programs, regional meetings and national conferences; discounts on products and services; an international network of business contacts; visibility and clout in political arenas; and procurement opportunities. Regional and national offices assisted in our research. We offer a special tribute to the Chicago, Lexington, and Philadelphia chapters.

San Francisco Renaissance Entrepreneurship Center, which since 1985 has offered the training and support that aspiring entrepreneurs need to start and successfully grow their small businesses. Through its intensive business planning course, the center seeks to reduce the mortality rate of small businesses, specifically targeting minority and women entrepreneurs. Claudia Vieke, Executive director, envisions the challenge of the center as the creation of public and private sector partnerships to increase small business ownership, create new jobs and revenues, and thereby strengthen the urban community.

Winston-Salem Business and Technology Center offers cost-effective space for small to midsized businesses. Services available include front-desk receptionist, postage, and fax and copy machines. Tenants are billed monthly based on usage of equipment.

Women Entrepreneurs, Inc., of Cincinnati, Ohio, seeks to promote self-employment as a viable alternative to achieving financial self-sufficiency through training, technical assistance, one-on-one counseling, networking, personal development, and assistance with access to financing. It is particularly designed to address barriers to the low-income community and women. Within this center, special appreciation goes to facilitators Peg Moertl and Sandy Evers.

The Women's Business Development Center (WBDC) is a not-for-profit organization of Chicago. It is a full-service business resource that helps entrepreneurs start and expand their businesses. The WBDC provides entrepreneurial services including management, financial, and marketing assistance; entrepreneurial training; vendor development; WBE certification; subsidized employment programs; major conferences; and advocacy. The codirectors, S. Carol Dougal and Hedy M. Ratner, were especially helpful.

Conference Rooms Facilities at
Businesses and Universities

Accent Chicago, Inc., Karen Kline, president
BECCA et al, Philadelphia
Boston University
Patty M. Breeze
The Citadel, Department of Business Administration
DePaul University, Department of Management
EBC Conference Center, Atlanta Financial Center (furnished by Tom Dye, president,
        and arranged by Bernie Mercer, Atlanta)
Just Brakes Corporation, Dallas, Deborah Hueppeler
Massachusetts Mutual Life Insurance Company, Lexington, Kentucky
MICHAUL'S Live Cajun Music Restaurant, Michele Babineaux, owner
Nurses Today, Inc., Dallas, Anita Porco, president
Pizel & Associates Commercial Real Estate, Pam Pizel, owner
Public Library, Orlando, Florida
University of New Orleans School of Business, Professor Michael Cusack and Alice
        Kennedy at the Small Business Development Center, School of Management
Wake Forest University
Winston-Salem Business and Technology Center, North Carolina

Facilitators in
Identifying Business Owners

Andrea Coates, president, New England Women Business Owners
Linda De Cuir, Data Collection Research Company and Women Entrepreneurs for
        Economic Development (WEED), New Orleans
Jill Martin Fugaro, San Francisco
Alice Kennedy, Small Business Development Center, University of New Orleans
Bernie Mercer, president, Bernie Mercer & Company, Atlanta
Mary Swinson, Swinson's Communications, Dallas

Other Information Providers

Chambers of commerce (in all states where interviews conducted)
Charleston Trident Chamber of Commerce, Ginger Norvell
Council for Entrepreneurial Development, North Carolina, Monica Doss,
        administrative director
Enterprise Development, Governor's Office, South Carolina

Female and Minority Business Incubator, Cincinnati, Ohio, Cassandra Middleton
Georgia Department of Industry and Trade (Atlanta)
Louisiana Small Business Development Center, Professor Ronald Schroeder,
    Loyola University, New Orleans
Piedmont Entrepreneurs Network
Mayor Joe Riley's Office, City of Charleston
Society of Association of Executives, South Carolina
South Carolina Chamber of Commerce
State Development Board, South Carolina
Teresa Taylor, *Post and Courier,* Charleston, South Carolina
Senator Strom Thurmond's and Fritz Holling's offices, Phil Black, business assistant
    official
United States Small Business Administration (regional and national offices)
University of Cincinnati Small Business Development Center, Nancy Rogers
Women's Chamber of Commerce, Atlanta

Biographical Sketches Furnished by
Cited Entrepreneurs in Focus Sessions

Lisa B. Adkinson, partner in the Strategic Eight Consulting Group of Greater Cincinnati, delivers the Planning Process to small businesses with the Cincinnati and Columbus Chambers of Commerce. She is the owner and a former CEO of Inner Applications, a total workplace design firm. Lisa served as president and board chair of Women Entrepreneurs, Inc. (WEI), received the Entrepreneur of the Year award in 1992, served on Ohio's Small Business and Entrepreneurship Council in 1994, and was selected as one of the area's top 40 business leaders under 40.

Ann Shelton Angel is president of Technologies Training of the Triad, Inc. (TTT), Winston-Salem, North Carolina, a computer training and consulting company. TTT serves large companies including Wachovia Bank and Thomasville Furniture as well as more than 250 small businesses in the Triad. Ann served as a delegate to the 1995 White House Conference on Small Business in Washington, D.C.

Lorena M. Blonsky, president and owner of LMB, an executive/professional search firm based in Chicago, specializes in information systems recruitment. Lorena has placed professionals in a variety of systems roles. For the past 12 years, she has been a member of the University of Chicago Women's Business Group, serving on the board of directors from 1987 to 1991 and as president in 1990.

Patty M. Breeze has an insurance practice, Mass Mutual, The Kentucky-West Virginia Agency, in Lexington. She works with professionals and business owners in the areas of life, health, and disability insurance; annuities; and mutual funds. She is a charter member and past president of the Lexington chapter of the National Association of Women Business Owners.

Susan O'Connor Brown of The Avalon Consulting Group, Rosemont, Pennsylvania, spent 18 years in the financial services arena as a senior executive managing growth and change. She formed her own consulting firm in 1991 and consults to organizations and executives primarily in the areas of strategic planning, change management, and leadership development.

Rebecca Carney is owner of BECCA et al, a Philadelphia-based company. She is an experienced professional in the fields of sales, marketing, and management. After more than 25 years in the corporate world, in 1989 she started BECCA et al, which provides gifts, promotional products, premiums, and incentives to local and multinational companies. Since 1995, BECCA et al has been in the industry's Multi-Million Dollar Roundtable.

Alice Collier Cochran, The Cochran Group, San Rafael, California, is a planning process and meeting facilitator who helps organizations manage change successfully through collaborative approaches. She is working on a book to "feminize" business meetings, *Roberta's Rules of Order*.

Sherie Conrad, owner of Conrad Consulting, New Orleans, is a human resource and small business management expert specializing in contingency and retained searches, temporary and contract technical staffing, training, customized seminar development, business and marketing planning, evaluation/assessment, needs forecasting, and job analyses. Her corporate background includes Pembo & Associates and Common Sense Consulting.

Ethel Cook, owner of Corporate Improvement Group, Bedford, Massachusetts, is a trainer and consultant on increasing personal productivity in the workplace. Founder of Do It! Day, a day to fight procrastination, she is frequently quoted in business, trade, and consumer publications and has been interviewed on radio and television throughout the United States, Canada, Australia, and the United Kingdom.

Eileen Duignan-Woods, P.E. of E.D.W. Associates, Inc., a Chicago and North Carolina Engineers & Construction Consultants based firm, has successfully owned and operated design and construction services. A licensed professional engineer in five states, she received her B.S. in mechanical and aerospace engineering from the Illinois Institute of Technology. She has published articles and held seminars on mechanical systems in building and construction management.

Evelyn Eskin is president of Health Power Associates, Inc., Philadelphia. Founded in 1987, the firm provides practice management, educational, and planning services to physicians, hospitals, academic health centers, and other health care organizations with commitments to physician practice success. She is a frequent speaker and writer for pharmaceutical companies, health care systems, universities, medical and other professional societies, and health care journals.

Patt Gallagher, owner of Evergreen Supply Company in Chicago, started selling electrical supplies out of the basement of her home in 1986. Pat did everything. Her customers knew her in a suit and a hard hat. Gallagher now has a sales volume of $7 million annually, employs close to 20 people, and recently started a second company that recycles fluorescent bulbs and ballasts.

Wendy Norden Ginn is CEO of Convert!, Inc., a San Francisco firm nationally recognized for superior quality data conversion services for 5,000 different computer and software formats. Prior to founding Convert! in 1987, she spent 12 years in technical and marketing management at Xerox Corporation. In 1990, she won the San Francisco Chamber of Commerce Business Plan Competition.

Janet Goldman, owner of Fragments, New York, New York, manufactures a private label of jewelry for Banana Republic, Ann Taylor, and other outlets and has a retail store in Soho, New York. Her mission as owner is that of discovering new talent and bringing it to a high-end market, such as Saks Fifth Avenue and Neiman Marcus. In 1996, she graduated from the O.P.M. program at Harvard University.

Diane C. Hanson has been president of her own consulting firm, Creative Resource Development, West Chester, Pennsylvania, for more than 10 years. The firm specializes in training, team development, organizational change, and creating innovation in organizations. Prior to being in her own business, she was a pioneering female in pharmaceutical sales, reaching the level of district manager by 1980.

Vickie L. Henry, chairman and CEO of Feedback Plus, Inc., known as "America's Mystery Shopper," conducts market research with 100,000 field representatives on behavioral patterns that affect service quality, customer satisfaction, retention, and improved sales. Author of the book *Feedback on Sales*, she has been vice president of the North Dallas Chamber of Commerce, president of Executive Women of Dallas, and director of the National Association of Women Business Owners. She was named Small Business Entrepreneur of the Year in 1994.

Joan M. Holliday is one of four partners of Women in Process Consulting, Chadds Ford, Pennsylvania, founded in 1988. Women in Process is a developmental organization dedicated to helping systems become more effective through the use of a holistic approach. The organization works to improve diversity, enable strategic processes, and encourage authentic leadership toward a fuller expression of potential for the individual and the system.

Lisa Jacobson founded Stanford Coaching, Inc., a one-on-one private SAT preparation firm based in Manhattan. She is a member of the executive committee of the American Women's Economic Development Corporation and has appeared on *The Today Show*, *NBC Nightly News*, and CNBC and in *The Wall Street Journal*, the *New York Times*, and *Inc.*

Karen Kline is president of Accent Chicago, Inc., which she launched in 1979. It has grown to five stores and includes an advertising specialty distributorship, Accent Promotions, and a wholesale distributorship, Sunburst Souvenirs. She is active on several boards, including that of the Lutheran School of Theology at Chicago. She received the Chicago Woman Business Owner of the Year award in 1992 and served as governor of Rotary International District #6440 in 1996-1997.

Susie Marshall is owner of CompuTactics, Inc., a Dallas firm that designs and develops computerized management information systems, with particular emphasis on Internet Web sites. Her new company, Technology Interchange Resources, is establishing an electronic commerce resource center in Dallas to teach business-people how to do business electronically and assist them in conducting electronic commerce.

Ruth Ann Menutis is president and Owner of *The Grove,* Natural Energy Unlimited, Inc., a natural snack retail and wholesale specialty fruit and nut business with more than $15 million in volume, operating in 18 major airports in the United States. She has built three previous successful companies and twice served as Louisiana chairperson to the National White House Conference on Small Business. She served as president of the French Market Corporation for 8 years and is the recipient of the Chamber of Commerce Person of the Year award. She is the mother of three children.

Laurie Moore-Moore is a partner in Real Trends, a Dallas-based communications and publishing company serving the residential real estate industry. In addition to producing a monthly subscription newsletter, the firm publishes industry research, runs CEO brainstorming groups, and hosts weekly television shows broadcast across North America. Laurie speaks to about 100 audiences annually.

Elizabeth Morris is a consulting economist specializing in economic development issues. She is president and founder of Insight Research Corporation, which provides economic, employment, tax impact, and cost/benefit analyses for public and private sector clients. Insight now performs approximately 300 such analyses each year and has contributed to location decisions affecting the workplace of more than 1.3 million workers.

Terri Parker-Halpin, principal in International ISO Group, Cincinnati, Ohio, is the author of more than 100 technical books and numerous technical articles. She has spoken nationally on technical writing and documentation management. She is cofounder of the Cincinnati chapter of the National ISO 9000 User Support Group. To date, all of her clients have achieved registration on their first attempt.

Susan L. Pickman is president of The Pickman Group, Inc., Orlando, Florida. She is a management consultant and licensed private investigator in Orlando, Florida. For the last 11 years, she owned Tuscawalla Travel. In 1994, she ran for the Florida legislature.

Joanne Pratt, president of Joanne H. Pratt Associates, holds degrees from Oberlin and Harvard University. She operates a consulting firm specializing in the virtual office, including telecommuting, home-based businesses, and other new work patterns. She is a recognized futurist and authority on home-based work, including business impacts, transportation implications, family issues, and impacts on corporate work patterns. She is the author of *Tele-commuting—Checking Into It* and *Myths & Realities of Working at Home*.

Anne Sadovsky, CEO of Anne Sadovsky & Company, a Dallas-based marketing consulting and seminar firm, provides counseling, training, and speeches to a variety of industries. *Mirabella* has listed her as one of the 1,000 women of the 1990s. Her books *101 Thoughts to Make You Think* and *101 Thoughts for Becoming the Real You* can be found in bookstores nationally.

Linda Sahagian founded Sahagian & Associates, Inc., in 1971, in Oak Park, Illinois. The firm manufactures specialty snack foods and confections under its own brand name and private labels. Her trademark packaging and designs, *A Yard Of* and *A Foot Of,* are sold throughout the United States and overseas.

Carol A. Scarano established Helping Hands Network, Inc., New York, New York, in 1990. The firm conducts assessment and placement of job candidates and consults with small and start-up companies to establish administrative and accounting support departments.

Kris Schaeffer, founder of Kris Schaeffer & Associates, San Francisco, has had 24 years of professionally challenging responsibilities. She has built entire training departments from scratch and has developed a long list of "first-evers" including sales training, product knowledge training, plant supervisor training, and team building. For 14 years, her company has provided comprehensive human resource programs for a wide range of industries.

Dianne Semingson, owner of DLS International, Inc., and its affiliate New Source Management, in Philadelphia, provides business development, marketing, community relations, and corporate philanthropy consulting services to businesses and foundations including Bell Atlantic, The Barnes Foundation, and The William Penn Foundation. Prior to founding DLS International, she served as a member of the mayor of Philadelphia's cabinet and as chamber of commerce regional director for the Mid-Atlantic states.

Honi Stempler of Chamblee, Georgia, has 18 years of experience in layout, design, production, copy editing, proofreading, and project management. Her first company was voted one of Atlanta's top five in the prepress field. She still contributes these skills but devotes the majority of her time to *Simple Solutions to Better Health* with natural body balancing and immune system strengthening foods.

Mary Louis Stott of Bioplans, Inc., Winston-Salem, North Carolina, is a chartered financial consultant (ChFC) who began her career in insurance sales in 1982. She and her husband own Bioplans, which assists small businesses and individuals in putting together their life, medical, and disability insurance packages.

Julie Coulter Thomas of Thomas & Thomas Architects, Ltd., Evanston, Illinois, is a licensed architect and interior designer whose work has been featured in *Art by Architects*. Winner of the Charlotte Danstrom Woman of Achievement National and Regional Award in 1993, she has served as a role model for the annual Futures Unlimited Conference, which encourages young women to pursue careers in math and science. She received second place in the Burnham Prize Competition in 1985 and first place in the "Late Entries to the Sears Tower."

Janee Tucker, president and CEO, Tucker & Associates (TAI), and vice president of Integrated Logistical Support, Inc. (ILSI), New Orleans, is a specialist in marketing, planning, and financial systems. She has received numerous awards for success as a business owner and service to the community, including the New Orleans Woman Business Owner of the Year, Best of Black Business Award, National Council of Negro Women/Quaker Oats as Community Leader, and Employer of the Year by the Business and Professional Women's organization. She is included in 1996/97 Strathmore's *Who's Who Registry of Business Leaders*.

Susan Weiner of West Newton, Massachusetts, is editor of the leading weekly trade publication on the mutual fund business. She formerly designed and led customized training programs for Americans on "How to Do Business with the Japanese." She has also managed Japanese business development and marketing communications for an investment management firm.

Catherine White, FinArc LLC, Lexington, Massachusetts, manages stock, bond, and mutual fund portfolios for individuals and institutions on a fee-only basis. The firm offers social screening of investments and solutions to clients' financial problems.

Dale Whitmer, a wife, mother, artist, writer, and entrepreneur, is the executive director of The Colin A. Ross Institute for Psychological Trauma in Dallas, Texas.

Gale P. Wise, B.C.S.W., Center for Change, Inc., is a clinical social worker in New Orleans with 15 years of experience in the specialty areas of child abuse, sexual abuse, and domestic violence. She received her M.S.W. from Atlanta University.

Pauline Yeats is a designer of "home couture" and interiors. Her collection of furniture and fabrics is sold at the Pauline Yeats' Interior Design Shop in New York and through architects and designers nationwide and internationally.

Other Participants Who Elected to Be Acknowledged by Name

Michele Babineaux, proprietor, MICHAUL'S on St. Charles, New Orleans, Louisiana

Janet Bensu, BENSU, Inc., San Francisco, California

Marie M. Clesi, State Farm Insurance Agency, Kenner, Louisiana

Andrea Coates, ChiroCare Plus, Brookline, Massachusetts

Lillian Coury, Pineapple Printing, Inc., New York, New York

Darlene Drake, president, Fitness Pro Health & Exercise Equipment, Lexington, Kentucky

Patricia A. Droppelman, CPN, president, Pediatric Nursing Care, Inc., Cincinnati, Ohio

Barbara Ullman Gerla, attorney-at-law, Cincinnati, Ohio

Jo Anne Gibbons, president, The Gibbons Group, Cincinnati, Ohio

L. Elaine Green, president, Video Features, Inc., Cincinnati, Ohio

Jackie Griffith, general manager, Hunter Management Group, Inc., Lexington, Kentucky

Gloriann Harris, CPA, Northbrook, Illinois

Carol Hecht, CLA, president, BarriCorp, Inc., Dallas, Texas

Deborah Hueppeler, financial consultant, Dallas, Texas

Hattie Hill, CEO, Hattie Hill Enterprises, Dallas, Texas

Linda Horn, L.R. Horn Capital Concepts, Inc., Harrison, Ohio

Fran (Raglin) Johnson, Elite Travel Services, Cincinnati, Ohio

Roberta Gose Kelley, Jim Kelley Associates, Atlanta, Georgia

Suzan B. Kotler, Certified Financial Planner, Money Concepts, Cincinnati, Ohio

Saralyn Levine, Delectable Dining, Chamblee, Georgia

Catherine L. Marrs, Liaison, Inc., Dallas, Texas

Janet McCann, interior designer, Wilmette, Illinois

Renee Peyton, Atlanta, Georgia

Pamela (Pam) Pizel, Pizel & Associates Commercial Real Estate, Dallas, Texas
Anita L. Porco, president, Nurses Today, Inc., Dallas, Texas
Debra Rust, president, Alpha Communications Technologies, Inc., Warrenville, Illinois
Patricia S. Sayre, Fiber-Seal, Cincinnati, Ohio
Shirley F. Schwaller, owner, Horizon Communications Group, Dallas, Texas
Marilyn O. Sifford, Marilyn Sifford Organizational Change, Philadelphia,
    Pennsylvania
Nancy Smerz, president, Air Comfort Corporation, Broadview, Illinois
Deborah Stange, president, West Fuels, Inc., Westchester, Illinois
Jeanne P. Tighe, Blue Grass Advertising Specialties, Lexington, Kentucky
Lauren Verdich, president, Lauren's Catering, Inc., Chicago, Illinois
Gale P. Wise, M.S.W., B.C.S.W., Center for Change, Inc., Counseling &
    Psychotherapy Associates, New Orleans, Louisiana

References

Adler, N. J. (1993). Competitive frontiers: Women managers in the triad. *International Studies of Management & Organization, 23*(2), 3-23.

Aldrich, H. (1989). Networking among women entrepreneurs. In O. Hagan, C. Rivchun, & D. Sexton (Eds.), *Handbook of organizational behavior* (pp. 190-222). Englewood Cliffs, NJ: Prentice Hall.

Aldrich, H., Birley, S., Dubini, P., Greve, A., Johannisson, B., Reese, P. R., & Sakano, T. (1991, April). *The generic entrepreneur? Insights from a multinational research project.* Summary in N. C. Churchill, W. D. Bygrave, J. G. Covin, D. L. Sexton, D. P. Slevin, K. H. Vesper, & W. E. Wetzel, Jr. (Eds.), *Frontiers of entrepreneurship research* (pp. 593-594). Babson Park, MA: Center for Entrepreneurial Studies, Babson College.

Aldrich, H., Rosen, B., & Woodward, W. (1986). Social behavior and entrepreneurial networks, summary. In W. D. Bygrave, S. Birley, N. C. Churchill, E. Gatewood, F. Hoy, R. H. Keeley, & W. E. Wetzel, Jr. (Eds.), *Frontiers of entrepreneurship research* (pp. 239-240). Wellesley, MA: Center for Entrepreneurial Studies, Babson College.

Aldrich, H., Rosen, B., & Woodward, W. (1987). The impact of social networks on business foundings and profit: A longitudinal study. In W. D. Bygrave, S. Birley, N. C. Churchill, E. Gatewood, F. Hoy, R. H. Keeley, & W. E. Wetzel, Jr. (Eds.), *Frontiers of entrepreneurship research* (pp. 154-168). Wellesley, MA: Center for Entrepreneurial Studies, Babson College.

Alpander, G., Carter, K., & Forsgren, R. (1990). Managerial issues and problem-solving in the formative years. *Journal of Small Business Management, 28*(2), 9-19.

Ando, F. (1990). Women in Business. In S. E. Rix (Ed.), *The American woman 1990-1991* (pp. 222-230). New York: W. W. Norton & Company.

Andre, R. (1995). Diversity in executive networks: A national study of women's representation in private sector economic development. *Journal of Managerial Issues, 7*(3), 306-322.

Antal, A. B. (1992). Trapped in the ice. *International Management, 47*(3), 42, 45.

Anthes, G. H. (1995, April 3). Small firms get low-cost on-line access. *Computerworld,* p. 28.

Appelbaum, S., & Shapiro, B. (1993). Why can't men lead like women? *Leadership & Organization Development Journal, 14*(7), 28-34.

Astin, H. (1984). The meaning of work in women's lives: A sociopsychological model of career choice and work behavior. *Counseling Psychologist, 12,* 117-126.

Barrett, M., & Christie, M. (1994). *Survey of selected business owners.* School of Management, Human Resources & Industrial Relations, Queensland University of Technology, Brisbane, Australia.

Bart, B. (1983, November). Educational interests of small business. *Journal of Business Education,* pp. 82-85.

Bass, B. (1985). *Leadership and performance beyond expectations.* New York: Free Press.

Bass, B. (1990). From transactional to transformational leadership: Learning to share the vision. *Organizational Dynamics, 18,* 19-31.

Bass, B., Avolio, B. J., & Atwater, L. E. (1996). The transformational and transactional leadership of men and women. *Applied Psychology: An International Review, 45,* 5-34.

Baucus, D. A., & Human, S. E. (1994). Second-career entrepreneurs: A multiple case study analysis of entrepreneurial processes and antecedent variables. *Entrepreneurship Theory and Practice, 19*(2), 41-71.

Baye, T. M. (1995, Spring). Relationship marketing: A six-step guide for the business start-up. *Small Business Forum,* pp. 26-41.

Beggs, J. M., Doolittle, D., & Garsombke, D. (1994, August). *Diversity in entrepreneurship: Integrating issues of sex, race, and class.* Paper (abstract) presented at the annual meeting of The Academy of Management Conference, Dallas, TX.

Belcourt, M. (1991). From the frying pan into the fire: Exploring entrepreneurship as a solution to the glass ceiling. *Journal of Small Business and Entrepreneurship, 8*(3), 49-55.

Belenky, M., Clinchy, B., Goldberger, N., & Tarule, J. (1986). *Women's ways of knowing: The development of self, voice, and mind.* New York: Basic Books.

Beutell, N., & Brenner, O. C. (1986). Sex differences in work values. *Journal of Vocational Behavior, 28,* 29-41.

Bigoness, W. (1988). Sex differences in job attribute preferences. *Journal of Organizational Behavior, 9,* 139-147.

Bilimoria, D., & Piderit, S. K. (1994). Board committee membership: Effects of sex-based bias. *Academy of Management Journal, 37*(6), 1453-1477.

Bird, B. J. (1988). Implementing entrepreneurial ideas: The case for intention. *Academy of Management Review, 13,* 442-453.

Bird, B. J. (1992). The operation of intentions in time: The emergence of the new venture. *Entrepreneurship Theory and Practice, 17*(1), 11-20.

Bird, B. J., & Jelinek, M. (1988). The operation of entrepreneurial intentions. *Entrepreneurship Theory and Practice, 13*(2), 21-29.

Birley, S. (1985). The role of networks in the entrepreneurial process. *Journal of Business Venturing, 1,* 107-117.

Birley, S. (1989). Female entrepreneurs: Are they really any different? *Journal of Small Business Management, 27*(1), 32-37.

Birley, S. J., Cromie, S., & Myers, A. (1991). Entrepreneurial networks: Their emergence in Ireland and overseas. *International Small Business Journal, 10*(1).

Birley, S., & Westhead, P. (1993). A taxonomy of business start-up reasons and their impact on firm growth and size. *Journal of Business Venturing, 9,* 7-31.

Blum, T. C., Fields, D. L., & Goodman, J. S. (1994). Organization-level determinants of women in management. *Academy of Management Journal, 37*(2), 241-268.

Boissevain, J. (1974). *Friends of friends, networks, manipulators and coalitions.* Oxford, UK: Basil Blackwell.

Bowen, D. D., & Hisrich, R. D. (1986). The female entrepreneur: A career development perspective. *Academy of Management Review, 11*(2), 393-407.

Bowers, B. (1994, January 10). Work-at-home deals help create new entrepreneurs: Distance can strain employee-boss relationships, spur independence. *Wall Street Journal* (Eastern Edition), p. B2.

Brass, D. J. (1985). Men's and women's networks: A study of interaction patterns and influence in an organization. *Academy of Management Journal, 28*, 327-343.

Brass, D. J. (1992). Power in organizations: A social network perspective. In G. Moore & J. Whitt (Eds.), *Research in politics and society* (pp. 295-323). Greenwich, CT: JAI Press.

Brenner, O., & Tomkiewicz, J. (1979). Job orientation of males and females: Are sex differences declining? *Personnel Psychology, 32*, 741-749.

Brenner, O., Tomkiewicz, J., & Schein, V. (1989). The relationship between sex role stereotypes and requisite management characteristics revisited. *Academy of Management Journal, 32*, 662-669.

Brockhaus, R. H., Sr. (1987). Entrepreneurial research: Are we playing the correct game? *American Journal of Small Business, 11*(3), 43-49.

Brockhaus, R. H., Sr., & Horwitz, P. A. (1986). The psychology of the entrepreneur. In D. A. Sexton & R. W. Smilor (Eds.), *The art and science of entrepreneurship* (pp. 25-48). Cambridge, MA: Ballinger.

Brodsky, M. A. (1993). Successful female corporate managers and entrepreneurs: Similarities and differences. *Group & Organization Management, 18*(3), 366-378.

Brophy, A. (1959). Self, role, and satisfaction. *Genetic Psychology Monographs, 59*, 263-308.

Broverman, I. K., Vogel, S. R., Broverman, D. M., Clarkson, F. E., & Rosenkrantz, P. S. (1972). Sex-role stereotypes: A current appraisal. *Journal of Social Issues, 28*(2), 59-78.

Brown, B., & Butler, J. E. (1995). Competitors as allies: A study of entrepreneurial networks in the U.S. wine industry. *Journal of Small Business Management, 33*(3), 57-66.

Brown, C. M. (1995). A network of opportunities. *Black Enterprise, 25*(12), 40.

Brush, C. G. (1992). Research on women business owners: Past trends, a new perspective and future directions. *Entrepreneurship Theory and Practice, 16*(4), 5-30.

Brush, C. G., & Hisrich, R. D. (1988). Women entrepreneurs: Strategic origins impact on growth. In B. Kirchhoff, W. Long, W. E. McMillan, K. Vesper, & W. Wetzel, Jr. (Eds.), *Frontiers of entrepreneurship research, proceedings of the Babson College Conference on Entrepreneurship Research* (pp. 612-625). Wellesley, MA: Center for Entrepreneurial Studies, Babson College.

Brush, C. G., & Hisrich, R. D. (1991). Antecedent influences on women-owned businesses. *Journal of Managerial Psychology, 6*(2), 9-16.

Burke, R. J., Belcourt, M. L., & Lee-Gosselin, H. (1989). *Work and family in the lives of female entrepreneurs: Having it all?* (Working Papers Series No. NC 89-27). Western Business School, University of Western Ontario.

Burke, R. J., & McKeen, C. A. (1994). Training and development activities and career success of managerial and professional women. *Journal of Management Development, 13*(5), 53-63.

Burke, R. J, Rothstein, M. G., & Bristor, J. M. (1995). Interpersonal networks of managerial and professional women and men: Descriptive characteristics. *Women in Management Review, 10*(1), 21-27.

Burt, R. S. (1982). *Toward a structural theory of action.* New York: Academic Press.

Burt, R. S. (1992). *Structural holes: The social structure of competition.* Cambridge, MA: Harvard University Press.

Buttner, E. H., & Gryskiewicz, N. (1993). Entrepreneurs' problem-solving styles. *Journal of Small Business Management, 31*(1), 22-31.

Buttner, E. H., & Moore, D. P. (1996). How do they measure success? Former corporate women entrepreneurs' responses. In M. Schnake (Ed.), *Southern Management Association Proceedings, New Orleans* (pp. 318-322). University, MS: Mississippi State University.

Buttner, E. H., & Moore, D. P. (1997). Women's organizational exodus to entrepreneurship: Self-reported motivations and correlates with success. *Journal of Small Business Management, 35*(1), 34-36.

Buttner, E. H., & Rosen, B. (1988a). Bank loan officers' perceptions of the characteristics of men, women, and successful entrepreneurs. *Journal of Business Venturing, 3*(3), 249-258.

Buttner, E. H., & Rosen, B. (1988b). The influence of entrepreneur's gender and type of business on decisions to provide venture capital. In D. F. Ray (Ed.), *Southern Management Association Proceedings, Atlanta* (pp. 314-317). University, MS: Mississippi State University.

Buttner, E. H., & Rosen, B. (1989). Funding new business ventures: Are decision makers biased against women entrepreneurs? *Journal of Business Venturing, 4*(4), 249-261.

Bycio, P., Hackett, R. D., & Allen, J. S. (1995). Further assessments of Bass's (1985) conceptualization of transactional and transformational leadership. *Journal of Applied Psychology, 80,* 466-478.

Capowski, G. S. (1992). Be your own boss? Millions of women get down to business. *Management Review, 81*(3), 24-30.

Chaganti, R. (1986). Management in women-owned enterprises. *Journal of Small Business Management, 24*(October), 18-29.

Chaganti, R., & Schneer, J. (1994). A study of the impact of owners' mode of entry on venture performance and management patterns. *Journal of Business Venturing, 9,* 243-260.

Chandler, G. N., & Hanks, S. H. (1991). How important is experience in a highly similar field? In N. C. Churchill, C. Neil, W. D. Bygrave, J. A. Hornaday, D. F. Muzyka, K. H. Vesper, & W. E. Wetzel, Jr. (Eds.), *Frontiers of entrepreneurship research* (pp. 1-10). Wellesley, MA: Center for Entrepreneurial Studies, Babson College.

Chandler, G. N., & Hanks, S. H. (1994). Founder competence, the environment, and venture performance. *Entrepreneurship Theory and Practice, 18*(3), 77-89.

Chodorow, N. (1974). Family structure and feminine personality. In M. Z. Rosaldo & L. Lamphere (Eds.), *Women, culture, and society* (pp. 43-66). Stanford, CA: Stanford University Press.

Chodorow, N. (1978). *The reproduction of mothering.* Berkeley: University of California Press.

Cianni, M., & Romberger, B. (1995). Perceived racial, ethnic, and gender differences in access to developmental experiences. *Group & Organization Management, 20*(4), 440-459.

Cooper, A. C. (1981). Strategic management: New ventures and small business. *Long Range Planning, 14*(5), 39-45.

Cooper, A. C. (1985). The role of incubator organizations in the founding of growth-oriented firms. *Journal of Business Venturing, 1*(1), 75-86.

Cooper, A. C. (1986). Entrepreneurship and high technology. In D. L. Sexton & R. W. Smilor (Eds.), *The art and science of entrepreneurship.* Cambridge, MA: Ballinger.

Cooper, A. C. (1993). Challenges in predicting new firm performance. *Journal of Business Venturing, 8,* 241-253.

Cooper, A. C., & Bruno, A. (1977). Success among high-technology firms. *Business Horizons, 20*(2), 16-22.

Cooper, A. C., & Dunkelberg, W. C. (1981). A new look at business entry: Experiences of 1805 entrepreneurs. In K. Vesper (Ed.), *Frontiers of entrepreneurship research* (pp. 1-20). Wellesley, MA: Center for Entrepreneurial Studies, Babson College.

Cooper, A. C., & Dunkelberg, W. C. (1986). Entrepreneurship and paths to business ownership. *Strategic Management Journal, 7,* 53-68.

Cooper, A. C., & Dunkelberg, W. C. (1987). Entrepreneurial research: Old questions, new answers and methodological issues. *American Journal of Small Business, 11*(3), 11-23.

Cooper, A. C., Woo, C., & Dunkelberg, W. (1989). Entrepreneurship and the initial size of firms. *Journal of Business Venturing, 4,* 317-332.

Coppolina, Y., & Seath, C. B. (1987). Women managers: Fitting the moulding or moulding the fit. *Equal Opportunity International, 6*(3), 4-10.

Cravens, D., Shipp, S. H., & Cravens, K. S. (1994). Reforming the traditional organization: The mandate for developing networks. *Business Horizon, 37*(4), 19-28.

Cromie, S., & Birley, S. (1992). Networking by female business owners in Northern Ireland. *Journal of Business Venturing, 7*(3), 237-251.

Cromie, S., & Hayes, J. (1988). Towards a typology of female entrepreneurs. *The Sociological Review, 36*(1), 87-113.

Cromie, S., & Hayes, J. (1991). Business ownership as a means of overcoming job dissatisfaction. *Personnel Review, 20*(1), 19-24.

Cuba, R., DeCenzo, D., & Anish, A. (1983). Management practices of successful female business owners. *American Journal of Small Business, 8*(2), 40-46.

Daily, C., & Dalton, D. (1992). Financial performance of founder-managed versus professionally managed small corporations. *Journal of Small Business Management, 30*(April), 25-34.

Davidson, P. (1989). Entrepreneurship—And after? A study of growth willingness in small firms. *Journal of Business Venturing, 4*(3), 211-226.

Deal, T. E., & Kennedy, A. A. (1982). *Corporate cultures: The rites and rituals of corporate life.* Reading, MA: Addison-Wesley.

Demarest, J. L. (1977). *Women minding their own businesses: A pilot study of independent business and professional women and their enterprises.* Unpublished doctoral dissertation, University of Colorado, Boulder.

Denison, D., & Alexander, J. (1986). Patterns and profiles of entrepreneurs: Data from entrepreneurship forums. In R. Ronstadt, R. J. Hornaday, R. Peterson, & K. Vesper (Eds.), *Frontiers of entrepreneurship research* (pp. 578-593). Wellesley, MA: Center for Entrepreneurial Studies, Babson College.

Desjardins, C. (1989, June). Gender issues in community college leadership. *American Association of Women in Community and Junior College Journal,* 5-11.

Devine, T. J. (1994). Characteristics of self-employed women in the United States. *Monthly Labor Review, 117*(3), 20-34.

Diffley, J. H. (1983). Important business competencies for the woman entrepreneur. *Business Education Forum, 37*(3), 31-33.

Dingwall, J. (1992). The woman weapon. *D&B Reports, 40*(6), 60-61.

Dipboye, R. (1987). Problems and progress of women in management. In K. Kaziora, M. Moskow, & L. Tannern (Eds.), *Working women: Past, present, future* (pp. 118-154). Washington, DC: Bureau of National Affairs.

Dipboye, R. L., Arvey, R. D., & Terpstra, D. E. (1977). Sex and physical attractiveness of raters and applicants as determinants of resume evaluations. *Journal of Applied Psychology, 62,* 288-294.

Dobrzynski, J. H. (1996, December 12). Women pass milestone in the board room. *The New York Times,* p. C4.

Drucker, P. F. (1985). *Innovation and entrepreneurship.* New York: Harper and Row.

Druskat, V. U. (1994). Gender and leadership style: Transformational and transactional leadership in the Roman Catholic Church. *Leadership Quarterly, 6,* 413-450.

Dubini, P. (1988). The influence of motivations and environment on business startups: Some hints for public policies. *Journal of Business Venturing, 4,* 11-26.

Duchesneau, D. A., & Gartner, W. B. (1990). A profile of new venture success and failure in an emerging industry. *Journal of Business Venturing, 5*(5), 297-312.

Dugan, I. J. (1996, September 30). Small business is big business. *Business Week,* p. 117.

Dyer, W. G. (1986). *Cultural change in family firms.* San Francisco: Jossey-Bass.

Dyer, W. G., Jr. (1994). Toward a theory of entrepreneurial careers. *Entrepreneurship Theory and Practice, 19*(2), 7-21.

Dyke, L. S., Fischer, E. M., & Reuber, A. R. (1992). An inter-industry examination of the impact of owner experience on firm performance. *Journal of Small Business Management, 30*(4), 72-87.

Eagley, A., & Johnson, B. (1990). Gender and leadership style: A meta-analysis. *Psychological Bulletin, 108*(2), 233-256.

Ely, R. (1995). The power in demography: Women's social construction of gender identity at work. *Academy of Management Journal, 38*, 589-634.

Emory, C. W., & Cooper, D. R. (1991). *Business research methods* (4th ed.). Homewood, IL: Irwin.

Fabowale, L., Orser, B., & Riding, A. (1995). Gender, structural factors, and credit terms between Canadian small businesses and financial institutions. *Entrepreneurship Theory and Practice, 19*(4), 41-65.

Fagenson, E. (1986). Women's work orientations: Something old something new. *Group and Organization Studies, 11*, 75-100.

Fagenson, E. (1990, August). *The values of organizational and entrepreneurial men and women: Occupational role and/or gender-related differences?* Paper presented at the annual meeting of the Academy of Management Conference, San Francisco.

Fagenson, E. (1993). Personal value systems of men and women entrepreneurs versus managers. *Journal of Business Venturing, 8*(5), 409-430.

Fagenson, E. A., & Marcus, E. (1991). Perceptions of the sex role characteristics of entrepreneurs. *Entrepreneurship Theory and Practice, 15*(4), 33-47.

Families and Work Institute. (1995). *Women: The new providers.* New York, NY.

Feeser, H. R., & Willard, G. E. (1989). Incubators and performance—A comparison of high- and low-growth high-tech firms. *Journal of Business Venturing, 4*, 429-442.

Fischer, E. M., Reuber, A. R., & Dyke, L. S. (1993). A theoretical overview and extension of research on sex, gender, and entrepreneurship. *Journal of Business Venturing, 8*(2), 151-168.

Ford, J., MacCallum, R., & Tait, M. (1986). The application of exploratory factor analysis in applied psychology: A critical review and analysis. *Personnel Psychology, 39*, 291-314.

Foss, L. (1993). Resources, networks and entrepreneurship: A survey of 153 starters and 84 non-starters in the cod farming industry in Norway. In N. C. Churchill, S. Birley, W. D. Bygrave, J. Doutriaux, E. J. Gatewood, F. S. Hoy, & W. E. Wetzel, Jr. (Eds.), *Frontiers of entrepreneurship research* (pp. 355-369). Babson Park, MA: Center for Entrepreneurial Studies, Babson College.

Freeman, S. J. (1990). *Managing lives: Corporate women and social change.* Amherst, MA: University of Massachusetts Press.

Fried, L. I. (1989). A new breed of entrepreneur—women. *Management Review, 78*(12), 18-25.

Gabor, A. (1994). Cracking the glass ceiling in R & D. *Research-Technology Management, 37*(5), 14-19.

Gallos, J. (1989). Exploring women's development. In M. Arthur, D. T. Hall, & B. S. Lawrence (Eds.), *Handbook of career theory* (pp. 110-132). New York: Cambridge University Press.

Gartner, W. B. (1985). A conceptual framework for describing the phenomenon of new venture creation. *Academy of Management Review, 10*(4), 696-706.

Gilligan, C. (1982). *In a different voice.* Cambridge, MA: Harvard University Press.

Gilson, E., & Kane, S. (1987). *Unnecessary choices: The hidden life of the executive woman.* New York: Paragon House.

Goffee, R., & Scase, R. (1983). Business ownership and women's subordination: A preliminary study of female proprietors. *Sociological Review, 31*, 625-648.

Goodwin, V., & Whittington, J. L. (1996, August). *A field study of a cognitive approach to understanding transformational and transactional leadership.* Paper presented at the meeting of The Academy of Management, Cincinnati, OH.

Googins, B., & Burden, D. (1987). Vulnerability of working parents: Balancing work and home roles. *Social Work, 32,* 295-300.

Greenberger, D. B., & Sexton, D. L. (1988). An interactive model of new venture initiation. *Journal of Small Business Management, 26*(3), 1-7.

Greenglass, F. R. (1985). Psychological implications of sex bias in the workplace. *Academic Psychology Bulletin, 7,* 227-240.

Greenglass, F. R. (1987). Anger in type A women: Implications for coronary heart disease. *Personality and Individual Differences, 8,* 639-650.

Gregg, G. (1985). Woman entrepreneurs: The second generation. *Across the Board,* 10-18.

Grusec, J. E., & Lytton, H. (1988). *Social development: History, theory, and research.* New York: Springer-Verlag.

Gutman, D. L. (1975). Parenthood: A key to the comparative study of the life cycle. In N. Datan & L. H. Ginsburg (Eds.), *Life span developmental psychology: Normative life crises* (pp. 167-184). New York: Academic Press.

Guy, M. E. (1994). Organizational architecture, gender and women's careers. *Review of Public Personnel Administration, 14*(2), 77-90.

Haberfeld, Y. (1992). Employment discrimination: An organizational model. *Academy of Management Journal, 35*(1), 161-180.

Hale, M., & Kelly, R. M. (1989). *Gender, bureaucracy, and democracy.* Westport, CT: Greenwood Press.

Hall, D. T. (1987). Careers and socialization. *Journal of Management, 13*(2), 301-321.

Hambrick, D. C., & Crozier, L. M. (1985). Stumblers and stars in the management of rapid growth. *Journal of Business Venturing, 1,* 31-45.

Handley, J. (1994). Women, decision making and academia: An unholy alliance. *Women in Management Review, 9*(3), 11-16.

Hansen, E. L., & Allen, K. R. (1992). The creation corridor: Environmental load and pre-organization information-processing ability. *Entrepreneurship Theory and Practice, 17*(1), 57-65.

Hansen, E. L., & Wortman, M. S. (1989). Entrepreneurial networks: The organization in vitro. In F. Hoy (Ed.), *Academy of Management Best Paper Proceedings: 49th meeting* (pp. 69-73). Atlanta, GA: Darby.

Hardesty, S., & Jacobs, N. (1986). *Success and betrayal: The crisis of women in corporate America.* New York: Franklin Watts.

Harding, F. (1996, May). How to build a network. *Journal of Accountancy,* pp. 79-82.

Harvey, M., & Evans, R. (1995). Strategic windows in the entrepreneurial process. *Journal of Business Venturing, 10*(5), 331-347.

Helgesen, S. (1990). *The female advantage: Women's ways of leadership.* New York: Doubleday.

Helgesen, S. (1995). *The web of inclusion.* New York: Currency Doubleday.

Hennig, M., & Jardim, A. (1977). *The managerial woman.* New York: Anchor/Doubleday.

Higgins, C., & Duxbury, L. (1994). "Supportive" managers can change your life and the company's bottom line. *Western Business School's National Center for Management Research and Development's Women in Management Program newsletter, 5*(1), 4.

Hill, R. J. (1993). Women and work—Is the glass ceiling coming down? *Risk Management, 40*(7), 26-34.

Hill, S. (1990). Changing the technological trajectory: Addressing the trailing edge of Australia's historical culture. *Futures (UK), 22,* 272-297.

Hisrich, R. D. (1990). Entrepreneurship/intrapreneurship. *American Psychologist, 45*(2), 209-222.

Hisrich, R. D., & Brush, C. G. (1984). The woman entrepreneur: Management skills and business problems. *Journal of Small Business Management, 22*(1), 30-37.

Hisrich, R., & Brush, C. (1987). Women entrepreneurs: A longitudinal study. In N. C. Churchill, J. A. Hornaday, B. A. Kirchhoff, O. J. Krasner, & K. H. Vesper (Eds.), *Frontiers of entrepreneurship research* (pp. 187-199). Wellesley, MA: Center for Entrepreneurial Studies, Babson College.

Hisrich, R. D., & O'Brien, M. (1981). The woman entrepreneur from a business and sociological perspective. In K. Vesper (Ed.), *Frontiers of entrepreneurship research* (pp. 21-29). Wellesley, MA: Center for Entrepreneurial Studies, Babson College.

Hisrich, R. D., & O'Brien, M. (1982). The woman entrepreneur as a reflection of the type of business. In K. Vesper (Ed.), *Frontiers of entrepreneurship research* (pp. 54-67). Wellesley, MA: Center for Entrepreneurial Studies, Babson College.

Holland, J. L. (1973). *Making vocational choices: A theory of careers.* Englewood Cliffs, NJ: Prentice Hall.

Hood, J. N., & Koberg, C. S. (1994). Patterns of differential assimilation and acculturation for women in business organizations. *Human Relations, 47*(2), 159-181.

Hornaday, J. A., & Aboud, J. (1971, Summer). Characteristics of successful entrepreneurs. *Personnel Psychology,* pp. 141-153.

Hudson Institute. (1987). *Workforce 2000: Work and workers for the 21st century.* Indianapolis: Hudson Institute.

Humphreys, M., & McClung, J. (1981). Women entrepreneurs in Oklahoma. *Review of Regional Economics and Business, 6*(2), 13-20.

Ibarra, H. (1993). Personal networks of women and minorities in management: A conceptual framework. *Academy of Management Review, 18*(1), 56-87.

Ibarra, H. (1995). Race, opportunity, and diversity of social circles in managerial networks. *Academy of Management Journal, 38*(3), 673-703.

Ibarra, H., & Andrews, S. B. (1993). Power, social influence, and sense making: Effects of network centrality and proximity on employee perceptions. *Administrative Science Quarterly, 38*, 277-303.

Ireland, R. D., & Van Auken, P. M. (1987). Entrepreneurship and small business research: An historical typology and directions for future research. *American Journal of Small Business, 11*(4), 9-20.

Jick, T. D., & Mitz, L. (1985). Sex differences in work stress. *Academy of Management Review, 10*, 408-420.

Johannisson, B. (1986). New venture creation—A network approach. In R. Ronstadt, J. Hornaday, R. Peterson, & K. Vesper (Eds.), *Frontiers of entrepreneurship research* (pp. 236-238). Wellesley, MA: Center for Entrepreneurial Studies, Babson College.

Johnston, W. B., & Packer, A. E. (1987). *Workforce 2000, work and workers for the 21st century.* Indianapolis: Hudson Institute.

Kalleberg, A. L., & Leicht, K. T. (1991). Gender and organizational performance: Determinants of small business survival and success. *Academy of Management Journal, 34*(1), 131-161.

Kamm, J. B., Shuman, J. C., Seeger, J. A., & Nurick, A. J. (1990). Entrepreneurial teams in new venture creation: A research agenda. *Entrepreneurship Theory and Practice, 14*(4), 7-17.

Kanter, R. M. (1977). *Men and women of the corporation.* New York: Basic Books.

Kanter, R. M. (1989). *When giants learn to dance: Mastering the challenge of strategy, management, and careers in the 1990s.* New York: Simon & Schuster.

Kaplan, E. (1988). Women entrepreneurs: Constructing a framework to examine venture success and failure. In B. Kirchhoff, W. Long, W. McMullen, K. Vesper, & W. Wetzel, Jr. (Eds.), *Frontiers of entrepreneurship research* (pp. 643-653). Wellesley, MA: Center for Entrepreneurial Studies, Babson College.

Katz, J. A. (1994). Modeling entrepreneurial career progressions: Concepts and considerations. *Entrepreneurship Theory and Practice, 19*(2), 23-39.

Katz, J., & Gartner, W. B. (1988). Properties of emerging organizations. *Academy of Management Review, 13*(3), 429-441.

Kelly, K. (1994, April 18). A landmark in women's networking. *Business Week*, pp. 106-107.

Kelly, R. M. (1991). *The gendered economy: Work, careers, and success.* Newbury Park, CA: Sage.

Kent, C. A., Sexton, D., & Vesper, K. (1982). *Encyclopedia of entrepreneurship.* Englewood Cliffs, NJ: Prentice Hall.

Kerlinger, F. N. (1986). *Foundations of behavioral research.* Fort Worth, TX: Holt, Rinehart & Winston.

Kilduff, M., & Krackhardt, D. (1994). Bringing the individual back in: A structural analysis of the internal market for reputation in organizations. *Academy of Management Journal, 37*, 87-108.

Klinkerman, S. (1996, May/June). Banking on female entrepreneurs. *Bank Management*, pp. 20-25.

Knight, R. M. (1987). Can business schools produce entrepreneurs? In N. C. Churchill, J. A. Hornaday, B. A. Kirchhoff, O. J. Krasner, & K. H. Vesper (Eds.), *Frontiers of entrepreneurship research* (pp. 603-604). Wellesley, MA: Center for Entrepreneurial Studies, Babson College.

Koberg, C., Feldman, H., & Sarason, Y. (1992). Minority men and women small business owners: Similarities and differences. In D. Naffziger & J. Hornsby (Eds.), *United States Association of Small Business and Entrepreneurship Proceedings* (pp. 41-52). Chicago: Ball State University.

Konek, C., & Kitch, S. (1994). *Women and careers: Issues and challenges.* Newbury Park, CA: Sage.

Korabik, K. (1981, March). *Androgyny and leadership: An integration.* Paper presented at the meeting of the Association for Women in Psychology, Boston, MA.

Korabik, K. (1982). Sex-role orientation and leadership style. *International Journal of Women's Studies, 5*, 328-336.

Korabik, K. (1990). Androgyny and leadership style. *Journal of Business Ethics, 9*(4), 283-290.

Kotkin, J., & Friedman, D. (1995). Why every business will be like show business. *Inc., 17*(3), 64-77.

Kouzes, J. M., & Posner, B. Z. (1987). *The leadership challenge.* San Francisco: Jossey-Bass.

Krippendorff, K. (1981). *Content analysis.* Beverly Hills, CA: Sage.

Krueger, N. F., Jr., & Brazeal, D. V. (1994). Entrepreneurial potential and potential entrepreneurs. *Entrepreneurship Theory and Practice, 18*(3), 91-104.

Kuratko, D., & Hodgetts, R. (1989). *Entrepreneurship: A contemporary approach.* Chicago: Dryden Press.

Larson, A., & Starr, J. A. (1993). A network model of organization formation. *Entrepreneurship Theory and Practice, 17*(2), 5-15.

Larwood, L., & Gattiker, U. E. (1989). A comparison of the career paths used by successful men and women. In B. A. Gutek & L. Larwood (Eds.), *Women's career development* (pp. 129-156). Newbury Park, CA: Sage.

Lavoie, D. (1984/1985, Winter). A new era for female entrepreneurship in the 80's. *Journal of Small Business, Canada*, pp. 34-43.

Lawler, J. (1994). Executive exodus. *Working Woman, 19*(11), 38-41.

Learned, K. E. (1992). What happened before the organization? A model of organization formation. *Entrepreneurship Theory and Practice, 17*(1), 39-48.

Lee-Gosselin, H., & Grise, J. (1990). Are women owner-managers challenging our definitions of entrepreneurship? An in-depth survey. *Journal of Business Ethics, 9,* 423-433.

Leonard-Barton, D. (1983). Interpersonal communication patterns among Swedish and Boston-area entrepreneurs. In J. Hornaday, J. Timmons, & K. Vesper (Eds.), *Frontiers of entrepreneurship research* (pp. 538-563). Wellesley, MA: Center for Entrepreneurial Studies, Babson College.

Lindsay, C., & Pasquali, J. (1993). The wounded feminine: From organizational abuse to personal healing. *Business Horizons, 36*(2), 35-41.

Linn, S. (1990). Master the art of mingling. *Entrepreneurial Woman, 90*(July/August), 92.

Litvan, L. M. (1995). Selling to Uncle Sam: New, easier rules. *Nation's Business, 83*(3), 46-48.

Loudermilk, K. (1987, May). *Sex discrimination in the workplace as reported by Wichita, KS area professional women.* Paper presented at the meeting of the Fourth Annual Women and Work Conference, Arlington, TX.

Louis, M. R. (1980). Surprise and sense making: What newcomers experience in entering unfamiliar organizational settings. *Administrative Science Quarterly, 25,* 226-251.

Luthans, F. (1986, August). *Fifty years later: What do we really know about managers and managing?* Presidential speech at the Academy of Management annual meeting, Chicago, IL.

Mainiero, L. A. (1994). On breaking the glass ceiling: The political seasoning of powerful women executives. *Organizational Dynamics, 22*(4), 5-20.

Maltby, S. (1995, October 11). *Banks and the woman business owner.* Speech delivered to University of Chicago Graduate School of Business, Chicago, IL.

Martin, P. (1993). Feminist practices in organizations. In E. Fagenson (Ed.), *Women in management* (pp. 274-296). Newbury Park, CA: Sage.

Masters, R., & Meier, R. (1988). Sex difference and risk-taking propensity of entrepreneurs. *Journal of Small Business Management, 26*(1), 31-35.

McCauley, C. D., Ruderman, M. R., Ohlott, P. J., & Morrow, J. E. (1994). Assessing the developmental components of managerial jobs. *Journal of Applied Psychology, 79*(4), 544-560.

McClelland, D. (1985). *Human motivation.* Glenview, IL: Scott, Foresman.

McKeen, C., & Burke, R. (1990). *Work experiences and career success of managerial and professional women* (Working Paper No. 90-44). Western Business School, University of Western Ontario.

McKeen, C., & Burke, R. (1992). Supporting the career aspirations of managerial women: Desired developmental opportunities. *Women in Management Review, 7*(5), 16-23.

Miles, B. M., & Huberman, A. M. (1984). *Qualitative data analysis.* Beverly Hills, CA: Sage.

Miles, R. E., & Snow, C. C. (1984). Fit, failure and the hall of fame. *California Management Review, 26*(3), 10-28.

Miller, J. B. (1986). *Toward a new psychology of women.* Boston: Beacon Press.

Mintzberg, H. (1973). *The nature of managerial work.* New York: Harper & Row.

Mitton, D. (1984). No money, know-how, know-who: Formula for managing venture success and personal wealth. In J. Hornaday, F. Tarplay, J. Timmons, & K. Vesper (Eds.), *Frontiers of entrepreneurship research* (pp. 414-428). Wellesley, MA: Center for Entrepreneurial Studies, Babson College.

Moore, D. P. (1987a). First and second generation female entrepreneurs—identifying the needs and differences. In D. F. Ray (Ed.), *Southern Management Association Proceedings* (pp. 175-177). Mississippi: Mississippi State University.

Moore, D. P. (1987b). *Identifying the needs of women entrepreneurs in South Carolina* (Technical Report No. 2). Charleston: South Carolina Development Board.

Moore, D. P. (1988). Female entrepreneurs: New methodologies and research directions in the 1990s. *Research Methodology Conference Proceedings, 38* (pp. 1-44). Nova Scotia: Mount Saint Vincent University.

Moore, D. P. (1990). An examination of present research on the female entrepreneur—suggested research strategies for the 1990's. *Journal of Business Ethics, 9*(4/5), 275-281.

Moore, D. P., Buttner, E. H., & Rosen, B. (1992). Stepping off the corporate track: The entrepreneurial alternative. In U. Sekaran & F. Leong (Eds.), *Womanpower: Managing in times of demographic turbulence* (pp. 85-110). Newbury Park, CA: Sage.

Moore, D. P., & Rust, P. (1984). Attributional changes and occupational perceptions, 1974-1982. In R. Robinson and J. Pearce (Eds.), *Academy of Management Proceedings* (pp. 363-366). Columbia: University of South Carolina College of Business Administration.

Moore, L. (1986). *Not as far as you think: The realities of working women.* Lexington, MA: Lexington Books.

Morgan, R., & Hunt, S. (1994, July). The commitment trust theory of relationship marketing. *Journal of Marketing, 58,* 20-38.

Morrison, A., White, R., & Van Velsor, E. (1987). *Breaking the glass ceiling: Can women reach the top of America's largest corporations?* Reading, MA: Addison-Wesley.

Murphy, A. (1992). The start-up of the '90s. *Inc., 14*(3), 32-40.

Naffziger, D. W., Hornsby, J. S., & Kuratko, D. F. (1994). A proposed research model of entrepreneurial motivation. *Entrepreneurship Theory and Practice, 18*(3), 29-42.

National Foundation for Women Business Owners. (1992). *Women owned businesses.* Washington, DC: Author.

National Foundation for Women Business Owners. (1994). *Styles of success.* Washington, DC: Author.

National Foundation for Women Business Owners. (1996). *Capital, credit and financing: Comparing women and men business owners' sources and uses of capital.* Silver Springs, MD: Author.

National Foundation for Women Business Owners, and Dun & Bradstreet Information Services. (1995, April). *Women-owned businesses: Breaking the boundaries—The progress and achievement of women-owned enterprises.* Silver Springs, MD: National Foundation for Women Business Owners.

Neider, L. (1987). A preliminary investigation of female entrepreneurs in Florida. *Journal of Small Business Management, 25*(3), 22-29.

Neugarten, B. (1968). *Middle age and aging: A reader in social psychology.* Chicago: University of Chicago Press.

Newman, M. A. (1993). Career advancement: Does gender make a difference? *American Review of Public Administration, 23*(4), 361-384.

Noble, B. P. (1986, July). A sense of self. *Venture,* pp. 34-36.

Noble, B. P. (1993, October 17). Reforming the talk on labor reform. *The New York Times,* p. F25.

Ohlott, P. J., Ruderman, M. N., & McCauley, C. D. (1994). Gender differences in managers' developmental job experiences. *Academy of Management Journal, 37*(1), 46-67.

O'Leary, V., & Ickovics, J. (1987, April). *Who wants a woman boss? Only those who have them.* Paper presented at the meeting of the Eastern Psychological Association, Arlington, VA.

Olm, K., Carsrud, A., & Alvey, L. (1988). The role of networks in new venture funding for the female entrepreneur: A continuing analysis. In B. Kirchhoff, W. Long, W. McMullen, K. Vesper, & W. Wetzel, Jr. (Eds.), *Frontiers of entrepreneurship research* (pp. 658-659). Wellesley, MA: Center for Entrepreneurial Studies, Babson College.

Olson, A. A. (1994, April). Long-term networking: A strategy for career success. *Management Review,* pp. 33-35.

Olson, S. F., & Currie, H. M. (1992). Female entrepreneurs: Personal value systems and business strategies in a male-dominated industry. *Journal of Small Business Management, 30*(1), 49-56.

Ornstein, S., & Isabella, L. A. (1990). Age vs. state models of career attitudes of women: A partial replication and extension. *Journal of Vocational Behavior, 36*, 1-19.

Ornstein, S., & Isabella, L. A. (1993). Making sense of careers: A review 1989-1992. *Journal of Management 19*(2), 243-267.

Ostgaard, T. A., & Birley, S. (1994). Personal networks and firm competitive strategy—A strategic or coincidental match? *Journal of Business Venturing, 9*(4), 281-305.

Ostgaard, T. A., & Birley, S. (1996). New venture growth and personal networks. *Journal of Business Research, 36*, 37-50.

Parsons, T. (1960). *Structure and process in modern societies*. New York: Free Press.

Pellegrino, E., & Reese, B. (1982). Perceived formative and operational problems encountered by female entrepreneurs in retail and service firms. *Journal of Small Business Management, 20*(2), 15-24.

Perkins, D. N. T., Nieva, V. F., & Lawler, E. E. (1978). *Causal forces in the creation of a new organization*. Ann Arbor, MI: ISR.

Peters, T. (1990). The best new managers will listen. Motivate. Support: Isn't that just like a woman? *Working Woman, 15*(9), 142-143, 216-217.

Phelps, S., & Mason, M. (1991). When women lose their jobs. *Personnel Journal, 70*(8), 64-69.

Powell, G. (1993). *Women and men in management* (2nd ed.). Newbury Park, CA: Sage.

Powell, G., & Mainiero, L. (1992). Cross-currents in the river of time: Conceptualizing the complexities of women's careers. *Journal of Management, 18*(2), 215-238.

Protzman, F. (1993, October 17). In Germany, the ceiling's not glass, it's concrete. *The New York Times*, p. F16.

Ragins, B. R., & Sundstrom, E. (1989). Gender and power in organizations. *Psychological Bulletin, 105*, 51-88.

Reuber, A. R., & Fischer, E. M. (1993). The learning experiences of entrepreneurs. In N. C. Churchill, S. Birley, J. Doutriaux, E. J. Gatewood, F. S. Hoy, & W. E. Wetzel, Jr. (Eds.), *Frontiers of entrepreneurship research* (pp. 234-245). Wellesley, MA: Center for Entrepreneurial Studies, Babson College.

Riding, A., & Swift, C. (1990). Women business owners and terms of credit: Some empirical findings of the Canadian experience. *Journal of Business Venturing, 5*(5), 327-340.

Ries, P., & Stone, A. J. (1992). *The American woman 1992-1993*. New York: W. W. Norton.

Robertson, I. T., & Sadri, G. (1993). Managerial self-efficacy and managerial performance. *British Journal of Management, 4*(1), 37-45.

Rosen, B., & Jerdee, T. (1973). The influence of sex-role stereotypes on evaluations of male and female supervisory behavior. *Journal of Applied Psychology, 57*, 44-48.

Rosen, B., & Jerdee, T. (1974). Influence of sex-role stereotypes on personnel decisions. *Journal of Applied Psychology, 59*, 9-14.

Rosener, J. (1989, August). *"Corporate flight" and female entrepreneurs: Is there a connection?* Paper presented at the Annual Meeting of the Academy of Management, Washington, DC.

Rosener, J. (1990, November-December). Ways women lead. *Harvard Business Review*, pp. 119-125.

Rosener, J. (1995). *America's competitive secret: Utilizing women as a management strategy*. New York: Oxford University Press.

Rosin, H., & Korabik, K. (1990). Marital and family correlates of women managers' attrition from organizations. *Journal of Vocational Behavior, 37*, 104-120.

Rosin, H. M., & Korabik, K. (1991). Workplace variables, affective responses, and intention to leave among women managers. *Journal of Occupational Psychology, 64*, 317-330.

Rush, B., Graham, J., & Long, W. (1987). The use of peer networks in the start-up process. In N. Churchill, J. Hornaday, B. Kirchhoff, O. Krasner, & K. Vesper (Eds.), *Frontiers of entrepreneurship research* (pp. 169-183). Wellesley, MA: Center for Entrepreneurial Studies, Babson College.

Sadovsky, A. (1991). *101 thoughts to make you think*. Dallas: Taylor.

Sadovsky, A., & Rice, A. (1991). *101 thoughts for becoming the real you*. Dallas: Taylor.

Sadri, G. (1994). *Self-efficacy questionnaire*. Unpublished manuscript, California State University, Fullerton, CA.

Salancik, G., & Pfeffer, J. (1978). The external control of organizations: A social information processing approach to job attitudes and task design. *Administrative Science Quarterly, 23*, 224-253.

Sashkin, M. (1984). *The leader behavior questionnaire*. King of Prussia, PA: Organization Design and Development.

Sashkin, M., & Burke, W. (1990). Understanding and assessing leadership. In K. Clark & M. Clark (Eds.), *Measures of leadership* (pp. 297-325). Greensboro, NC: Center for Creative Leadership.

Sathe, V. (1985). *Culture and related corporate realities*. Homewood, IL: Richard D. Irwin.

Schein, E. H. (1978). *Career dynamics: Matching individual and organizational needs*. Reading, MA: Addison-Wesley.

Schein, E. H. (1983). The role of the founder in creating organizational culture. *Organizational Dynamics, 12*(1), 13-28.

Schein, E. (1985). *Organizational culture and leadership: A dynamic view*. San Francisco: Jossey-Bass.

Schein, E. H. (1990). *Career anchors: Discovering your real values* (Rev. ed.). San Diego, CA: Pfeiffer & Company.

Scheinberg, S., & MacMillan, I. C. (1988). An 11 county study of motivations to start a business. In B. A. Kirchhoff, W. A. Long, W. E. McMillan, K. H. Vesper, & W. E. Wetzel, Jr. (Eds.), *Frontiers of entrepreneurship research* (pp. 669-687). Wellesley, MA: Center for Entrepreneurial Studies, Babson College.

Schreier, J., & Komives, J. (1973). *The entrepreneur and new enterprise formation: A resource guide*. Milwaukee, WI: Center for Venture Management.

Schwartz, E. B. (1976). Entrepreneurship: A new female frontier. *Journal of Contemporary Business, 5*(1), 47-76.

Scott, C. (1986). Why more women are becoming entrepreneurs. *Journal of Small Business Management, 24*(4), 37-44.

Seidel, J. V., Kjolseth, R., & Seymour, E. (1988). *The Ethnograph, a user's guide*. Corvallis, OR: Qualis Research Associates.

Selz, M. (1993, December 29). Small manufacturers display the nimbleness the times require. *Wall Street Journal* (Eastern Edition), pp. A1-A2.

Sexton, D., & Bowman-Upton, N. (1990). Female and male characteristics and their role in gender-related discrimination. *Journal of Business Venturing, 5*(1), 29-36.

Sexton, D., & Smilor, R. (Eds.). (1986). *The art and science of entrepreneurship*. Cambridge, MA: Ballinger.

Shane, S., Kolvereid, L., & Westhead, P. (1991). An exploratory examination of the reasons leading to new firm formation across country and gender (Part 1). *Journal of Business Venturing, 6*(6), 431-446.

Shapero, A. (1982). Social dimensions of entrepreneurship. In C. Kent, D. Sexton, & K. Vesper (Eds.), *The encyclopedia of entrepreneurship* (pp. 72-90). Englewood Cliffs, NJ: Prentice Hall.

Shaver, K. G., Gatewood, E. J., & Gartner, W. B. (1991). Attributions for new venture creation: An experimental comparison. In N. C. Churchill, W. D. Bygrave, J. G. Covin, D. L. Sexton, D. P. Slevin, K. H. Vesper, & W. E. Wetzel, Jr. (Eds.), *Frontiers of entrepreneurship research* (pp. 32-49). Babson Park, MA: Center for Entrepreneurial Studies, Babson College.

Shipper, F. (1994). A study of managerial skills of women and men and their impact on employees' attitudes and career success in a nontraditional organization [Abstract]. In D. P. Moore (Ed.), *Academy of Management Best Papers Proceedings, 54* (p. 471). Madison, WI: OmniPress.

Shuman, J., Seeger, J., Kamm, J., & Teebagy, N. (1986). An empirical test of ten entrepreneurial propositions. In R. Ronstadt, R. Hornaday, R. Peterson, & K. Vesper (Eds.), *Frontiers of entrepreneurship research* (pp. 187-198). Wellesley, MA: Center for Entrepreneurial Studies, Babson College.

Smart, G. M., Jr. (1991, January). Building a chain of contacts. *Training and Development Journal*, pp. 21-27.

Smirchich, L. (1983). Concepts of culture and organizational analysis. *Administrative Science Quarterly, 28*, 339-358.

Snavely, B. K. (1993). Managing conflict over the perceived progress of working women. *Business Horizons, 36*(2), 17-22.

Sonnenberg, F. K. (1990, January/February). How to reap the benefits of networking. *The Journal of Business Strategy*, pp. 59-62.

Spotlight on women directors. (1992). *Directors & Boards, 16*(4), 66-68.

Stevenson, L. (1986). Against all odds: The entrepreneurship of women. *Journal of Small Business Management, 24*(3), 30-36.

Stewart, L. P., & Gudykunst, W. B. (1982). Differential factors influencing the hierarchical level and number of promotions of males and females within an organization. *Academy of Management Journal, 25*(3), 586-597.

Stroh, L., Brett, J., & Reilly, A. (1992). All the right stuff: A comparison of female and male managers' career progression. *Journal of Applied Psychology, 77*(3), 251-260.

Stuart, R. W., & Abetti, P. A. (1990). Impact of entrepreneurial and management experience on early performance. *Journal of Business Venturing, 5*(3), 151-162.

Tabachnick, B. G., & Fidell, L. S. (1996). *Using multivariate statistics* (3rd ed.). New York: Harper & Row.

Taylor, A. (1986, August 18). Why women managers are bailing out. *Fortune*, pp. 16-23.

Terpstra, D., & Olson, P. (1993). Entrepreneurial start-up and growth: A classification of problems. *Entrepreneurship Theory and Practice, 17*(3), 5-20.

Tharenou, P., Latimer, S., & Conroy, D. (1994). How do you make it to the top? An examination of influences on women's and men's managerial advancement. *Academy of Management Journal, 37*(4), 899-931.

Thompson, J., & Hood, J. (1991, August). *A comparison of corporate social performance in female-owned and male-owned small business.* Paper presented at the Academy of Management meetings, Miami, FL.

Tjosvold, D., & Weicker, D. (1993). Cooperative and competitive networking by entrepreneurs: A critical incident study. *Journal of Small Business Management, 31*(1), 11-21.

Trost, C. (1990, May 16). Women managers quit not for family but to advance their corporate climb. *Wall Street Journal*, pp. B1, B4.

Uchitelle, L., & Kleinfield, N. R. (1996, March 3). On the battlefields of business, millions of casualties. *The New York Times*, pp. Y1, Y14-17.

U.S. Bureau of the Census. (1991). *Characteristics of business owners in 1987* (CSB087). Washington, DC: Government Printing Office.

U.S. Congress, House of Representatives. (1988). *New economic realities: The rise of women entrepreneurs* (Committee on Small Business, Report 100-736). Washington, DC: Government Printing Office.

U.S. Department of Commerce. (1986a, July). *The state of small business White House Conference on small business—A report to the President of the United States.* Washington, DC: Government Printing Office.

U.S. Department of Commerce. (1986b). *Women and business ownership, an annotated bibliography.* Washington, DC: Government Printing Office.

U.S. Department of Commerce, Bureau of the Census. (1986). *Current population reports* (Series P-23, No. 146). Washington, DC: Government Printing Office.

U.S. Department of Commerce, Bureau of the Census. (1991). *The statistical abstract of the United States.* Washington, DC: Government Printing Office.

U.S. Department of Labor, Bureau of Labor Statistics. (1995, November). BLS releases new 1994-2005 employment projections [Entire issue]. *Monthly Labor Review, 13*(11).

U.S. Small Business Administration. (1985). *State of small business.* Washington, DC: Government Printing Office.

U.S. Small Business Administration. (1995). *The state of small business: A report of the president 1994.* Washington, DC: Government Printing Office.

U.S. Small Business Administration Office of Advocacy Report. (1995). *The third millennium: Small business and entrepreneurship in the 21st century.* Washington, DC: Government Printing Office.

van de Ven, A. H., Hudson, R., & Schroeder, D. M. (1984). Designing new business startups: Entrepreneurial, organizational, and ecological considerations. *Journal of Management, 10*(1), 87-107.

van Oldenborgh, M. (1992). Making it to the executive suite. *International Business, 5*(7), 54-60.

Vesper, K. H. (1983). *Entrepreneurship and national policy.* Chicago: Walter E. Heller International Corp., Institute for Small Business.

Vesper, K. H. (1990). *New venture strategies.* Englewood Cliffs, NJ: Prentice Hall.

Vokins, N. (1993). The minerva matrix women entrepreneurs. In S. Allen & C. Truman (Eds.), *Women in business: Perspectives on female entrepreneurs* (pp. 46-56). New York: Routledge.

Weber, M. (1947). *The theory of social and economic organizations.* A. M. Henderson & T. Parsons (Trans. and Eds.). Glencoe, IL: Free Press.

Westley, F., & Mintzberg, H. (1989). Visionary leadership in strategic management. *Strategic Management Journal, 10*(Summer), 17-32.

Whisler, T. L. (1988). The role of the board in the threshold firm. *Family Business Review, 1,* 309-321.

White, B., Cox, C., & Cooper, C. (1992). *Women's career development: A study of high flyers.* Cambridge, MA: Blackwell.

Willard, G. E., Krueger, D. A., & Feeser, H. R. (1992). In order to grow, must the founder go: A comparison of performance between founder and non-founder managed high-growth manufacturing firms. *Journal of Business Venturing, 16,* 181-194.

Williams, M. J. (1988). Women beat the corporate game. *Fortune, 118,* 128-138.

Winn, J., & Stewart, K. (1992). The modern entrepreneurial woman. *United States Association of Small Business and Entrepreneurship Proceedings* (pp. 192-201). Chicago, IL: United States Association of Small Business and Entrepreneurship.

Wolfman, B. (1984). *Women and their many roles* (Stone Center Working Paper, No. 7). Wellesley, MA: Wellesley College.

Wortman, M. S., Jr. (1987). Entrepreneurship: An integrating typology. *Journal of Management, 13*(2), 259-279.

Yammarino, F. J., Dubinsky, A. J., Comer, L. B., & Jolson, M. A. (1997). Women and transformational and contingent reward leadership: A multiple-levels-of-analysis perspective. *Academy of Management Journal, 40*(1), 205-222.

Zhao, L., & Aram, J. D. (1995). Networking and growth of young technology-intensive ventures in China. *Journal of Business Venturing, 10*, 349-370.

Name Index

Abetti, P. A., 67, 77, 172
Aboud, J., 26
Adler, N. J., 4, 9
Aldrich, H., 30, 115, 117, 149, 165
Alexander, J., 14, 52, 194
Allen, J. S., 100
Allen, K. R., 115, 149
Alpander, G., 83, 90, 92, 195
Alvey, L., 139
Ando, F., xiii, 2
Andre, R., 175
Andrews, S. B., 116, 117
Anish, A., 90, 165
Antal, A. B., 10
Anthes, G. H., 187
Appelbaum, S., 101, 102, 173, 195
Aram, J. D., 139
Arvey, R. D., 41
Astin, H., 157
Atwater, L. E., 100
Avolio, B. J., 100

Barrett, M., 52, 76, 173, 194, 200
Bart, B., 12
Bass, B., 100
Baucus, D. A., 15, 52, 77, 116, 172
Baye, T. M., 68

Beggs, J. M., 14, 15
Belcourt, M., 4, 70, 158, 200
Belenky, M., 99, 112
Beutell, N., 157
Bigoness, W., 157
Bilimoria, D., 116, 147
Bird, B. J., 66, 67, 167, 174
Birley, S., 3, 4, 9, 14, 15, 16, 17, 19, 52, 67,
    69, 115, 116, 117, 118, 128, 134,
    148, 149, 150, 194, 200
Blum, T. C., 60
Boissevain, J., 117
Bowen, D. D., 2, 12
Bowers, B., 17
Bowman-Upton, N., 20
Brass, D. J., 116
Brass, D. P., 134, 185
Brazeal, D. V., 66
Brenner, O., 9, 157
Brett, J., 9
Bristor, J. M., 141
Brockhaus, R. H., Sr., 12, 52
Brodsky, M. A., 27, 70, 79, 169, 194, 200
Brophy, A., 104
Broverman, D. M., 39
Broverman, I. K., 39
Brown, B., 126
Brown, C. M., 118, 134

Bruno, A., 53
Brush, C., 3, 4, 15, 16, 17, 30, 52, 53, 68,
    69, 83, 90, 92, 99, 117, 134, 161,
    185, 195, 200
Burden, D., 47
Burke, R., 38, 59, 141, 158, 161
Burke, W., 100, 102, 173, 195
Burt, R. S., 116, 134, 185
Butler, J. E., 126
Buttner, E., 2, 5, 16, 31, 88, 94
Bycio, P., 100

Capowski, G. S., 79, 194
Carsrud, A., 139
Carter, K., 83, 90, 92, 195
Chaganti, R., 3, 14, 19, 89
Chandler, G. N., 69, 99
Chodorow, N., 101, 161
Christie, M., 52, 76, 173, 194, 200
Cianni, M., 69
Clarkson, F. E., 39
Clinchy, B., 99, 112
Comer, L. B., 101, 114, 170
Conroy, D., 26
Cooper, A. C., 3, 4, 14, 20, 52, 53, 55, 67,
    68, 69, 70, 77, 78, 115, 149, 157,
    172, 173, 194
Cooper, C., 111, 157
Cooper, D. R., 190
Cooper, K., 201n.1
Coppolina, Y., 101
Cox, C., 111, 157
Cravens, D., 186
Cravens, K. S., 186
Cromie, S., 26, 70, 78, 79, 117, 200
Crozier, L. M., 68, 77, 172
Cuba, R., 90, 165
Currie, H. M., 3

Daily, C., 67, 68, 70
Dalton, D., 67, 68, 70
Davidson, P., 156
Deal, T. E., 6, 7
DeCenzo, D., 90, 165
Demarest J. L., 2
Denison, D., 14, 52, 194
Desjardins, C., 101
Devine, T. J., 1, 3, 15, 17

Diffley, J. H., 2
Dingwall, J., 1, 7, 30
Dipboye, R., 7, 41
Dobrzynski, J. H., 7, 18
Doolittle, D., 14, 15
Drucker, P. F., 2, 68
Druskat, V. U., 100
Dubini, P., 52, 194
Dubinsky, A. J., 101, 114, 170
Duchesneau, D. A., 68, 77, 172
Dugan, I. J., 170
Dun & Bradstreet Information Services, xiii,
    2, 14, 161
Dunkelberg, W. C., 3, 14, 20, 52, 53, 55, 67,
    69, 172, 194
Duxbury, L., 114, 170
Dyer, W. G., 70
Dyer, W. G. Jr., 52
Dyke, L. S., 4, 15, 52, 70, 77, 172, 173

Eagley, A., 101
Ely, R., 27
Emory, C. W., 190
Evans, R., 116, 149

Fabowale, J., 94
Fagenson, E., 10, 14, 19, 25-26, 27, 62, 68,
    70, 79, 101, 157, 161, 194, 200
Families and Work Institute, 47, 101
Feeser, H. R., 52, 67, 70
Feldman, H., 14, 19
Fidell, L. S., 196
Fields, D. L., 60
Fischer, E. M., 4, 15, 52, 69, 70, 77, 172,
    173
Ford, J., 196
Forsgren, R., 83, 90, 92, 195
Foss, L., 116, 118
Freeman, S. J., 41
Fried, L. I., 2, 109
Friedman, D., 115, 149

Gabor, A., 29, 194
Gallos, J., 109
Garsombke, D., 14, 15
Gartner, W. B., 12, 52, 66, 68, 77, 78,
    172

Gatewood, E. J., 52.
Gattiker, U. E., 153
Gilligan, C., 101, 107, 152
Gilson, E., 27, 35, 39
Goffee, R., 94, 95
Goldberger, N., 99, 112
Goodman, J. S., 60
Goodwin, V., 114, 170
Googins, B., 47
Graham, J., 115
Greenberger, D. B., 167
Greenglass, F. R., 36
Gregg, G., 2
Grise, J., 15
Grusec, J. E., 161
Gryskiewicz, N., 31, 88
Gudykunst, W. B., 116, 148
Gutman, D. L., 108
Guy, M. E., 60

Haberfeld, Y., 116, 148
Hackett, R. D., 100
Hale, M., 109
Hall, D. T., 52
Hambrick, D. C., 68, 77, 172
Handley, J., 116
Hanks, S. H., 69, 99
Hansen, E. L., 66, 115, 149, 174
Hardesty, S., 44, 109, 157, 158
Harding, F., 128
Harvey, M., 116, 149
Hayes, J., 26, 70, 78, 79, 200
Helgesen, S., 99, 100, 102, 103, 112, 134,
     173, 185, 195
Hennig, M., 101
Higgins, C., 114, 170
Hill, R. J., 60
Hill, S., 7
Hisrich, R. D., 2, 3, 4, 12, 14, 16, 17, 52, 53,
     69, 83, 90, 92, 93, 94, 115, 149, 195,
     200
Hodgetts, R., 83, 93, 195
Holland, J. L., 52
Hood, J., 161
Hood, J. N., 4
Hornaday, J. A., 26
Hornsby, J. S., 67
Horwitz, P. A., 52
Huberman, A. M., 198

Hudson Institute, 1
Hudson, R., 52, 149
Human, S. E., 15, 52, 77, 116, 172
Humphreys, M., 83, 90, 92, 96, 195
Hunt, S., 68, 78, 173

Ibarra, H., 35, 116, 117, 134, 148, 185
Ickovics, J., 114, 170
Ireland, R. D., 3, 53
Isabella, L. A., 52

Jacobs, N., 44, 109, 157, 158
Jardim, A., 101
Jelinek, M., 66, 67, 174
Jerdee, T., 41
Jick, T. D., 47
Johannisson, B., 115, 116
Johnson, B., 101
Johnston, W. B., 2
Jolson, M. A., 101, 114, 170

Kalleberg, A. L., 4, 200
Kamm, J., 14, 127
Kane, S., 27, 35, 39
Kanter, R. M., 38, 42, 114
Kaplan, E., 9
Katz, J., 52, 66, 70, 78, 79, 167, 169
Kelly, R. M., 39, 109, 161
Kennedy, A. A., 6, 7
Kent, C. A., 12
Kerlinger, F. N., 190
Kilduff, M., 125, 130
Kitch, S., 41, 99, 100, 109
Kjolseth, R., 197
Kleinfield, N. R., 51, 52
Klinkerman, S., 170
Knight, R., 52
Koberg, C., 4, 14, 19
Kolvereid, L., 11, 14, 15, 52, 70, 79, 194
Komives, J., 2
Konek, C., 41, 99, 100, 109
Korabik, K., 9, 27, 47, 101, 112, 170
Kotkin, J., 115, 149
Kouzes, J. M., 100
Krackhardt, D., 125, 130
Krippendorff, K., 198
Krueger, D. A., 70

Krueger, N. F., Jr., 66
Kuratko, D., 67, 83, 93, 195

Larson, A., 117, 134, 185
Larwood, L., 153
LaSota, 13
Latimer, S., 26
Lavoie, D., 13
Lawler, E. E., 52
Lawler, J., 39
Learned, K. E., 52, 66, 174
Lee-Gosselin, H., 15, 158
Leicht, K. T., 4, 200
Leonard-Barton, D., 115
Lindsay, C., 27
Linn, S., 115, 149
Litvan, L. M., 187
Long, W., 115
Loudermilk, K., 41
Louis, M. R., 7
Luthans, F., 114, 170
Lytton, H., 161

MacCallum, R., 196
McCauley, C. D., 36, 116, 148
McClelland, D., 26
McClung, J., 83, 90, 92, 96, 195
McKeen, C., 38, 59, 161
MacMillan, I. C., 11, 14, 15, 52, 194
Maier, R., 14, 19
Mainiero, L., 28, 30, 52, 69, 116, 163
Maltby, S., 170
Marcus, E., 200
Martin, P., 109
Mason, M., 30, 200
Masters, R., 14, 19
Miles, B. M., 198
Miles, R. E., 126
Miller, J. B., 106, 109, 111
Mintzberg, H., 99, 100, 112, 173
Mitton, D., 116
Mitz, L., 47
Moore, D. P., 3, 4, 6, 8, 11, 14, 16, 52
Morgan, R., 68, 78
Morrison, A., 9, 18, 22
Morrow, J. E., 36
Murphy, A., 1, 3, 16, 53

Myers, A., 117

Naffziger, D. W., 67
National Foundation for Women Business
    Owners (NFWBO), xiii, 2, 14, 93,
    156, 157, 190
Neider, L., 26, 90
Neugarten, B., 112
Newman, M. A., 60
Nieva, V. F., 52
Noble, B. P., 4, 15, 154
Nurick, A. J., 127

O'Brien, M., 2, 3, 14, 93, 94
Ohlott, P. J., 36, 116, 148
O'Leary, V., 114, 170
Olm, K., 139
Olson, A. A., 128
Olson, P., 83, 195
Olson, S. F., 3
Ornstein, S., 52
Orser, B., 94
Ostgaard, T. A., 69, 115, 117, 118, 128, 134,
    148, 149, 150

Packer, A. E., 2
Parsons, T., 100
Pasquali, J., 27
Pellegrino, E., 2, 93
Perkins, D. N. T., 52
Peters, T., 114, 173
Pfeffer, J., 116, 117
Phelps, S., 30, 200
Piderit, S. K., 116, 147
Posner, B. Z., 100
Powell, G., 28, 30, 39, 52, 99, 103, 163
Protzman, F., 9

Ragins, B. R., 56
Reese, B., 2, 93
Reilly, A., 9
Reuber, A. R., 4, 15, 52, 69, 70, 77, 172,
    173
Rice, A., 160
Riding, A., 94

Ries, P., 1
Robertson, I. T., 195
Romberger, B., 69
Rosen, B., 2, 6, 16, 41, 94, 115, 117
Rosener, J., 2, 3, 25, 39, 99, 101, 102, 103, 109, 195
Rosenkrantz, P. S., 39
Rosin, H. M., 9, 27, 47
Rothstein, M. G.
Ruderman, M. N., 36, 116, 148
Rush, B., 115

Sadovsky, S., 160
Sadri, G., 104, 195
Salancik, G., 116, 117
Sarason, Y., 14, 19
Sashkin, M., 100, 102, 173, 195
Sathe, V., 6
Scase, R., 94, 95
Scheinberg, S., 10, 14, 15, 52, 194
Schein, E. H., 6, 9, 52, 67, 70, 78, 79, 99, 100, 167, 168, 169
Schneer, J., 89
Schreier, J., 2
Schroeder, D. M., 52, 149
Schwartz, E. B., 2
Scott, C., 2, 52, 70, 79, 93
Seath, C. B., 101
Seeger, J., 14, 127
Seidel, J. V., 197
Selz, M., 17
Sexton, D., 12, 20, 167
Seymour, E., 197
Shane, S., 11, 14, 15, 52, 70, 79, 194
Shapero, S., 66, 167
Shapiro, B., 101, 102, 173, 195
Shaver, K. G., 52
Shipper, F., 101
Shipp, S. H., 186
Shuman, J., 14, 127
Smart, G. M., Jr., 138
Smilor, R., 12
Smirchich, L., 7
Snavely, B. K., 38
Snow, C. C., 126
Sonnenberg, F. K., 131
Starr, J. A., 117, 134, 185
Stevenson, L., 2, 13, 96

Stewart, K., 3, 116, 148
Stone, A. J., 1
Stroh, L., 9
Stuart, R. W., 67, 77, 172
Sundstrom, E., 56
Swift, C., 94

Tabachnick, B. G., 196
Tait, M., 196
Tarule, J., 99, 112
Taylor, A., 4, 18
Teebagy, N., 14
Terpstra, D., 41, 92, 195
Tharenou, P., 26
Thompson, J., 161
Tjosvold, D., 125, 132
Tomkiewicz, J., 9, 157
Trost, C., 9, 18

Uchitelle, L., 51, 52
U.S. Bureau of the Census, 51
U.S. Congress, House of Representatives, xiii, 2
U.S. Department of Commerce, Bureau of the Census, 2, 4, 12, 13, 14
U.S. Department of Labor, Bureau of Labor Statistics, 51
U.S. Small Business Administration, 12, 51

Van Auken, P. M., 3, 53
van de Ven, A. H., 52, 149
van Oldenborgh, M., 60
Van Velsor, E., 9, 18, 22
Vesper, K., 2, 70, 77, 172
Vogel, S. R., 39
Vokins, N., 101

Weber, M., 30
Weicker, D., 125, 132
Westhead, P., 11, 14, 15, 52, 70, 79, 194
Westley, F., 99
Whisler, T. L., 67, 70
White, B., 111, 157
White, R., 9, 18, 22

Whittington, J. L., 114, 170   Wortman, M. S., 12, 66, 115, 174
Willard, G. E., 52, 67, 70
Williams, J. J., 41
Winn, J., 3   Yammarino, F. J., 101, 114, 170
Wolfman, B., 111
Woo, C., 20, 42, 53, 55, 69, 172
Woodward, W., 115, 117   Zhao, L., 139

Subject Index

Academy of Management, Entrepreneurial Division of, 12
Adams, Janet S., xviii
Adkinson, Lisa:
  biographical sketch of, 221
  on creativity and flexibility, 88
  on the decision point, 49
  on hiring skills, 184
  on visionary attitudes, 111
Alumnae Resources Centers of San Francisco, 13, 218
American Women's Economic Development Corporation (AWED), 218
Anderson, Christian, xviii
Angel, Ann Shelton:
  biographical sketch of, 221
  on corporate politics, 42
  on incubator experience, 32, 56
  on teamwork and collaboration, 106
Art and Science of Entrepreneurship, The (Sexton, Smilor), 12
Autonomy and freedom:
  departure decision and, 10, 15, 26-27, 79, 168, 194
  of entrepreneurship, 10, 15
  success measure of, 160
AWED (American Women's Economic Developent Corporation), 218

Babineaux, Michele, 57, 227
Baird, Lynn, xviii
Bensu, Janet, 227
  on corporate experience, 8
  on risk-taking, 44
Blonsky, Lorena M.:
  biographical sketch of, 221
  on differentiation, 90
  on networking, 132
  on reinforcement, 96
Breeze, Patty M.:
  biographical sketch of, 221-222
  on caretaking vs. decision-making, 108
  on compensation, 45
  on networking, 127, 134
Brown, Susan O'Connor:
  biographical sketch of, 222
  on corporate politics, 31-32
  on internal success measure, 159-160
  on self-esteem, 28
  on teamwork and collaboration, 105-106
Bureau of Labor Statistics, 13, 14
Buttner, Doug, xviii
Buttner, E. Holly, xviii
Buttner, Sally, xviii

Career frustration:

of corporate climbers, 3-4
departure decision and, 49-50
vs. family responsibilities, 23, 23t,
    47-48, 169
See also Career transition challenges
Career transition challenges:
    appreciation and, 82
    management skills and, 82-83
    personal experiences of, 81-82
    risk-taking and, 81-82
    summary regarding, 169-170
    See also Survey: career transition
        challenges
Carney, Rebecca:
    biographical sketch of, 222
    on employee caretaking, 107
    on identity, 28
    on incubator confidence, 59
    on success measures, 156
Catalyst women's research group, 7
Census of Women-Owned Business, 13
Challenge of entrepreneurship, 23, 24t, 25
    accomplishment recognition, 34-35, 37,
        45
    controlling one's destiny, 36-37
    definitions and, 12, 13
    leadership opportunity, 35-36, 79
    regaining excitement, 37
    respect, 34-35
Citadel Development Foundation, xvi, xvii,
    189
Clesi, Marie, 227
    on being realistic, 178
    on networking, 134
    on success measures, 164
Coates, Andrea, 227
    on ethics, 26
    on networking, 138
Cochran, Alice Collier, 222
Compensation. *See* Financial considerations
Conrad, Sherie:
    on being realistic, 178
    biographical sketch on, 222
    on corporate politics, 43-44
    on networking, 128-129, 133
    on self-fulfillment measure, 158
    on support systems, 182
Cook, Ethel:
    biographical sketch on, 222
    on corporate experience, 11

on corporate politics, 42-43
on flexibility, 88
on networking, 139
Corporate advancement frustration, 22,
    23-24, 24t, 37
    career barriers, 25, 39-40
    competence demonstration, 39
    discrimination, 7, 8, 9, 18, 40-42, 60, 169
    as incubator push factor, 60
    not fitting in, 38
Corporate climbers, xiv, 3-4, 18, 52, 70-71
    experience or training programs,
        perceptions of, 69-70, 74t, 76-77
    financial expertise, perception of, 69, 73t
    managerial experience, perception of,
        68, 71, 73t, 74t, 76-78, 167-168
    marketing and technical experience,
        perception of, 68-69, 71, 73t, 76, 78,
        172, 173
    networking and, 120, 121t-124t
    post hoc analysis of, 76
    profiles of, 72t
    self-determination, concept of, 70-71,
        72, 75t, 76, 78
Corporate experience:
    career barriers and, 39-40, 153
    competition from entrepreneurs and, 17
    corporate climbers and, xiv, 3-4, 18, 52,
        70-71, 167-168
    in European Community, 10
    financial discrimination and, 7-8, 9, 18
    frustrations of, 3-4, 6, 9, 10, 18, 30-34
    in Germany, 9-10
    glass ceiling concept and, 9, 18, 22, 25,
        60
    male management barrier and, 7, 8, 9,
        22
    networking within, 116-117, 171
    organizational change and, 6-7
    organizational politics of, 7, 8, 9, 31-32,
        42-44, 61
    research areas regarding, 18-19
    See also Departure reasons; Sexual
        harassment; Survey: departure
        reasons
Corporate incubator:
    advancement discrimination and, 60-61
    career transition from, 51-53
    confidence, credibility, creativity
        transfer and, 58-60, 95, 170

contact importance and, 55, 56, 67,
   115-116, 120, 123t, 140-148, 170
corporate climbers and, 52, 68, 70-71,
   167-168
corporate flight and, 70-71
corporate politics and, 61-62
female stereotyping and, 62-64
financial considerations and, 64-65
financial expertise perception and, 69
gestation period and, 53-58
information transfer and, 52, 53-58
intentional entrepreneurs and, xiv, 18,
   66, 67-68, 168, 174
literature review on, 52, 67-68
managerial experience perception and,
   68, 71, 73t, 74t, 76-78, 170, 173
marketing and technical experience
   perception and, 68-69, 71, 73t, 74t,
   76, 78, 172
negative lessons learned from, 16
organizational experience perception
   and, 69-70
push factor concept and, 54
research issues in, 19
self-determination perceptions and, 72,
   75t, 76, 78
skills acquisition and, 3, 11, 16, 56-57,
   67, 73t, 170
special training programs perceptions
   and, 69-70, 74t, 76-77, 174
summary regarding, 170
   See also Survey: corporate incubator
Corporate power and politics, 23, 24, 24t,
   42-44
of bureaucracy, 31-32
compensation equity, 44-46
as incubator push factor, 61, 169
organization structure and, 40
Coury, Lillian, 227
Cox, Beth, xviii
Crawfords Directory, 10
Current Population Reports, 14

Decision factors. *See* Departure reasons
Departure reasons:
autonomy and freedom, 10, 15, 79, 168,
   194
compensation, 15
congenial working environments, 17-18

downsizing, 17, 18, 39
job freedom, 10, 15
perceived opportunities, 15
personal development, 10, 15
research literature on, 15
respect and recognition, 15, 34-35, 37, 45
success measurement and, 153-154, 155t
summary regarding, 167-169
welfare considerations, 15
   See also Survey: departure reasons
Discrimination:
in advancement, 7, 8, 9, 18, 40-41, 60,
   169
in bank financing, 94
by clients, 64, 95
female stereotypes and, 45-46, 63-64
financial, 7-8, 9, 18, 41, 45
in information dissemination, 146-147
not being taken seriously and, 41-42
sexual harassment and, 25, 41
token status and, 38
Downsizing, 17, 18, 39, 51, 147, 174
Drake, Darlene, 227
on emotional support, 181
on family responsibilities, 179
on networking and gender, 129-130
Droppelman, Patricia, 227
on networking, 126-127, 131
Duignan-Woods, Eileen:
biographical sketch of, 222
on client discrimination, 178
on economic caution, 179
on finances, 94
on multiple roles, 113
Dun & Bradstreet Information Services, xiii
Duncan, Melinda, 218

Employment and Earnings (Bureau of Labor
   Statistics), 14
Encyclopedia of Entrepreneurship (Kent,
   Sexton, Vesper), 12
Entrepreneurship. *See* Career transition
   challenges; Challenge of
   entrepreneurship
Eskin, Evelyn:
biographical sketch of, 222-223
on bureaucracy, 31
on client empowerment, 110
on discrimination, 42

on self-fulfillment measure, 159

FACNET (Federal Acquisition Computer
    Network), 187
Family:
    vs. career frustrations, 23, 24t, 169
    success measures and, 153, 162-163
    work links with, 15-16, 47-48
Federal Acquisition Computer Network
    (FACNET), 187
Federal Acquisition Streamlining Act, 187
Feldman, Howard D., xviii
Female employment statistics, 1, 9
Female entrepreneurs. *See* Women
    entrepreneurs
Financial considerations:
    challenge of, 170
    compensation inequity experiences and,
        44-46
    corporate incubation and, 64-65
    pay equity discrimination and, 7-8, 9,
        18, 41, 45
    tax reduction and, 15
Finch, Holmes, xviii
Flemming, Marquita, xviii
Focus group data. *See* Survey: departure
    reasons
Freedom. *See* Autonomy and freedom
Frontiers of Entrepreneurship Research, The
    (Babson Conference papers), 12

Gallagher, Patt, 223
Gender differences:
    in leadership style, 100, 101, 171
    in networking, 145-147
    occupational labeling study and, 11
    in organizational networks, 116-117
    typical entrepreneurial traits, 14-15,
        19-20
Gerla, Bert, 227
    on success measures, 164
Gibbons, Jo Anne, 227
Ginn, Wendy:
    biographical sketch of, 223
    on corporate politics, 42
    on female stereotyping, 62-64
Glass ceiling concept, 9, 18, 22, 25, 60
Goldman, Janet, 223

Gose, Bert:
    on isolation, 97
    on self-fulfillment measure, 159
Green, L. Elaine, 227
    on corporate climbing, 57
    on creating opportunities, 37
    on entrepreneurial vs. managerial
        experience, 70-71
Griffith, Jackie, 227
Grogan, Ann, 8
Gryskiewicz, Nur, xviii

Habeeb, Patricia Ann (Patty), 218-219
Hanson, Diane C., 175, 223
Harper, Jeanette, xviii
Harris, Gloriann, 227
    on support, 96
Hecht, Carol, 227
    on emotional support, 182
    on employee empowerment, 162
    on objectivity, 184
Henry, Vickie L., 32, 223
Hill, Hattie, 227
    on choosing a business, 176
    on finances, 179
    on hiring experts, 183
    on networking, 134-135
    on personal time, 185
Holliday, Joan M.:
    biographical sketch of, 223
    on business definition, 89
    on competence, 37
    on integration of work and values, 112
    on internal success measure, 160
Hopple, Mary B.:
    on choosing a business, 178
    on recognition, 37
Horn, Linda, 227
    on caretaking vs. decision-making, 108
    on networking, 144
    on self-projection, 87-88
Hub effect. *See* Interactive leadership;
        Survey: interactive leadership
Hueppeler, Deborah, 227
    on incubator experience, 55
    on male-dominated industry, 64

Ibex (International Business Exchange), 187

Implementation:
  be realistic, 178-180
  the business plan, 180-181
  employees and, 184
  leadership and operations, 183-184
  personal life and, 184-185
  a personal plan, 176-178
  selling oneself, 182-183
  spouse and support, 181-182
  support systems use and, 182
Independence. *See* Autonomy and freedom
Intentional entrepreneurs:
  concept of, xiv, 18, 66
  experience or training programs,
    perceptions of, 69-70, 74t, 76-77, 174
  financial expertise, perception of, 69,
    73t, 168
  managerial experience, perception of,
    68, 71, 73t, 74t, 76-78
  marketing and technical experience,
    perception of, 68-69, 71, 73t, 76, 78,
    172, 173
  networking and, 120, 121t-124t, 168
  post hoc analysis of, 76
  profiles of, 72t
  self-determination concept of, 70-71, 72,
    75t, 76, 168
Interactive leadership:
  interpersonal orientation and, 83
  key role of, 99
  male-oriented style and, 99, 100
  summary regarding, 170
  survey focus regarding, 101-102
  transactional style of, 100
  transformational style of, 100, 102-103,
    114
  web leadership style of, 99, 100-101, 114
  See also Survey: interactive leadership
Internal Revenue Service, 14
International Business Exchange (Ibex), 187
Interview sites, xiv

Jacobson, Lisa, 224
Job freedom. *See* Autonomy and freedom
Johnson, Fran (Raglin), 227
  on information access, 146-147
  on intentional entrepreneur concept,
    66-67
  on networking, 135, 145

Journal of Business Venturing, The, 12

Kearns, Sharon, xviii
Kelley, Roberta Gose, 227
Kline, Karen:
  biographical sketch of, 224
  on business focus, 90
  on networking, 131-132
  on risk-taking, 81-82
Kotler, Suzan B., 227
  on business plan importance, 180
  on caretaking, 106
  on finances, 181
  on flexibility, 88
  on making it happen, 175-176
  on powerlessness, 48
  on value added networking, 131

Leader Assessment Inventory, 102
Leadership Assessment Instrument, 173
Leadership issues:
  opportunity for, 35-36, 79
  research on, 19
  See also Interactive leadership; Survey:
    interactive leadership
Leverton, Mary Margaret, xviii
Levine, Saralyn, 227
  on being realistic, 179
  on flexibility, 90
  on individuality, 31

Marrs, Catherine, 227
  on being the boss, 184
  on being prepared, 181
  on corporate politics, 62
  on marketing skills, 183
Marshall, Susie:
  on authority, 28-29
  biographical sketch of, 224
  on organization structure, 40
Martin Fugaro, Jill:
  background on, 4
  business launched by, 5-6
  departure reason of, 6
McCann, Janet, 227
  on drive to succeed, 87
  on incubator experience, 57

Megalowomanitis concept, 128
Menutis, Ruth Ann:
    biographical sketch of, 224
    on networking, 131
    on women's strides, 21-22
Michael J. Coles School of Business,
    Kennesaw State University, xviii
Miles, Bud, xviii
Moore, Dorothy P., xviii
Moore, Jamie L., xviii
Moore, Jamie W., xviii
Moore-Moore, Laurie:
    on authority, 35
    on being prepared, 179
    biographical sketch of, 224
    business of, 15
    on buying a business, 181
Morris, Elizabeth:
    on autonomy, 26, 27
    biographical sketch of, 224
    on bureaucracy, 30-31
    on information transfer, 54-55
    on strategic alliances, 126
Myth of the Unlimited Potential concept,
    158

National Association of Women Business
    Owners (NAWBO):
    acknowledgement to, 219
    networking with, 139, 144, 150, 171,
        175
    NFWBO founding and, 13
    participant selection and, xiv, 189, 190
National Foundation for Women Business
    Owners (NFWBO), xiii
    founding of, 13
    study by, 161
NAWBO. See National Association of
    Women Business Owners (NAWBO)
Networking:
    formal vs. informal, 116
    gender differences in, 116-117
    impact of, 115
    sources of, 115-116, 186-187
    strategies of, 117-118
    summary regarding, 171
    web nature of, 161, 185
    See also Personal networks; Survey:
        networking

New York University Stern Center for
    Entrepreneurial Studies, xvi, xvii, 189
NFWBO (National Foundation for Women
    Business Owners), xiii, 13, 161
Norden Ginn, Wendy, 33

Occupational gender labeling study, 11
101 Thoughts for Becoming the Real You
    (Sadovsky and Rice), 160
101 Thoughts to Make You Think
    (Sadovsky), 160
Organizational incubator. See Corporate
    incubator
Organizational life. See Corporate
    experience
Outsourcing, 51

Parker-Halpin, Terri:
    on being realistic, 178
    biographical sketch of, 224-225
    on hiring skills, 184
    on networking, 134
    on promotion discrimination, 46
Pennathur, Sudha:
    background of, 4-5
    business launched by, 6
    frustrations of, 8
Performance measures, 17
    congenial working environments and,
        17-18
    research issues of, 19
    work and family links and, 15-16
Personal networks:
    acquiring new channels and, 186-187
    context of, 185
Peyton, Renee, 227
    on client empowerment, 162
    on recognition, 37
    on role modeling, 111
Pickman, Susan L., 225
Pizel, Pamela, 228
    on choosing a business, 176
    on networking, 128
Porco, Anita, 228
    on unethical practices, 46
Pratt, Joanne:
    on being realistic, 178
    biographical sketch of, 225

on corporate politics, 43
on success measures, 156

Rathburn, Jude, xviii
Recognition of accomplishments, 15, 34-35, 37, 45
Renaissance Entrepreneurship, 13
Robinson, Sanford, xviii
Rust, Debra, 228
    on business plan importance, 180
    on finances, 93, 178-179
    on incubation transfer, 59

Sadovsky, Anne:
    on advancement discrimination, 60
    biographical sketch of, 225
    on freedom and autonomy, 160
    on selling oneself, 182
Sahagian, Linda:
    background of, 5
    biographical sketch of, 225
    business launched by, 6
    on difficulties, 177
San Francisco Renaissance
        Entrepreneurship Center, 219
Sayre, Patricia, 228
    on being flexible, 180
    on caretaking, 106, 107
    on multiple roles, 113
Scarano, Carol:
    biographical sketch of, 225
    on previous organizational
        environments, 30
Schaeffer, Kris:
    biographical sketch of, 225
    on corporate politics, 62
Scherer, Robert F., xviii
Schwaller, Shirley, 228
    on client commitment, 181
    on departure reason, 48
Self-determination, 23, 24t
    autonomy and freedom and, 25, 26-27, 79, 168
    bureaucracy frustration and, 30-34
    content analysis of, 25
    corporate incubator experience and, 71, 72, 75t, 76, 78, 168
    scaled ratings of, 23-24, 24t

See also Self-esteem
Self-esteem:
    decision-making authority and, 29
    departure decision and, 27-30, 34, 168
    identity and, 27-28
    regaining excitement and, 37
    self-confidence and, 28, 43
Self-reliance:
    controlling one's destiny and, 36-37
    prevalence of, 16
Semingson, Dianne:
    biographical sketch of, 225-226
    on the decision point, 49
    on information transfer, 54
Sexual harassment:
    decision factor of, 25
    legislation against, 9
Sifford, Marilyn, 228
    on business definition, 89
    on competence demonstration, 39
    decision factor for, 50
    on decision-making, 29-30
    on integration of work and values, 112
    on nonprofit networking, 186
    on not fitting in, 38
    on success measures, 156
Simple Solutions to Better Health, 6
Small Business Administration, Office of
        Women's Business Ownership of, 14
Small Business Administration, xiv, 4
Small Business Development Center, Wright
        State University, xviii
Small business statistics, 1, 18, 51
Smerz, Nancy, 228
    on employee retention, 162
    on personal planning, 176
    on workmanship, 129
Sobczak, A. J., xviii
Stange, Deborah:
    on credibility, 96
    on isolation, 97
*State of Small Business White House
        Conference on Small Business - A
Report to the President of the United States*
        (U.S. Department of Commerce), 12
*Statistics of Income for Sole
        Proprietorships*, 13
Stempler, Honi:
    background of, 5
    biographical sketch of, 226

on recognition, 34-35
Stott, Mary Louise:
    biographical sketch of, 226
    on credibility, 95
    on innovation, 88
Strange, Deborah, 228
Success measurement. *See* Survey: success
    measurement
Survey: on career transition challenges:
    conclusions regarding, 98
    credibility issues and, 94-96
    delegation issue and, 86, 87t, 90-92,
        169
    expectations and, 84, 86, 86t, 87t
    financial considerations and, 86, 87t,
        92-94, 169
    focus vs. flexibility paradox and, 169,
        8990
    hiring skills and, 90, 91, 169
    industry turbulence and, 84t, 85, 85t
    innovation and, 88-89
    management skills ratings and, 83, 84t,
        86, 87t
    perspective changes and, 86-88
    problems and issues and, 83, 85t
    role definition and, 89
    summary regarding, 169-170
    support vs. isolation and, 84, 86t, 96-98,
        140
    survey focus interviews on, 198
    survey methods on, 195
    time in business and, 83-85, 86t
Survey: on corporate incubator:
    corporate climbers profile and, 71, 72,
        72t, 73t, 167-168
    discussion and conclusions regarding,
        76-80
    intentional entrepreneurs profile and, 71,
        72, 72t, 73t, 76, 168
    post hoc analysis and, 75
    similar organization background profile
        and, 71, 74t
    special training program profile and, 71,
        74t, 174
    summary regarding, 170
    survey methods on, 194-195
    transition intention profile and, 71, 75t
Survey: on departure reasons, 24-25
    autonomy, 26-27, 79, 168-169, 194
    career barriers, 39-40

career and family balancing, 23, 23t,
    47-48, 169
compensation inequity, 44-46
competence demonstration, 39
content analysis of, 25
controlling one's destiny, 36-37
discrimination, 36, 40-42, 169
freedom, 26-27, 168-169, 194
leadership opportunity, 23, 23t, 35-36,
    79, 168-169
not fitting in, 38
organizational politics, 42-44, 169
other reasons, 48-50
questions regarding, 21-22
rank order of, 22-23, 23t
recognition, 34-35, 37, 45
regaining excitement, 23, 23t, 37
respect, 34-35
scaled ratings of, 23-24, 24t
self-esteem, 27-30, 154, 194
stifing bureaucracy effects, 30-34
summary regarding, 50, 167-169
survey focus interviews on, 197-198
See also Survey: questionnaire
Survey: implications of:
    future research recommendations and,
        172-173
    on organizational dimensions, 174
    on starting a business, 172
Survey: on interactive leadership:
    caretaking vs. decision-making and,
        106-108, 114
    conclusions regarding, 113-114
    creativity and, 104
    employee welfare and satisfaction and,
        103-104, 114, 161
    empowering clients and, 110, 161
    empowering subordinates and, 109-110,
        170
    exploratory analysis of, 104
    gender differences in, 100, 101, 171
    loss of freedom and, 104
    multiple role integration and, 113
    operational support and, 104
    power attitudes and, 103, 108-109
    role modeling and, 102, 103, 110-111
    scale ratings of, 102-104
    self-efficacy and, 104
    summary regarding, 170-171
    survey focus interviews on, 198-199

self-efficacy and, 104
summary regarding, 170-171
survey focus interviews on, 198-199
survey methods on, 195
teamwork and collaboration and, 103,
105-106, 171
Survey: methodology of:
contact protocol, 190-192, 191t
corporate exit and incubator experience
interviews analysis, 197-198
focus session format, 190
grouping variable for incubator analysis
measures, 194-195
instrumentation, 192, 201-217
leadership interviews analysis, 198-199
leadership measures, 195
limitations of, 199-200
networks analysis, 199
networks measures, 195
organizational exit measures, 193-194
pilot test of instrument, 193
questionnaire data analysis, 196
respondent profile, 192, 192t, 193t
selection criteria, 189-190
success analysis, 199
success measures, 195-196
transition problems and strategies
interviews analysis, 198
transition problems and strategies
measures, 195
Survey: on networking:
contacts, teams, teamwork and
credibility and, 120, 125, 126-130,
137, 174, 175
content analysis and, 137
as cooperative-integrative strategy,
125-126, 132-133
corporate contacts and, 115-116, 120,
123t, 126-130, 140-149, 171
corporate/entrepreneurial difference and,
141-142
entrepreneurial role of, 124t
exclusion from, 145-148, 171
gender differences regarding, 145-147
impact of, 147-148
minuses, limits and pluses of, 142-145
network association and performance
perceptions and, 125, 130
network centrality and, 117, 118, 119t,
120, 121t, 125-126, 148

networks as extension, 118, 135
networks as inclusion, 118, 134-135, 185
operational support and, 136
personal support system and, 136-137,
148
questionnaire data and, 135-137
questionnaire responses and, 118-120,
119t
as resource access, 125, 136-137, 139,
150
as sanity check, 137, 139, 149, 150
as sounding boards, 137, 138-139, 149,
150
summary regarding, 148-151, 171
support systems and, 118, 119-120, 119t,
122t, 125, 135-139, 148
survey focus interviews on, 199
survey methods on, 195
transitional functions of, 119t, 120, 123t,
140-149
value added dimension of, 125, 131,
150, 185
See also Personal networks
Survey: purpose of:
issues studied by, 18-20
observations and, 18
Survey: questionnaire of, 203-217
confidentiality clause of, 202
focus group sessions and, xv
follow-up survey on, xv
participant selection criteria and, xv
privacy protection and, 201-202
Survey: on success measurement:
care ethic, 153, 160-162
conclusions regarding, 166
definitions regarding, 152-153, 163-164
departure factors and, 142, 153-154,
155t
financial profitability, 153, 154, 156,
166, 171
freedom and autonomy, 160
internal measure of, 159-160, 171,
174-175
self-fulfillment, 153, 157-159, 166, 171,
174-175
size and, 153, 164-165, 165t, 171
stability vs. growth, 153, 156-157, 166,
171-172
summary regarding, 171-172
survey data on, 153, 154t

survey focus interviews on, 199
survey methods on, 195-196
work and family balance, 153, 162-163

Tanner, Mary:
  on doing without, 177
  on family vs. career conflicts, 47-48
  on training experience, 56
Thomas, Julie:
  on being in charge, 36
  biographical sketch of, 226
  on hiring skills, 184
  on incubator security, 55
Tighe, Jeanne, 36-37, 228
Toivenon, Cynthia, 59
Token status concept, 39
Transactional leadership style, 100
Transformational leadership style, 100,
  102-103, 114
Tucker, Janee (Gee):
  biographical sketch of, 226
  on choosing a business, 176
  on confidence, 58-59
  on formal school training, 57
  on gender and corporate advancement,
  26-27

University of North Carolina at Greensboro,
  xvi, xvii, 189
University of Portland, xviii
U.S. Congress, House of Representatives,
  xiii

Verdich, Lauren, 228
Vozikis, George S., xviii

WBDC (Women's Business Development
  Center), 13, 219
Web leadership style, 99, 100-101, 114
Weiner, Susan:
  biographical sketch of, 226
  corporate experience of, 16
  on networking, 139
White, Catherine, 226

White House Conferences for Small
  Business, 175
Whitmer, Dale:
  biographical sketch of, 227
  on finances, 44-45
  on gender barriers, 38
Winston-Salem Business and Technology
  Center, 219
Wise, Gail, 228
  biographical sketch of, 227
  on choosing a business, 177
  on corporate networking, 140
Withers, Gail:
  on credibility, 95
  on finances, 65
  on networking, 146
  on role modeling, 111
Women and Business Ownership (LaSota),
  13
Women entrepreneurs: research field on:
  data sources on, 13-14
  definitions in, 11-12, 13
  fundamentals of, 12-13
  issues of, 18-19
  organizational interactions and, 16-18
  typical entrepreneurial values and, 14-16
  work and family linkages and, 15-16
Women entrepreneurs:
  corporate competition of, 17
  impact of, 1-2
  prevalence of, xiii, 1, 18
  second generation profile of (1980s), 2-3
  traditional profile of (before 1980), 2, 3
  values of, 3
  See also Career transition challenges;
    Implementation; Survey: specific
    subject
Women Entrepreneurs, Inc., 13, 219
Women's Business Development Center
  (WBDC), 13, 219
Women. See Female employment; Women
  entrepreneurs
Women's Entrepreneurial Advocates, xiv
Wonsavage, Nancy, 11

Yeats, Pauline:
  biographical sketch of, 227
  on client empowerment, 161-162

About the Authors

Dorothy P. Moore is Professor of Business Administration and Citadel Development Foundation Faculty Fellow at The Citadel, in Charleston, South Carolina. She holds a Ph.D. in management, human resource and organizational behavior from the University of South Carolina. Previously the co-owner and operator of a small business, she is the coauthor of two books and the author of articles in the areas of performance appraisal and selection processes, stress, entrepreneurship, culture, and organizational change. She served as Chair of the Women in Management Division of the Academy of Management in 1986-1987 and the editor of the *Academy of Management Proceedings* from 1993 to 1995. In 1993, she received the Women in Management Division's Sage Janet Chusmir Service Award for outstanding service as mentor, scholar, and role model.

E. Holly Buttner is Associate Professor of Management and Organizational Behavior in the Bryan School of Business and Economics at the University of North Carolina at Greensboro (UNCG). She received her MBA from the Wharton School at the University of Pennsylvania and her Ph.D. in organizational behavior from the University of North Carolina at Chapel Hill. Her authored and coauthored articles are on the topics of the influence of entrepreneurial gender on loan funding decisions, entrepreneurial problem-solving styles, female entrepreneurship, managerial assessment, and proce-

dural justice. Her coauthored work has won Best Paper Awards at the
Academy of Management and at the Southern Management Association. She
recently won the Woman of Distinction Award at UNCG for her research,
mentoring, and service to women. She has served on the Executive Committee and chaired the Dorothy Harlow Outstanding Paper Committee,
among others, for the Women in Management Division of the Academy of
Management.